Structure and Spontan
Clinical Prose

MW01069645

"A good writer who goes for the jugular, I mean the heart. Suzi Naiburg has a real feel for what writing is and can do, a blessing not all share."

Michael Eigen, *The Birth of Experience*

"*Structure and Spontaneity in Clinical Prose* is a rare find, a real gem that combines wisdom for writers and editors. Its multilayered analytic approach will assist would-be authors to find their voice and helps us all deepen our readings of clinical prose. Dr. Naiburg is a gifted teacher whose wealth of experience in guiding others is conveyed on every page. As an editor, I find her insights invaluable."

Joe Cambray, past president of the International Association for Analytical Psychology, former US editor of *The Journal of Analytical Psychology*

"Suzi Naiburg's book brings clinical writing alive as art and lived experience and offers a stunning understanding of what it takes to create good clinical prose. Her book is a splash of clear cold water on the familiar landscape of arid, artless clinical writing. Dr. Naiburg is a rare reader of clinical works, attentive to the word-by-word decisions writers make. Her skillful exegesis of a range of styles and structures invites readers to attend to nuances of language and appreciate how clinicians relive particular moments with their patients that cannot be summed up but only evoked through the art of that particular writer. Her writing exercises invite spontaneity and considered choices, creativity and constraint, micro decisions and macro structures of organization. This book is a vital resource for anyone interested in clinical writing, or for that matter, anyone interested in truly compelling writing."

Annie G. Rogers, *A Shining Affliction* and *The Unsayable*

Structure and Spontaneity in Clinical Prose will teach you to read gifted writers for inspiration and practical lessons in the craft of writing; apply the principles and techniques of the paradigmatic, narrative, lyric narrative, evocative, and enactive modes of clinical prose; and put what you learn immediately into practice in eighty-four writing exercises.

Each of the five modes uses different means to construct worlds out of language. The paradigmatic abstracts ideas from experience to build concepts and theories. The narrative mode organizes experience through time, creating meaningful relationships between causes and effects. Lyric narratives present events unfolding in an uncertain present. The evocative mode works by invitation and suggestion, and the enactive mode creates an experience to be lived as well as thought.

Structure and Spontaneity is fundamentally a book about reading and writing in new and different ways. It is an invaluable resource for new and experienced psychoanalysts and psychotherapists and for students, teachers, editors, and writers in the humanities and social sciences.

Suzi Naiburg is a graduate and faculty member of the Massachusetts Institute for Psychoanalysis in private practice in Belmont, MA. She is also a writing coach, teacher, and editor who taught expository writing at Harvard and more than fifty clinical writing workshops.

Structure and Spontaneity in Clinical Prose

A writer's guide for psychoanalysts and psychotherapists

Suzi Naiburg

Routledge
Taylor & Francis Group

NEW YORK AND LONDON

First published 2015
by Routledge
711 Third Avenue, New York, NY 10017

and by Routledge
27 Church Road, Hove, East Sussex BN3 2FA

*Routledge is an imprint of the Taylor & Francis Group,
an informa business*

Library of Congress Cataloging-in-Publication Data

A catalog record for this book has been requested.

ISBN: 978-0-415-88199-9 (hbk)
ISBN: 978-0-415-88200-2 (pbk)
ISBN: 978-0-203-84814-2 (ebk)

Typeset in Times
by Apex CoVantage, LLC

Printed and bound in the United States of America by Publishers Graphics,
LLC on sustainably sourced paper.

Credits

To the authors who inspired me; my writing clients, who taught me what they needed to know; and my patients, who are all my teachers.

Contents

Preface

Whether we are in our consulting room engaged with our patients or cloistered trying to write by ourselves, we are often searching for words to say what really matters. But rarely do sentences spill out easily on the page or gather themselves gracefully into paragraphs of clinical prose. Even if they did, how could they do justice to the unconscious depths, intimacy, and emotional complexity of psychoanalytic experience? As Thomas Ogden (2004) writes, "Psychoanalysis is a lived emotional experience. As such, it cannot be translated, transcribed, recorded, explained, understood or told in words" (p. 857). "One can no more say or write an analytic experience than one can say or write the aroma of coffee or the taste of chocolate" (Ogden, 2005a, p. 16).

Yet we need to write about our clinical work. We owe it to our patients,[1] colleagues, and ourselves and to those who want to learn more about psychoanalysis and psychotherapy.[2] Because you have opened this book, chances are you or the writers you mentor would like to write with more daring, confidence, clarity, and ease.

Structure and Spontaneity in Clinical Prose will teach you how to read gifted writers for inspiration and practical lessons in the craft of writing; apply the principles and techniques that characterize what I call the NARRATIVE, EVOCATIVE, ENACTIVE, LYRIC NARRATIVE, and PARADIGMATIC MODES of clinical prose; and put what you learn immediately into practice in eighty-four writing exercises. You will learn how to tell a clinical story in different ways; "recreate an emotional experience" (Bion, 1992b); evoke "*in the experience of reading* . . . 'the music of what happen[ed]' (Heaney, 1979, p. 173)" (Ogden, 2005a, p. 16); and employ language that invites readers to participate in what the analyst experiences *as the analysis unfolds*. Daring to write differently, you may make discoveries about your patients, your work, and yourself. Whether you are doing the exercises, drafting a paper, writing clinical notes, or preparing for supervision, experimenting with different modes of clinical prose will help you deepen your work and develop your voice.

If you are not a psychotherapist, you will also find much here. While *Structure and Spontaneity* is about clinical prose, it is fundamentally a book about reading,

---

[1] The patients you write about may be individuals, couples, families, groups, or organizations.
[2] Throughout my book, the words *psychoanalysis* and *psychotherapy* (and the like) are used interchangeably.

writing, and honoring different ways of organizing experience in words. Its lessons may be broadly applied and are relevant to writers in the humanities and social sciences.

Whatever your field, you may recognize yourself or the writers you teach in these profiles: Intuitive writers may get flummoxed sequencing ideas on paper, and thinking types may find it difficult to distance themselves from their own ideas to know if they have anything worthwhile to say. Class-A procrastinators, perfectionists, and other self-saboteurs find starting to write so painful they often give up. The best intentioned may get derailed thinking about writing for others, while prolific writers may produce publishable papers but tire of writing in the same old way. *Structure and Spontaneity in Clinical Prose* will address these issues and more.

Consider this book an extended writing seminar that is always open for you to drop in. I have field tested my approach in more than fifty clinical writing workshops for both new and experienced writers, unpublished and published alike. What you hold in your hands is the culmination of more than twenty years of teaching, coaching, and editing experience combined with my passion for literature, my respect for what words can do, and my training as a literary critic and psychoanalyst.

Each of the modes of clinical prose may be considered a form of persuasion. Naming and comparing the paradigmatic and narrative modes, Jerome Bruner (1986) explains that "arguments convince one of their truth, stories of their life-likeness. The one verifies by eventual appeal to procedures for establishing formal and empirical proof. The other establishes not truth but verisimilitude" (p. 11). Each could be considered "a specialization or transformation of simple exposition, by which statements of fact are converted into statements implying causality. But the types of causality implied in the two modes are palpably different" (p. 11). In Bruner's reading, the paradigmatic mode's "if x, then y" leads to "a search for universal truth conditions" (p. 12). "The King died, and then the queen died" leads to a story and its "particular connections between events—mortal grief, suicide, foul play" (p. 12). The paradigmatic mode uses details to establish principles at higher levels of abstraction. Its value lies in the explanatory power of principles, while the narrative mode favors the significance of the particulars and the meaning of their specific interconnections.

Each of the modes uses different means to construct worlds out of language. The paradigmatic mode *abstracts ideas from experience* to build concepts and theories. The narrative mode organizes experience *through time*, creating meaningful relationships between events, between human motivation and action, interactions and internal states, causes and effects. A story's plot is what separates a narrative from a list of events, the annals and chronicles of old from history (White, 1981). A plot creates coherence retroactively where little may be discernable as events unfold.

As you will see, I have reserved the term lyric narrative for a particular kind of clinical story that creates the illusion of events *unfolding in an uncertain present* before hindsight allots importance and anchors meaning. The evocative, enactive,

Pingvallavegur

Sissy Eiriksdottir

Aftenük lokkewe

and lyric narrative modes create an illusion of *opening up the present moment for reexperiencing*. The evocative mode works by invitation and suggestion. Christopher Bollas (1999) calls evocative description "a conjuring of the nominated" (p. 195), a phrase that is itself evocative and thus performs or enacts its meaning. The enactive mode creates an experience to be lived as well as thought. All of these differences will be explored in the chapters ahead. What follows is a glimpse of what's to come.

In Chapter 1, *A Writing Workshop*, you will find warm-up exercises that have proven effective in opening potential space in which to write and play. Chapter 2, *The Poetry of What We Do and the Playground of Clinical Prose*, elaborates the underlying philosophy of my book. You will learn about writing clinical narratives in Chapters 3 and 4. Chapters 5 and 6 will introduce you to the evocative and enactive modes respectively. Chapter 7 presents lyric narratives and demonstrates how they express a commitment to the priority of experiencing, the nonlinearity of clinical process, and the limitations of present knowledge. You will learn about the paradigmatic mode in Chapter 8 and be introduced to a versatile tool called *the levels of abstraction* (figure 8.1; p. 105). Chapter 9 looks at some of the narrative moves and interweaves you could make to bring the narrative and paradigmatic modes into close proximity. Chapter 10 will guide you to listen for the felt presence of the writer on the page, look for traces of the writer's mind at work, and gain confidence in developing your voice.

Chapter 11 lays out the key components of introductions. Chapter 12 focuses on the narrative axis of your paper, the story of your clinical work. Chapter 13 shows you how the links you make between clinical material and interpretations, concepts, and theory, etc., create a paper's conceptual or vertical axis. As an invitation to think about the myriad shapes arguments may take, in Chapter 14, I will show you how two writers present ideas in radically different ways. In Chapter 15, you will learn how to use sources effectively and artfully and write a literature review when one is called for. Chapter 16 teaches you how to handle conclusions to take full advantage of the opportunities they afford. Chapter 17 is about revising, and Chapter 18 deals with how to institute disguise to protect your patient's identity. The Afterword closes the book on a personal note.

Although each chapter builds on what comes before, you may read what's here in any order. Feel free to explore anything that catches your eye and return to what you need as often as you like. If you don't have the time or inclination to do the writing exercises as they come up, I strongly suggest you read them anyway, since they are an integral part of each chapter's conversation and will offer food for thought as well as suggestions for your writing practice.

While this book is rich in materials for your reading and writing life, I couldn't fit everything in. Case writing, for example, deserves separate attention. Yet what you learn here may be applied, and as you bring a literary sensibility to all that you write, more possibilities for expression will emerge. I trust the conversation I have started here will go on as I continue to write, teach, develop my website (www.SuziNaiburg.com), and work with some of you individually. I look forward to that.

Acknowledgements

It took a village to sustain me while I wrote this book. The supporting functions were many—safeguarding my psyche and soma; helping me care for my home and garden; providing counsel so I could focus on my writing and clinical practice; guiding me along the path to becoming a psychoanalyst; protecting the solitude I needed to write; reading my chapters; and shepherding my book through production. By providing more nurture than they required, my children, their partners, and my grandchildren played an important part. At the other end of life's continuum, my mother inspires me to live with grace and wit as age bestows its inevitable indignities.

Long before I started writing this book, many others contributed to my becoming its author. My associations reach back not only through decades but also careers and into almost everything I read. To trace my lineage requires more words than I am allowed. Writing clients and patients also offered me essential learning experiences. I trust each of you will recognize yourself as I point in your direction. I am grateful for all you have given me.

I also want to acknowledge five authors who gave me permission to quote from their unpublished work: Heather Craige, from early drafts of "Mourning Analysis: The Post-Termination Phase" (2002); Dianne Elise, email communication (2012); Sharon Manning, "My Father Is a River" (2013); Jade McGleughlin, from "Letter to a Patient or . . . " (2001) and "To Be Seen Is To Be Disappeared: When Recognition of Trauma Betrays the Trauma Itself" (2013); and Barbara Pizer, from " 'Eva, Get the Goldfish Bowl': Affect and Intuition in the Analytic Relationship" (2005b) and "Maintaining Analytic Liveliness: 'The Fire and the Fuel' of Growth and Change" (2007). All rights to these materials remain with these authors.

I am also grateful for permission to quote from the following previously published materials. Excerpts from Christopher Bollas, *Forces of Destiny: Psychoanalysis and the Human Idiom* © 1989 by Christopher Bollas. Used by permission of Free Association Books. Excerpts from Phillip M. Bromberg, *Standing in the Spaces: Essays on Clinical Process, Trauma & Dissociation* © 1998 by The Analytic Press, Inc., Publishers. Used by permission of The Analytic Press, Inc., Publishers. Excerpts from Heather Craige, "Mourning Analysis: The Post-Termination Phase." *Journal of the American Psychoanalytic Association 50*: 507–550 © 2002 by Heather Craige. Used by permission of SAGE Publications. Excerpts from

Michael Eigen, *Ecstasy* © 2001 by Michael Eigen. Used by permission of Wesleyan University Press. Excerpts from Michael Eigen, *The Sensitive Self* © 2004 by Michael Eigen. Used by permission of Wesleyan University Press. Excerpts from Samuel Gerson, "When the Third is Dead: Memory, Mourning, and Witnessing in the Aftermath of the Holocaust," *International Journal of Psychoanalysis 90*: 1341–1357 © 2009 by the Institute of Psychoanalysis, London. Used by permission of John Wiley & Sons, Ltd.

Excerpts from Leston Havens, *Coming to Life: Reflections on the Art of Psychotherapy*, pp. 1, 2, 6, 12, 59–63, 64, 71. Cambridge, MA: Harvard University Press © 1993 by Leston Havens. Used by permission of the publisher. Excerpt from André Gide, *The Counterfeiters* © 1973 Vintage Books/Random House. Used by permission of the publisher. Excerpts from Sue Grand, "Unsexed and Ungendered Bodies," *Studies in Gender and Sexuality 4*: 313–341 © 2003 by Taylor & Francis Group. Used by permission of the Taylor & Francis Group, LLC. Excerpts from Sue Grand, *The Hero in the Mirror: From Fear to Fortitude* © 2010 by Taylor & Francis Group, LLC. Used by permission of the Taylor & Francis Group, LLC. Excerpts from Sue Grand, "God at an Impasse: Devotion, Social justice, and the Psychoanalytic Subject," *Psychoanalytic Dialogues 23 (4)*: 449–463 © 2013 by the Taylor & Francis Group. Used by permission of the Taylor & Francis Group, LLC. Excerpts from Jeffrey C. Miller, *The Transcendent Function: Jung's Model of Psychological Growth through Dialogue with the Unconscious* © 2004 The State University of New York. Used by permission. All rights reserved. Excerpts used by permission of the publisher from "Penelope's Loom: Psychology and the Analytic Process" in *Relational Concepts in Psychoanalysis: An Integration* by Stephen A. Mitchell, pp. 271–273, Cambridge, MA: Harvard University Press © 1988 by the President and Fellows of Harvard College.

Excerpts from Thomas H. Ogden, *Conversations at the Frontier of Dreaming* © 2001 by Thomas H. Ogden. Used by permission of Jason Aronson, Inc. Excerpts from Thomas H. Ogden, "Reading Winnicott" *The Psychoanalytic Quarterly 70*: 299–323 © 2001 *The Psychoanalytic Quarterly*. Used by permission of John Wiley and Sons. Excerpts from Thomas H. Ogden, "On Psychoanalytic Writing" *International Journal of Psychoanalysis 66*: 15–29 © 2005 by the Institute of Psychoanalysis, London. Used by permission of John Wiley & Sons, Ltd. Excerpts from *The Beast in the Nursery: On Curiosity and Other Appetites* by Adam Phillips, © 1998 by Adam Phillips. Used by permission of Pantheon Books, an imprint of the Knopf Doubleday Publishing Group, a division of Random House LLC. All rights reserved. Excerpts from Adam Phillips, *Promises, Promises: Essays on Psychoanalysis and Literature* © 2001 by Adam Phillips. Used by permission of Perseus Books Group. Excerpts from Barbara Pizer, "When the Crunch is a (K) not: A Crimp in Relational Dialogue" *Psychoanalytic Dialogues 13 (2)*:171–192 © 2003 by the Taylor & Francis Group. Used by permission of the Taylor & Francis Group, LLC. Excerpts from Barbara Pizer, "Passion, Responsibility, and 'Wild Geese': Creating the Absence of Conscious Intentions" *Psychoanalytic Dialogues, 15 (1)*: 57–84 © 2005 by the Taylor & Francis Group. Used by permission of the Taylor & Francis Group, LLC.

Excerpts from Annie G. Rogers, *A Shining Affliction: A Story of Harm and Healing in Psychotherapy* © 1995 by Annie G. Rogers. Used by permission of Viking Penguin, a division of The Penguin Group (USA) LLC., and Dunow, Carlson & Lerner Literary Agency. Excerpts from Donnel B. Stern, *Partners in Thought: Working with Unformulated Experience, Dissociation, and Enactment* © 2010 by the Taylor & Francis Group. Used by permission of the Taylor & Francis Group, LLC. Excerpts from Joye Weisel-Barth, "Thinking and Writing about Complexity Theory in the Clinical Setting" *International Journal of Psychoanalytic Self Psychology, 1 (4)*: 365–388 © 2006 by the Taylor & Francis Group. Used by permission of the Taylor & Francis Group, LLC. Excerpts from Drew Westen, "The Language of Psychoanalytic Discourse" *Psychoanalytic Dialogues 12 (6)*:857–898 © 2002 by the Taylor & Francis Group. Used by permission of the Taylor & Francis Group, LLC.

1 A Writing Workshop

One does not discover new lands without consenting to lose sight of the shore for a very long time.

André Gide, *The Counterfeiters*

I remember my high school physics teacher describing how many important discoveries were made when scientists set out to investigate something else. About the same time, *serendipity* became one of my favorite vocabulary words. The sound of it was irresistible. The exercises in this chapter are designed to send you off in new directions so that writing itself becomes a discovery process and serendipity, your travel partner. But if losing sight of familiar shores prompts you to search for flotation devices, remember what you know as a psychotherapist: You can trust the process even if you don't know where you're headed. That's one way to welcome the unexpected.

In the exercises in this chapter, you may want to write about the same patient or clinical dilemma from different angles, because that focus creates a multiplying effect—call it *serendipity squared*. On the other hand, if you want to write about different patients, you may be led in other interesting directions. So feel free—anytime—to vary your sailing plan and chart your own course.

Portraits in a Sentence

Skilled writers can draw a striking portrait of a person or process with a few deft strokes. Here are three examples:

She wore guilt like an old sweater, familiar and all too comfortable. (Naiburg, a writing exercise)

He hurled his silence like a fast ball into a vacant lot. (Naiburg, a writing exercise)

Like watching the scattered shards of glass in a kaleidoscope suddenly cohere, all the many vital clues to her ancestry suddenly came together. (Pickering, 2012, pp. 589–590)

Exercise 1.1

a. For this exercise, try capturing in one or two sentences something evocative about a patient, clinical process, or your therapist self. The challenge is to create a vivid miniportrait using as few sentences as possible.
b. Create several more miniportraits. Consider jotting them down immediately after a session.

Mood Music

A seventeen-year-old patient called Andrew wrote the following self-portrait in the third year of his analysis:

> . . . My words are lost shouts in a dead prison,
> torn assemblages of thoughts in a mute body,
> Or dust in the air that breathed then.
> My words are stones sweeping the beach,
> The pebbles thrown carelessly by innocent children,
> Sinking
> Swept away
> By the tide.
> All worn and inadequate communications.
> Broken mirror: Darkened windows.
> Empty shells on the shore—You can hear the sea.
> But I who is words, untrained passion and solitude,
> I am unaccessible, unexpressable, floating unwritable thoughts,
> They are my movements and my body . . . (Sidoli, 1993, pp. 88–89)

Helen Grebow (2009) creates another version of mood music when she tells us how she felt at the end of a session with a new patient and imagines how her patient might feel:

> At the end of the session, she bolted out the door. I realized that my breathing had become shallow and tempered. I had been gripped by the recognition that any intense movement could send shock waves through the room, undoing her and us . . . ending our dance at the beginning. I felt that had been her experience in so many relationships before me. Now an inextricable player, I wrote my version of *her* patchwork story:

> I live my life in pieces—
>   ragged,
>   jagged,
>   frayed,
>   splayed,
>   quilted.
> Piecemeal I venture into the world

Running for cover or for a cover—
Hoping the threadbare seams hold
    as I gently pull my cover around me, over me—
        containing me,
            shaping me,
                shielding me,
                    cushioning me,
        concealing me.
Protecting the trailing threads—I step
        cautiously,
            tentatively,
                fearfully,
                    gingerly,
        vigilantly—
Aware that one misstep, one small catch
        and
            the slow unraveling will begin. (pp. 265–266)

Exercise 1.2

In this exercise I invite you to catch a feeling, sensation, or mood in words that capture something of your patient's experience or your experience with your patient. For Seamus Heaney (2002), a poem begins even before words are formed. We could say the same thing about evocative prose: "The crucial action is pre-verbal. . . . Frost put it this way: 'A poem begins as a lump in the throat, a homesickness, a lovesickness. It finds the thought and the thought finds the words' " (pp. 22–23).

a. Start this exercise by feeling into that preverbal place Frost identifies and let your feelings find the thought; the thought, words; and the words, their own form as you write a mood-music piece from that embodied place.
b. If you wrote in your patient's voice in *a*, try writing in your own voice or vice versa.

Writing from the Inside Out

In " 'Eva, Get the Goldfish Bowl': Affect and Intuition in the Analytic Relationship," Barbara Pizer (2005b) enacts the stinging shame she feels when her patient calls her out for lending him one of her papers:

The hour had come to an end and I felt helpless. I could not sit with the guilt and the pain that I felt Julian experiencing. I lend him a paper I have written about holding on and letting go; about freedom to feel one's feelings and still taking responsibility.

The next day Julian comes in to tell me that he read the paper as my relating to him my confusion, and having crossed a line! He is panicked. But not too panicked to talk about it.

"My mother," he tells me, "was always needing me—when what I wanted was to be taken care of."

Suddenly, sitting with Julian, I am seven years old, transported to my Grandmother's farm . . .

"Do you think," I say to Julian, "I am looking for you to take care of me?"

"Absolutely." Julian is locking on. "That is clear."

. . . . in the summer that my younger sister was about to be born. Ilse and I are sent away. We spend the entire month of July at Grandma's farm, which would be lots of fun if both my parents were along . . .

"I wanted unconditional love from you," Julian is telling me, "by a non-person. Being a person crossed the line."

A hideous Nanny is hired to accompany us. We hate her. She spends her time reading or on the phone.

"Being a person crosses the line."

. . . It is shockingly hot that summer at Grandma's farm. I can feel the heat in my cheeks. There's a stream in the front meadow where we are not supposed to go. We can see it from the window of the farmhouse. Ilse and I, we wriggle through the forbidden barb wire fence of that front meadow and we are walking through the high grass . . .

Julian asks me what this issue of intimacy that I write about is supposed to mean between him and me. What do I want from him? What am I really saying?

Silence is useless, Julian will not yield.

Ilse is balancing on a log across the stream when it happens . . .

"My mother paid more attention to my brothers and her best friend's kids. They were always at the house. When I ask her about it, she tells me that I seemed so happy as a child, so self-sufficient. Didn't need anything."

I must have stepped squarely in a nest of yellow jackets.

"I know my mother needs me. It looks like you do too but why won't you admit it? Why else would you give me that paper?"

Julian doesn't raise his voice. But he is fixed on me. He says he is certain that he knows what he is talking about. Why would I not admit what I need from him?

A nest of yellow jackets. A million of them. They swarm around me without mercy. Ilse is screaming bloody murder but even I can hardly hear her over the sound of the bees.

"She needs me. You do too."

I stand there frozen as the bees narrow in on me and settle on my skin. The more I try to brush them off, the harder they hunker down. I wonder if they know I'm shaking.

I make no argument with Julian. (pp. 27–29; italics in original)

Pizer quickly draws us into the emotional intensity and immediacy of two scenes, one narrative line on top of the other, climax on top of climax. Her present and past feelings build synergistically with each of Julian's accusations. Her interweave is masterful. Her internal drama undoubtedly erupted as affectively loaded, wordless images and body memories intensified by the stark contrast between the turmoil she experiences internally and the professional demeanor she must maintain interpersonally. The sensation of speed is created, in part, by her syntax. Frequent repetitions of simple, declarative constructions push the reader rapidly forward as the tension builds.

"Good writing is supposed to evoke sensation in the reader," E.L. Doctorow writes, "not the fact that it is raining, but the feeling of being rained upon" (quoted in Stein, 1995, p. 8). What Pizer feels as Julian "is locking on" is enacted in the story of her seven-year-old self as she enters forbidden territory and is stung by yellow jackets. It's a "shockingly hot" day, and she is a culpable child, bitten "without mercy" as she stands frozen and, unbeknownst to her attackers, shaking.

Exercise 1.3

Francine Prose (2006) suggests that when writers read "carnivorously," it is not "for what can be ingested, stolen, or borrowed, but rather for what can be admired, absorbed, and learned" (p. 31). I invite you to take what you learn from Pizer and apply her techniques to writing a clinical scene of your own, moving between your internal experience and what is happening between you and your patient, creating what Bruner (1990) calls a narrative's "dual landscape."

a. Let a scene of intense engagement with a patient come to mind.
b. Take a few minutes to recreate the memory of that experience in all its rich emotional complexity and let the feel of it reenter your body.
c. Writing from that embodied place, give your readers as rich a sense of what it is like for you to be in relationship with your patient *and yourself* in this moment by creating two, intertwined narrative lines as Pizer does. Using the present tense will help you create a sense of immediacy.

"Fetching"

Frost (1995) praises a writer who forms an "unmade word" or "takes a word from where it lies and moves it to another place" to create a phrase by a practice he calls "fetching" (p. 695). Start with everyday speech, Frost advises, "the hard everyday word of the street, business, trades, work in summer" (p. 694), "practical" and "unliterary" (p. 696). Then gave that word a new turn, "a figurative fetching of fresh words to your use" (p. 696). Frost takes a common phrase with its implicit sexuality—"Did you ever get it up?" (p. 695)—and uses its energy in a new way—"Are you contented to use the same old words all the time or do you ever get up a new one?" (p. 695).

In another example, he writes:

> Compare the use of the word 'alien,' a practical, everyday word with whose meaning you are familiar—a common word until a great poet, Keats, used it in his "Ode to the Nightingale."

> > "The self-same song that found a path
> > Through the sad heart of Ruth, when sick for home,
> > She stood in tears amid the alien corn." (Frost, 1995, p. 697)

Exercise 1.4

a. Select a feeling, therapeutic process, or personal attribute for your stem word that applies to you or one of your patients and pair it with an everyday word, fetching it from where it usually lies. To spark your creativity, try generating a few phrases using the same stem. As you do, let go of any impulse to be logical or consistent. For example:

> Empathy + furious = furious empathy
> Empathy + outrageous = outrageous empathy
> Empathy + blue = blue empathy
> Empathy + stingy = stingy empathy
> Empathy + . . .

b. Shift to another stem to create a new set of pairs, incorporating your phrase into a sentence if you like. For example:

> Her speech slowed to an alien speed.
> He couldn't reach her alien heart.
> He fell silent after taking an alien turn in the thicket of his mind.

One of the best times to do an exercise like this is when you're falling asleep or not yet awake. Then your associations are likely to be more unconventional as "the border guard of the prefrontal cortex is going off duty" (Kluger, 2013, p. 44) or hasn't yet been aroused. One of my workshop participants dubbed her early morning epiphanies "pillow thoughts."

Clustering

If you surrender to writing as a process and let the process carry you along, your implicit knowledge will guide you. Clustering is an exercise to help you discover what you haven't set out to find. My adaptation of Rico's (1983) exercise loosens things up a bit, but I won't stop to analyze that. Clustering, as Rico, Elbow and Belanoff (2003), and others explain, is essentially brainstorming on paper. Associative links don't have to pass logical inspection. I'll guide you through the steps. Try to do all of them in the same sitting to achieve that multiplying effect, serendipity squared.

Exercise 1.5

a. In the middle of a large sheet of unlined paper (as big as newsprint), write a word or short phrase (like "premature rejection") that you associate with a patient, your clinical work, or your clinical self. Circle that phrase.

b. Using what you've circled as a prompt, brainstorm on paper by writing down as many words and phrases that come to mind. For example, I wrote "leaves therapy before her time is up," "leaves the party early," "better to reject than be rejected," "vulnerable to hurt," "easily bruised," "narcissistic vulnerability," "hidden desire," "despairing," "my sadness." Scatter your associations anywhere on the paper. Your mind will probably cluster them without your conscious direction. Don't judge, censor, or question what you write.

c. Some people prefer doing this exercise quickly; others would rather take their time. Either way, let your associations fall where they may. Don't worry about moving words around or trying to connect the dots. Let this process run its course for a while.

d. With clustering completed, look for patterns and sequences of thoughts that may be emerging. Identify the affect and what's at stake for you and your patient.

e. Imagine that you're going to tell a colleague about the ideas you discovered. To prepare, put numbers next to the notes you want to talk about, numbering them in the order in which you would present them. Talking to a colleague or imagining you will may help you organize your thoughts.

"Freewriting"

In "freewriting," introduced by Ken Marcorie in the 1950s, championed by Peter Elbow (1973, 2000), and a key feature in Natalie Goldberg's (1986) writing practices, you are encouraged to write as quickly as possible without stopping or looking back, without fear of judgment, criticism, or exposure. Elbow (2000) calls freewriting "private, nonstop writing." You may digress, forget rules that govern writing (like grammar), and let go of the need to write well or make sense (p. 85). Goldberg (1986) encourages writers in timed freewriting exercises to "lose control" and "go for the jugular." For Goldberg (1986), the goal of freewriting "is to burn through to first thoughts, to the place where energy is unobstructed by social politeness or the internal censor, to the place where you are writing what your mind actually sees and feels, not what it *thinks* it should see or feel" (p. 8). Elbow later modified his approach to encourage writers to work at their own pace rather than against the clock.

Exercise 1.6

a. In this freewriting exercise, give yourself time to write paragraphs and pages about anything that has come up in the previous exercises or recently in your clinical work. Start anywhere and let thoughts, feelings, and words emerge without stopping, looking back, editing, or wondering where you're headed or if you are making sense.

b. When you're ready to stop writing, read what you have and notice what is compelling. Circle any finders and keepers and save them.

c. When you want to do more freewriting, you may start with the same prompt and see where it leads or begin with something new.

Exercise 1.7

Gather what you have written for this chapter, give yourself time to read it in one sitting, and see what you notice. Here are a few questions you might consider:

a. What have you learned about your patients, your clinical work, your writing process, and yourself?

b. Are you more at home in one kind of thinking or writing than another? Which ones?

c. Is it easy for you to lose sight of familiar shores when you write? If not, what might help you to be more adventurous?

2 The Poetry of What We Do and the Playground of Clinical Prose

I do not think I am under any illusion that what can be conveyed in a paper . . . represents the 'reality' of what happened in the consulting-room. . . . It is like trying to convey poetry in prose—impossible, and painful too because we know something is being lost or spoilt in the attempt.

Barbara Wharton, "Response to Plaut: 'The Writing of Clinical Papers: The Analyst as Illusionist' "

. . . experimenting with literary form used in analytic writing is part and parcel of the effort to develop fresh ways of thinking analytically. A fresh idea demands a fresh form in which to say it.

Thomas Ogden, "On Psychoanalytic Writing"

. . . propositions are not *the basic units of human meaning and thought. Meaning traffics in patterns, images, qualities, feelings, and eventually concepts and propositions.*

Mark Johnson, *The Meaning of the Body: Aesthetics of Human Understanding*

Do you remember the playground slides you climbed up as a kid? At the top of the ladder, you could see over grownups and feel tall as a tree. Coming down, you could build momentum and shoot into the dirt. Scrambling back up along the slide's incline, you could commandeer the next slide down. Instead of sitting up, you might angle your body and find ways to put on the brakes or stretch out, hands or feet first. Your imagination was free to soar, but the repertoire of moves you could make on an old-fashioned slide was limited by the structure itself.

Playgrounds have changed since I was a regular. Even in the 1970s when my children were young, integrated designs afforded multiple approaches to platforms, tire swings, and sliding planes, all of which could accommodate more than one person. Social engagement, perspective taking, and a wide range of activities were encouraged by the structure's design. Today, innovative playgrounds continue to encourage exploration, discovery, social involvement, and a wide range of activities. Some designs incorporate elements of the landscape, building sliding planes into hills and outfitting expansive approaches with ropes and foot grips. Others come with movable parts that invite children to alter their environment as they play.

Our field has changed too, especially over the last generation, but the structures of clinical prose that we use the most have "maintained a more or less familiar look" (Altman & Davies, 2001, p. 823). Serviceable primarily for predictable activities, they may be constraining like the standard-issue slide. You can see the influence of the research template in social work, psychotherapy, and psychoanalytic journal articles alike. An idea is presented in context of theory, followed by a literature review, more theory, the presentation of narrative summaries and possibly a clinical vignette, a discussion of the writer's ideas, ending perhaps with a summary of what's already been said. Same approach, same slide down, most of the time.

But there are exceptions. The playground of clinical prose, as I conceive it, includes an array of structures that invite spontaneity, open vistas for discovery, and encourage a much greater range of play, individual expression, and collaboration with readers. I call these structures *modes of clinical prose*. They are the NARRATIVE, EVOCATIVE, ENACTIVE, LYRIC NARRATIVE, and PARADIGMATIC. Before we explore them in the chapters ahead, I want to suggest another way to enter this playground to appreciate it as a whole.

"An analytic experience—like all other experiences," Ogden (2005a) notes, "does not come to us in words. An analytic experience cannot be told or written; an experience is what it is" (p. 16). In the language of William James, "our experience is rich and deep, characterized by 'much at once' blending together in a continuous flow" (quoted in Johnson, 2007, p. 89), which Johnson (2007) describes as "an ongoing flow of qualities and qualitative changes" felt as a qualitative whole (p. 72). How "much at once" there is in an analytic interaction or micromoment—let alone a single session or entire analysis. For John Dewey, this "unity [of experience] is neither emotional, practical, nor intellectual" (quoted in Johnson, 2007, p. 74). These distinctions, or any others, Johnson (2007) explains, arise "after the fact" (p. 74). Experience—"the total overwhelming impression comes first" (Dewey quoted in Johnson, 2007, p. 75), comes before discriminations are made, conceptualizing begins, and meanings are cocreated.

One of your challenges as a clinical writer is to translate analytic and qualitative experience and the poetry of what we do (and feel and intuit . . .) with our patients into prose, knowing how inadequate any translation might be. Frost said "that poetry is what is lost in translation. It is also what is lost in interpretation" (quoted in Bromberg, 2011, p. 2). A dream brought into analysis is not the same as the dreamer's nocturnal experience (Ogden, 2005a, p. 16). "An experience is what it is" (Ogden, 2005a, p. 16). Psychic realities "cannot in fact be seen or smelled or heard . . . cannot be sensuously apprehended" (Bion, 2004/1964, p. 132).

We may carve concepts out of experiencing, but "qualities are not reducible to the abstractions by which we try to distinguish them" (Johnson, 2007, p. 70). Nor can we "capture qualitative experience in propositions with subject-predicate structure" (Johnson, 2007, p. 70), although we need both concepts and propositions as ways of knowing, forms of "worldmaking" (Goodman, 1978), "kinds of constructions that lead to the creation of worlds" (Bruner on Goodman in Bruner, 1990, p. 97). I feel at home with Goodman's notion that "there is an irreducible plurality of 'worlds'" (Bruner, 1990, p. 98) or symbol systems, however small, like a poem, or large, like the arts and sciences. For Goodman, "the difference . . . is *not* that the arts are 'subjective' and science 'objective'" (Bruner, 1990, p. 101) or, in our vocabulary, that the narrative, evocative, enactive, and lyric narrative modes are subjective, and the paradigmatic and its conceptual structures are more objective. "Rather each constructs its world differently, and objectivity versus subjectivity is not the distinction at issue" (Bruner, 1990, p. 101).

Danielle Klinenberg's watercolor "All Souls" (cover image) is not representational art, but it speaks to me of worldmaking. As a painting, it is a specific *act* of worldmaking that also depicts the creative *process* of worldmaking. Out of the "much at once" of color, form, process, flow, and the feelings they evoke, patterns like the emerging blue arc may be found or made.

For Goodman (1978), "worlds are made not only by what is said literally but also by what is said metaphorically, and not only by what is said either literally or metaphorically but also by what is exemplified and expressed—by what is shown as well as by what is said" (p. 18). I think of the modes of clinical prose as worlds in Goodman's sense of symbol systems that are made in different ways. Each affords opportunities for vision, construction, creativity, and play. Each uses language to create a different kind of experience for its readers. Welcome to the playground of clinical prose.

3   Narrative Meaning and Technique

When I settle into a place, listening and watching, I don't try to fool myself that the stories of individuals are themselves arguments. I just believe that better arguments, maybe even better policies, get formulated when we know more about ordinary lives.

Katherine Boo, *Behind the Beautiful Forevers*

Narrative Meaning

We are all storytellers—therapists and patients alike, in and out of our consulting rooms. With stories in their myriad forms, we make sense of the world and our experiences in it. We create meaning and give wings to our imagination. For many of our patients, the creation of narrative coherence is a courageous and meaningful act in itself. We also know from attachment research that a mother's autobiographical competence is a predictor of her infant's security of attachment. Even in young children's creations of narratives, the linking of events is more than an ordering of them in time. It is also a way of knowing.

Bruner (1990) comments on the bedtime soliloquies of a toddler (Nelson, 1989): "Her early accounts began by stringing together happenings by the use of simple conjunctions, moved then to reliance upon temporals like *and then*, and passed finally to the use of causals like her ubiquitous *because*" (Bruner, 1990, p. 90). Other markers of time, like "*sometimes*" and "*always*," revealed how narrative organization was used to distinguish "the canonical or ordinary from the unusual" (p. 91). Soon after the obligatory ("got to") enters her vocabulary, she begins to distinguish "between her own doubts (*I think maybe . . .*) and states of uncertainty in the world (*sometimes Carl come play*)" (pp. 91–92).

Bruner (1990) observes that Emily's narrative creativity is multidimensional: "The engine of all this linguistic effort is not so much a push toward logical coherence, though that is not absent. It is, rather, a need to 'get the story right': who did what to whom where, was it the 'real' and steady thing or a rogue happening, and how do I feel about it" (p. 92). Talking to herself in her crib at night, Emily "seemed to be in search of an integral structure that could encompass what she had *done* with what she *felt* with what she *believed*" (p. 89). "She was not simply reporting," Bruner notes. "She was trying to make sense of everyday life" (p. 89), and she was using narratives to do that.

When Bruner (1986) compares the narrative mode with the paradigmatic, he notes that each is governed by different principles. We judge stories by how real or imaginative they are, not by the standards of argument or empiricism. Narrative favors the particulars of experience rather than the generalities of the paradigmatic. Characterization is best achieved by the use of selected details that are individualized, even idiosyncratic and surprising. Bruner (1990) emphasizes that a well-written story is open to multiple interpretations. "To make a *story* good, it would seem, you must make it somewhat uncertain, somehow open to variant readings, rather subject to the vagaries of intentional states, undetermined" (pp. 53–54). A story's "uncertainty or subjunctivity . . . what the Russian Formalist critics referred to as its 'literariness' " makes it easier "to enter into . . . easier to identify with," to try on "for psychological size" (Bruner, 1990, p. 54). I would add that its literariness also makes it truer to the complexities of human nature and the world.

An Indeterminate Beginning

"Light filters down among the stacks inside the library's cool vault. Dust motes swirl in the air, tiny particles of color in the muted light" (Rogers, 1995, p. 3). These two sentences could easily be the beginning of a poem but are instead the first lines of Annie G. Rogers' remarkable book-length clinical narrative, *A Shining Affliction: A Story of Harm and Healing in Psychotherapy*. Her first chapter is a one-page story of a vision of a young girl Rogers sees in the university stacks. Rogers' memory of this child is clear, but her vision is fleeting. Once seen, she vanishes into thin air and "spinning light" (p. 4).

This beginning puts readers on notice that Rogers' narrative is undetermined; its meaning cannot always be pinned down:

> I tell you this light stays. I can't separate the light from the silence—it burnishes my skin, a memory like a photograph—and leaves in my ears a roar of silence, deafening. You could say, "The child did not exist, or if she did, she did not vanish as you imagine." And perhaps this is so. On the other hand, some angels yearn to be recognized, but can't bear to be exposed too long in the light they themselves cast over the human world. (p. 4)

Where do you stand, dear reader? With a willing suspension of disbelief? Luckily, you don't have to choose, because there is no argument. What you will find instead is a set of nested autobiographical stories that are full of resonant images, told from a particular point of view, and open to variant readings. The outer frame begins and ends with spinning particles of light, an allusion to the author's shining affliction, itself an ambiguous term. Within that frame is the story of her treatment of a young boy, and within that is an even more courageously told story of Rogers' ruptured therapy with Melanie, Rogers' mental breakdown, and her healing analysis with Dr. Blumenfeld. Literary narratives, like good poetry and analysis itself, create structures of experiencing in which potential space may be opened between participants. In all these arts, writer and reader, analysand and analyst cocreate meaning that is subject to multiple interpretations and iterations.

Practicing Technique

Prose (2006) advises writers to read widely and attentively and reread books they love: for the "wells of beauty and pleasure" they provide and as "private lessons in the art of fiction" (p. 3). *A Shining Affliction* offers many such lessons in clinical writing as a narrative, reflective, and scenic art. Careful readings of a handful of scenes from Rogers' book will show you narrative techniques up close and in action. Paired writing exercises will help you put what you learn into practice. Practicing technique, Gardner (1991/1983) assures aspiring writers, is a sure way to build mastery and confidence, step by guided step (p. 125).

Narrative as Immediate Scene

The second chapter of *A Shining Affliction* is different from the first and is even cast in a different light. To track these changes, we shall use Stein's (1999) distinctions between backstory, description, narrative summary, and immediate scene. Backstory refers to "the characters' lives before the story, novel, or film began" (p. 237). Stein defines description as "a depiction of a locale or person. The Latin root of the word 'depiction,' *pingere*, means 'to picture' or to fashion a visual image" (p. 237). Narrative summary is defined as "the recounting of what happens offstage, out of the reader's sight and hearing, a scene that is told about rather than shown" (p. 239). An immediate scene "is an action that happens in front of the reader, that is shown rather than told about. If you can't film a scene, it is not immediate" (p. 238). Stein notes that most contemporary readers prefer visible scenes to description, narrative summary, and backstory thanks to the influence of film and television. Later, I will amend Stein's definition of an immediate scene to include the presentation of internal experience that can't be seen. Retaining his term, however, reminds us how scenic writing can bring experience to life and draw your readers in.

Creating an immediate scene requires a disciplined process of selection, keeping backstory and narrative summary to a minimum. Notice how Rogers has mastered the art of editing the narrative as an immediate scene as she recreates her first play-therapy session with Ben:

> Less than a week later, I walk down a dimly lit hallway in Glenwood, a residential and day treatment center for emotionally disturbed children just outside Chicago. This is to be my first psychotherapy session with the first child I will treat, the beginning of my one-year doctoral clinical internship. I extend my hand in a nonverbal invitation to a five-year-old, tense little boy with dark eyes and straight brown bangs. He follows me down to the playroom, without accepting my hand, without looking at me. I open the door and we enter.

Ben stands in the center of this small room, his back to me. He is a stranger to me and I no less a stranger to him. I sit down and wait for him to make the first move which will conduct this overture, our beginning.

He stands very still, alone, silent—then explodes into action. He runs once around the room, touching things deftly in his flight—the desk, the chair, the chalkboard, puppet box, toy shelves, sink. He jerks toys from the shelves, throwing them on the floor.

"I want to play with this and this and this" he says, pulling down clay, a puppet, Tinkertoys and a box of train tracks. He squats down on the floor and begins to put the tracks together. Without looking at me, he speaks again: "There's gonna be a big fire. There's gonna be a big explosion!"

He switches the focus abruptly, but continues to tell me about the same thing: "You and I, we go camping. I get lost in the woods. There is a big fire."

He dumps out the Tinkertoys and quickly sifts through a box of small plastic figures, pulling out six soldiers, then places them in a circle all around him. "They will protect me." He wraps his arms around his bare knees and sits perfectly still. Silence wraps itself around us.

"The woods are burning down, but you are safe now?" I ask. These are my first words to him.

He glances at me briefly, and, as if to show me how unsafe he really is, he says, "I am sick. They took me to a hospital. You are the nurse and you will give me a shot." He pulls two pillows under his head and lies down among the Tinkertoys and railroad tracks. He extends a fistful of long Tinkertoy pieces to me.

"These will be the shots. I have to get all of 'em." He looks away and a small shudder passes through his body. I see his fear and his bravery at once. I take one "shot" from him.

"Perhaps one shot will make you better." I roll up his sleeve and rub a spot on his arm. He watches me intently.

"It will sting just for a moment, then it will be over and you will sleep," I say. I touch the Tinkertoy to his arm. Ben winces, then closes his eyes and "sleeps," as I suggested.

Abruptly, he sits up and begins to pull more toys from the shelves.

"I am going to play store. We need this and this and this!"

He runs around the room again, picking up chalk, a cup, even the sign on the door. His words come out with quick breaths; his breathing carries the sound of fear. "I have my baby dragons, too, and baby Superman, and they are all very sick," he tells me. "Make them be well," he adds, without looking at me.

He rushes to the light switch before I can answer and turns the light off. Blackness. No text on child therapy has prepared me to work in the dark.

"How can I make them well, Ben?" I ask. But he ignores my question.

"I will sleep in the store alone. I am not afraid," he says.

Blackness and silence. I wait, not knowing what to do. "Turn on the light. It's morning now," he shouts. I grope for the light.

Ben sits up, blinking. "I had a bad dream."

"A bad dream?" I ask, feeling stupid, not in any way prepared for this child.

He nods and moves toward the pile of assorted toys he calls "the store," trying to line up the toys in rows, but he is unable to focus at all now. He runs back and forth across the small room, and then, suddenly, at the other end of the room, he flicks out the light.

"It is night now. You are my mommy now and I am your son, OK? So don't leave me alone at night." Then silence as he settles down to sleep.

"No, I won't leave you alone," I reiterate.

"Goodnight, Mommy."

"Goodnight, Ben."

The stillness lasts several minutes, then Ben switches on the light again. I glance at my watch. Our time is almost up.

"Morning again," he announces. "Now I will be the teacher." He moves toward my desk and uses the paper and crayons lying there.

"This is how to make an eight, little boy," he says. He draws a clumsy 8 in red crayon. "No, not like that, like this!"

I tell him our time for today is almost up, but that I will see him two times a week and he will come again and play as he likes. I ask him to help me put away the toys before we leave. Ben throws them at the toy shelves haphazardly.

"Where is my class?"

I touch his arms lightly. "You're worried about where your class is," I say. "You don't want to stay and clean up now."

He pauses and nods.

"Today, you can go, but tomorrow we'll clean up together, all right?"

He does not answer. He backs away from my touch until he reaches the door, then turns and runs. (pp. 5–7)

Ben is action oriented, but what makes this an immediate scene in Stein's terms is that Rogers stays very close to what you can visualize. The few exceptions are carefully enfolded into the action to guide your viewing. Rogers' text could easily be read as a script for a play. The opening sentences set the stage, orienting her readers in time and place. Clinical writers often fail to alert their readers to the passage of time as a treatment unfolds, leaving them in doubt about where the patient is in the treatment process. Rogers doesn't lose track of her readers' needs. She shows us exactly how her relationship with Ben begins. By sketching in just a few gestures, she reveals the tension between them, drawing us into the playroom to see what happens next.

In the second paragraph, Rogers not only introduces the metaphor of the stranger but also shows us how Ben plays the part by standing with his back to her. She also returns to the refrain of the first paragraph with the phrase "our overture, our beginning." Elsewhere Rogers gives voice to the silence and the dark. She comments on her internal state three times, augmenting what is intrinsically filmable. Her readers may feel as much in the present moment as she is, as much in the dark. With the exception of the first two sentences, these deviations from more visual writing are thematically linked to Rogers being open minded, fully present, and baffled.

Rogers writes this passage in the present tense, mostly in dialogue and with very little description or self-reflection. We are told that Ben is five and that he is tense and has "dark eyes and straight brown bangs." A few directional clues guide us to see what she sees: "Without looking at me, he speaks again." And later more interpretively, "He looks away and a small shudder passes through his body. I see his fear and his bravery at once. I take one 'shot' from him." Rogers uses mostly short, simple, and compound declarative sentences, which contribute to our sense of things happening quickly. A handful of sentences enact Ben's exploding into action as phrases are doubled and nouns spill out to name the toys Ben pulls into play. Rogers' execution of narrative as immediate scene keeps the emphasis on Ben's action orientation and throws us into the same commotion that Rogers experiences first hand.

Exercise 3.1

Narrative as Immediate Scene

Think of a relatively action-filled clinical moment and write it up as a film-able scene, using dialogue and as little backstory and narrative summary as possible.

A Reflective Self

Immediately after her first session with Ben, Rogers tries to make sense of what happened. This scene differs from the more visual writing of the play-therapy session, because it employs narrative summary and gives us greater access to Rogers' reflections:

> I sit alone in the playroom, trying to "see" clearly what this child has shown me, what he was telling me in his play. When a child does not know and cannot describe, in words or in play, what has happened to him, it dominates his life. I knew this from the beginning of my work with Ben.
>
> What did he show me in one hour? Running, being lost, and fire. Fear of being left alone, being controlled, or being touched.
>
> It's a confused story Ben enacts—a story line without a clear sequence or plot, a jumble of scenes—in the woods, in a hospital, in a room at night where he tries to sleep alone. He throws toys and runs around the playroom; his feelings shift quickly. Fear is uppermost among the feelings that come into the room. But there is bravery too, almost a stoicism about taking all the shots. The plot of his story shifts as rapidly as his emotions, and it's hard for me to follow; I stumble after, learning in darkness that he is searching for a mother to stay with him at night, and for a nurse who can make him "better." I know this only as I begin to respond and play my part with him. In the process of playing with Ben, following the pace and rhythm of his play, I feel he is running from haunting memories.
>
> Ben sits inside his circle of soldiers and tells me a story about the danger he feels with the woods burning all around him. There is a story behind this one, a room beyond this room, but neither he nor I know this consciously. In this beginning we are strangers to one another, telling stories and acting on a stage neither of us has constructed alone. Ben is a little boy who has come to be with me in this small room. He is my patient and I am his therapist. Yet from the beginning, different as we may be, we are engaged in a powerful human drama, a drama that neither one of us can play out (or even imagine) alone.

And what have I shown Ben? That I will wait for him to make a beginning. That I will play a part in the play that he began. And that I am willing to work in the dark. (p. 8)

In this passage, very little action in the traditional sense of plot occurs. What happens, happens in Rogers' mind. The only intrinsically filmable action is described in the scene's opening clause—"I sit alone in the playroom." Although Rogers' reflections are gleaned just outside the temporal and spatial boundaries of the therapy session, they are still within its affective range. Rogers abstracts themes from Ben's play, comments on his feelings and hers, voices intuitions, and introduces metaphors that become more lyrical. As she gathers bits of Ben's enacted story together, we can track how her mind creates larger clusters of ideas, framed by the passage's more philosophical first and last sentences. The balance between what is and is not filmable in this scene is the reverse of the previous one.

Rogers can be seen as lifting what she felt and observed out of the flow of experience, now held in memory, and transforming that material into something new at a higher level of abstraction. This process of abstraction may lead to ideas, interpretations, or new concepts that could become the building blocks of the paradigmatic mode, but in *A Shining Affliction*, Rogers' story takes precedence.

Exercise 3.2

A Reflective Self

Write a scene in which you let your readers track your process of reflecting on the meaning of what happens in the immediate scene you wrote for exercise 3.1. This new scene may not have much of a plot, because most of the action is internal.

Set side by side, the scene of Rogers' first session with Ben and the scene immediately following it illustrate two complementary functions of storytelling—to narrate one's experience or another's story and render its meaning. I see clinical narratives as interweaves of these elements laid down in different patterns with various hues, highlighting, and balance. When I separate out any of these activities—experiencing, narrating, reflecting, or rendering meaning—I do so for heuristic purposes. In our clinical work, these functions often occur simultaneously and are recursive.

However in studies of first-person narratives, an interesting distinction is drawn between the experiencing self and the narrating self (Cohn, 1983). In autobiography, the older, presumably wiser, narrating self may look back on the younger, experiencing self. The writer controls the distance between these two perspectives and can play up their differences. In the immediate scene of the therapy session, Rogers is both the narrating and experiencing self. In the next scene when she is alone in the playroom, she is the narrator who looks back and reflects on her experiencing self interacting with Ben.

In a first-person narrative, a writer makes any number of choices, for example, about the distance between her narrating and experiencing self; how much she reveals about herself; how self-reflective she will be. These choices, among others, constitute what I think of as a writer's narrative stance. We rarely mistake the narrator of fiction with the flesh-and-blood author. Intentionally unreliable narrators (Booth, 1961) are a reminder of how separate they can be. Even in autobiographies and memoirs, the narrator's stance is considered a construction that is influenced by the writer's effort to put the past in service of the present. But the distance between the *I* who is telling a clinical story and the clinical writer is negotiable. When you write about your clinical work, how close do you want that relationship to be?

I think it's time to amend Stein's definition of an immediate scene to include the analyst narrator's internal experience. Yet his language is worth keeping, because writing immediate scenes actively engages your readers in the cocreation of meaning rather than feeding it to them predigested in a narrative summary (my pp. 120–128). Narrative summaries rarely admit alternative readings. They don't show more than they tell, although some are more experience near than others. Let's use the term immediate scene to emphasize a written scene that is filmable but may also give readers access to what is happening in you as well as with you and your patient. Immediate scenes, in our vocabulary, may bring the internal worlds of the participants on stage.

"The Descriptive, Pictorial Touch" and a Reflective, Experiencing Self

In chapter 3 of *A Shining Affliction*, Rogers' description of her first meeting with her supervisor reveals her experiencing self in a more reflective state. We are privy to more of her feelings and observations and find more description than we did in the previous scenes. The sentence structure is more intricate, and this intricacy is mirrored in the more complex structure of the chapter itself, composed of three scenes, a memory, and the foreshadowing of Rogers' mental breakdown. As Rogers approaches Dr. Sachs' office and waits for her appointment, she conveys a mix of feelings and uses a technique Henry James calls "the descriptive, pictorial touch" (quoted in Miller, 1972, p. 171).

Good description, Stein (1995) writes, "is not static. It is part of the story telling. . . . [and] has more than one function" (p. 7). It is written from a particular point of view (Gardner, 1991/1983, p. 36) and reveals not only the object of someone's attention but something about the observer. Descriptive language may be evocative and/or enactive, communicating on both implicit and explicit levels. Notice how much each sentence in the opening paragraph of Rogers' third chapter accomplishes and reveals about her as narrator:

> At the end of the first week [at Glenwood], I drive to supervision in the hazy heat
> of the late afternoon, alert and prickly with anticipation, an odd contrast of feel-
> ings and weather. Crossing to the revolving doors of the Chicago Psychoanalytic
> Institute, I pass a man pushing a broom who looks up, but not at me. I follow his
> eyes to the other side of the parking lot where a teenage girl with short red hair
> clings to her father's arm, pulling him back toward a car. Grimly, he pulls her in
> the opposite direction. I am enchanted by her refusal to go into the building, to
> see a doctor here—but the strength of her misery and the embarrassment of her
> father's predicament make me hurry along, well ahead of them. (p. 11)

In the first sentence Rogers orients us in time and to the environment and her
narrator self's internal state. She also weaves outer and inner together, comments
on this "odd combination," punctuates her description with the wonderfully enactive sound of "prickly," and reveals herself as a self-reflective observer. Although
little happens in terms of plot—Rogers drives to the institute and enters—a sense
of movement is captured in the descriptions themselves, adding to the dynamic
quality of the scene and mirroring the liveliness of Rogers' mind.

Aristotle noted that description is heightened " 'by using expressions that represent things in a state of activity' " (quoted in McClanahan, 1999, p. 9). Rogers
shows us several people in such states and lets us track how she processes what
she sees. As Rogers moves toward the institute, she passes a man sweeping. We
see her look at him and follow his gaze to another drama unfolding between a
father and daughter. I have the greatest urge to diagram this paragraph using zig-
zags to illustrate how our attention follows Rogers' shifts of attention. Everything
in the paragraph seems to be in motion.

The whole paragraph is organized around three pairs of terms: hazy heat/alert
and prickly anticipation; the daughter, who is miserable and resisting/the grim,
embarrassed father pulling; the workman sweeping, looking/Rogers, the psychology intern, taking everything in and hurrying away. These images will be gathered up, repeated, and intensified a few paragraphs later as they mingle with new
ones. This paragraph's sense of movement will be offset by the later paragraph's
contrasting energies and images.

"Weather," Havens (1993) observes, "is the great Rorschach card, the great
vague stimulus on which we all, every day, project our wishes and furies"
(pp. 11–12). The other characters described in the scene, like those a patient
describes in a session or dream, may also be explored for their narrative and affective possibilities (Ferro & Basile, 2009). The father/daughter pair could symbolize
conflicting impulses Rogers has—to enter the institute or hold back. Two more self
states are represented respectively in the laborer, who looks at the father/daughter
drama without having to leave the scene, and Rogers, who hurries away. What
drives her? Her sense of their embarrassment or hers? Perhaps both. Not knowing
propels us into the next scene. Although more of Rogers' mind is revealed when
her narrating self is reflective, it is far from transparent, thus stimulating our curiosity and eliciting our participation in cocreating multiple readings of her text.

Exercise 3.3

Evocative Description

Gardner (1991/1983) suggests the following exercise to emphasize how description is always written from a particular point of view: "Describe a barn as seen by a man whose son has just been killed in a war. Do not mention the son, or war, or death. Do not mention the man who does the seeing" (p. 37). Such an exercise also demonstrates how description can convey emotions without naming them.

a. Imagine a particularly difficult or moving session with a patient and let yourself embody your feelings about that session.
b. From that embodied state, describe your office, something in it, or something that catches your eye that you can use to convey how you feel. Don't mention yourself as the therapist, your patient, or the qualities of the session. Like Gardner's exercise, let what you describe convey what you feel without naming your feelings.

Showing and Telling

The second paragraph of Rogers' third chapter (quoted below) moves the plot along, introduces us to her supervisor, describes the institute's waiting room, and presents a small dilemma, the resolution of which adds to our understanding of the young Rogers. Showing and telling are often combined as they are in this passage:

> I push through the doors, carrying a briefcase of the tapes and notes from my initial sessions with each of the children I have seen this week. I sit in the private waiting room just outside the office of Dr. Rachael Sachs, an eighty-four-year-old pioneer in the psychoanalytic treatment of children. A consultant at Glenwood, she has already agreed to supervise my work. There, in this tiny space, I find a pile of children's books and outdated magazines, with a painting of a Renaissance angel in one of them. It is uncannily quiet. I sit for several moments before I notice a buzzer with a little note typed beneath it that reads, "Please ring when you arrive for your appointment." I have arrived for an appointment, but I am not a patient. No, I am not. Should I ring or not? I decide to ring. I press the buzzer and hear nothing, and no one comes to answer. Should I ring again? I think not. (pp. 11–12)

Many teachers urge writers to show rather than tell. Stein (1995) defines showing as making something "visible to the reader as if it were happening before his eyes, moment by moment" (p. 307). Rogers shows us her dilemma and what she does about it. What's reported or described rather than played out in full view falls under the rubric of telling. When Rogers tells us about her supervisor and how "uncannily quiet" it is in the waiting room, we take her at her word. We don't expect everything to be dramatized. Prose (2006) notes how misleading it is to advise writers always to show rather than tell. Telling can be an economical way to provide information without pulling readers away from your story. In this scene, Rogers has conveyed a lot of information without distracting her readers from her experience. She has also slowed the narrative down, creating a plausible opening for a memory to arise that creates the scene that follows.

Exercise 3.4

A Clinical Adagio and a Clinical Scherzo

Depending on how the techniques of showing and telling are used, they may slow a narrative down or speed it up.

a. To get the feel of using these techniques to alter narrative tempo, experiment with showing something that slows your narrative's tempo as Rogers does in the waiting-room scene.
b. In another piece, show something that speeds your narrative up as Barbara Pizer (2005b) does when she writes about her memory of being stung by yellow jackets (my pp. 3–5).

Memory and Imagination

What does Rogers feel while she waits for Dr. Sachs? She doesn't tell us directly. Instead she gives us the story of how she mastered reading Freud:

> Three blocks from this building, in my neighborhood library, I discovered Freud at thirteen. The dense language of psychoanalysis confused me initially, but, not one to be put off, I discovered a way out of my confusion after reading Chaim Potok's *The Chosen*, in which Danny, a boy of fourteen, reads Freud. I read Freud as Danny did. I lined up a series of books on a library table: an English translation of Freud, Webster's *English Dictionary*, a German dictionary, a psychoanalytic dictionary, and my notebook, in which I assembled a glossary of terms and kept a running log of my questions and observations. After several months I began to know my way around in Freud's cases. I can still see myself pushing back my braids as I hovered over "Dora"—then flying to the other end of the table to look up *tussis nervosa* in my psychiatric dictionary—while all about me old men sat reading books and newspapers calmly. In this way, I began to explore a new landscape: the geography of psychic life. And from there I moved on to the library at this Psychoanalytic Institute as an undergraduate, using a professor's library card to get in. I read Jung and Erikson and Winnicott and other psychoanalysts. It was the thrill of entering another language, another country, that held me dancing at my library table Saturday mornings during all the years of my adolescence and early twenties. Now, as a graduate student, I feel as though I have cracked the code, I know the words, I discern the meanings behind

the words—this I believe. I have graduated from a library table of Freud's densely written early cases to my own cases and my own words. (p. 12)

At the heart of Rogers' story is an endearing picture of a young girl in braids flying to the end of the library table lined with heavy books. What makes this description work? Its lifelikeness, the use of specific details, the lively quality of that earnest teenager, and Rogers' use of contrasts—between hovering and flying; the young girl and old men; and the eager, experiencing self and the older, wiser, narrating self. The quality of the narrator's voice, claiming its victory and knowledge, and its tone of warmth and appreciation add resonance.

Rogers has a knack for sketching in enough visual detail to stimulate her readers' imagination and picking specific details that particularize her characters and make her scenes memorable. "It is not just detail that distinguishes good writing," Stein (1995) notes, "it is detail that individualizes. I call it 'particularity' " (p. 254). It's also important to "choose the most effective details and err on the side of too little rather than too much" (Stein, 1995, p. 186). Selecting particular, concrete details is an effective antidote to overwriting.

How do you read Rogers' association to mastering Freud? As a sign of her confidence as she waits for her supervisor or as compensation for her insecurity? Notice the text doesn't ask us to choose, which is one of the beauties of the narrative mode. Like experience itself, stories can be read in multiple ways.

Another Look at Description

"Words are angels, messengers—but suddenly, in this airless room, I have no words, no message, nothing to bring here" (Rogers, 1995, p. 12). With this sentence, Rogers skillfully links her memory of learning Freud to the present moment in the waiting room just as the memory itself is associatively linked to the psychoanalytic institute. While the library's world is full of language, the waiting room is suddenly and ominously empty of words. Rogers' description functions here as a "transitional device" (McClanahan, 1999) that marks a dramatic shift in her state. It also creates *tension*, a word that is "derived from the Latin *tendere*, meaning 'to stretch' " (Stein, 1995, p. 307). Rogers stretches out the description of what she lacks by giving us three variations—"no words, no message, nothing to bring here" (p. 12).

One of the ways McClanahan (1999) helps writers understand description is by pointing out what it is not:

- Description is not . . . "all that flowery stuff." It isn't mere embellishment. . . .
- Description isn't optional. . . .
- Description doesn't always mean detailing how something *looks*. . . . Evocative and memorable description is rooted not only in visual detail but in smells, tastes, textures and sounds of the world. . . .
- Description doesn't begin on the page. It begins in the eye and ear and mouth of the beholder. To write good description, we must look long, hard and honestly at the world. . . .

- Description is not a way to hide from the truth. . . .
- Writing descriptively doesn't always mean writing gracefully. . . . Some descriptions demand uneven syntax and plainspoken, blunt prose. Jagged, even. Fragments too. Slice of chin. Buzz saw.
- Description doesn't always require a bigger vocabulary. . . .
- Description rarely stands alone. . . . (pp. 7–8)

Exercise 3.5

Description as a Transitional Device

Following Rogers' example and with McClanahan's comments in mind, write a short descriptive passage to serve as a transitional device between two clinical moments that you could present as immediate scenes.

A Lyrical Ingathering

The following paragraph is a lyrical ingathering of images from earlier parts of Rogers' third chapter, intensified by the sudden shift in the narrator's mood. Here the tension is sustained, creating suspense:

> A man pushes his broom, a sweep of sound—a look, unspoken, toward a girl clinging to her father's arm—she skids along the pavement, dragging her feet—and I rush ahead of my own fear of seeing patients. The sky above us is an unbroken white-blue, the blue of impenetrable secrets. The terror of what I am doing suddenly takes my breath away, empties my mind of all words, while the angel in the magazine stares back at me, implacable. (pp. 12–13)

At first it may seem that we are outside the institute again until we realize we are inside the narrator's mind while she waits for Dr. Sachs. The syntax of the first sentence enacts in its structure the displacement and disturbance the narrator feels. The uncanny quiet of the waiting room has become a breathless, mind-emptying, terrifying surround. Instead of the zigzag movements and opposing pairs of the chapter's opening paragraph, the images in this paragraph coalesce around fear and terror. The sweeper's unspoken look, the sky's impenetrable secrets, the angel's implacable stare are all more ominous images.

Does reading this paragraph prompt you to revise your interpretation of how Rogers' memory of mastering Freud served her while she waited for Dr. Sachs? Clearly her anxiety has the upper hand here. Second readings, Iser (1980) explains, are always different from the first (p. 55). As we move through a text, the experience of reading is transformed by "anticipation" and "retrospection." We anticipate what is coming based on what we have read and revise what we thought based on what we discover. A narrative text is not something that is fixed but is "a living event" that is created and recreated in the process of reading (Iser, 1980, p. 64).

"Authenticating," "Particularizing" Details

The scene of Rogers' supervision, which comes next, is easily filmable, although Rogers is a self-reflective narrator who employs description and most of the action consists of talking. It is an immediate scene in Sol Stein's terms; dialogue is one of the markers. Action does not have to be big for the scene to be filmable. Think of Henry James or the movie *My Dinner with Andre*. As Rogers describes Dr. Sachs, she tells us about herself and creates a sense of immediacy, though it is a quiet, reflective kind:

> Promptly at 3:00 Rachael Sachs opens the door and invites me into her office. With gray-white hair, she is stooped but tall; she walks with a cane, leaning on the desk corner as she returns to her chair. She wears a blue dress with a tie around the middle, but has no waist to speak of: every contour has grown soft, padded into one bundle. As she settles herself behind her desk, I take the only chair in front of it. She leans down and opens a bottom drawer and takes out a box of hard candy.
>
> "Here, Annie, have a piece of candy. I get sleepy by midafternoon," she says, taking a piece for herself. I feel suddenly like a child in a doctor's office. Then she pulls out a pair of bedroom slippers from another drawer and puts them on, making me more at ease, strangely. Finally she sits back and looks at me, a long look. I know this look—it is the look my mother gave me when she discerned my intentions and feelings before I knew them myself. I want to squirm. Reserve, shyness, good sense perhaps, something in me I can't name, holds back the words I have rehearsed.
>
> "Tell me about this week with the children," she begins, rescuing me from wordlessness.
>
> I haul out my tapes and notes. "You have begun to write about the children already," Rachael notices. "No," she says as I hand her my notes. "Read them aloud to me; let's hear them."
>
> I begin by reading the summary of my first session with Ben, taken from my tape recording and my thoughts in the playroom when I was reading his file. My voice quivers a little as I read. Rachael nods. "Go on, read me everything you have." I read about the other three children I have begun to see. When I finally look up again, she nods and smiles.
>
> "I feel that I have a lot to learn from you" is her startling comment. I must have looked startled too, because she suddenly becomes intent, serious. "Trust yourself a little, trust this beginning," she says. These words, from a woman who has been treating children all her life, are a huge relief to me. (p. 13)

Although I have only quoted the first page of this three-page scene, we can see that Rogers' narrative is grounded in enough particulars of what happens to be able to make sense of her response and find the scene believable. We can feel our way into it and imagine Dr. Sachs, perhaps even wish to meet with her for supervision. Gardner (1991/1983) tells young writers that even true stories must convince readers of their authenticity, and when they do, "all effects, even the most subtle, have explicit or implicit causes" (p. 23).

One reason Rogers' scene is convincing is that she provides the emotional and interpersonal clues that make her reactions believable. Her first impression of her supervisor is shaped by Sachs' appearance and movements, by her offering candy and changing into slippers. The knowing look that makes Rogers squirm is quickly followed by Sachs' simple request that rescues Rogers. Later Sachs reassures her supervisee, encouraging her to trust herself. Although we may not initially notice it, we are implicitly prepared for Rogers' warm response to Sachs by the tone of Rogers' descriptions. "Soft" contours "padded into one bundle" and "no waist to speak of" are gentle, casual descriptions. Almost everything that happens or is noted puts the young intern at ease, except one "authenticating detail" as Gardner (1991/1983, p. 23) would call it—the look that makes her "want to squirm." That's the detail that makes the true story feel real.

Exercise 3.6

"Authenticating," "Particularizing" Details

Add a few authenticating, particularizing details to a scene you have written.

Narrative Summary and Foreshadowing

With a subtle, skilled, and varied use of narrative summary in the next paragraph, Rogers tells us about her work with Dr. Sachs as it develops over time while we remain in the narrative present with her. Rogers is thus able to inform us without distracting us from the immediate scene. Two thirds of the way into the scene of her supervision, Rogers writes: "Gradually, over a period of months, I will learn a way of thinking: a psychoanalytic way of thinking grounded in practice, a way to decipher the meanings of children's play and their responses to me—but I will retain my way of proposing alternative and even contradictory explanations" (pp. 14–15).

In another paragraph, we learn that Dr. Sachs will meet Rogers twice a week without charging her for supervision. In exchange, Sachs asks Rogers to "write down everything that you are thinking about these children, make it a practice you never shirk, and then bring it to me and we'll talk about it. You write what you really think, and I'll listen, all right?" (p. 15). Rogers closes chapter 3 with this foreshadowing: "And, for a long time, I do write exactly what I think about my own work. Until it begins to touch my own life too closely" (p. 15).

Backstory

In chapter 15, Rogers demonstrates how to use backstory effectively. First, let me establish the context. In a session recounted in chapter 12, Ben has gotten out of control and bites Rogers as she tries to restrain him. Chapter 14 presents another play-therapy session, an opportunity for repair. The chapter ends with the narrative stretching into the future (prospection): "But Ben does not repeat his tantrum—not in this session or ever again. He certainly will be tense, frustrated, disappointed and angry at times, but never again so overwhelmed. At home and at school his self-abusive behavior decreases, but does not disappear altogether" (p. 53).

In chapter 15, Rogers falls asleep wondering where Ben was when he was removed from his first foster home. She awakens the next morning to snow and a vague sense of a dream: "I remember the smell of paper-whites, a burning smell, and a question. I don't remember it clearly now, but it was about Ben" (p. 55). A few clinical terms float through her mind and leave her "muddled" (p. 55). She continues: "As I sweep off the car windshield, a line comes to me, whole, like a finished painting—'What you fear most has already happened.' I do not apply this line to myself but to Ben, and then I remember my question of the previous night" (p. 55). Implicitly we know that Winnicott's (1974) wisdom also applies to Rogers.

In the backstory, which Rogers gives us next, we find echoes of the intuitions she had after her first session with Ben. Notice how her deft handling of temporality informs her readers, moves the plot along, and packs a punch:

> That day, and consistently every day for the next two weeks, I call the Division of Children and Family Services about Ben's first foster placement. I get the runaround until finally, one day, a clerk in the record-keeping office gives me the missing information: Ben spent most of his first year and a half alone in a crib, locked in a small windowless room. When a fire broke out in the house, he was discovered there in his crib after the family had been evacuated and the fire extinguished. That was how he was removed from his first foster home. (p. 55)

Chapter 15 ends here, starkly. Rogers has now confirmed the missing links she had intuited, demonstrating that narrative is not only the sequencing of events in time but a fundamental way we come to understand how events are meaningfully related.

In the next scene, chapter 16, Rogers incorporates her new knowledge into her reflections about Ben's play and the ways he keeps repeating the trauma he could neither remember nor forget. We will leave Rogers' narrative at this point, before she evocatively depicts her own dissociative states and daringly tells the stories of the rupture with her therapist Melanie, her breakdown, her successful analysis with Dr. Blumenfeld, her recovery, and her continuing her work with Ben. Before we move on, however, I want to note that every time I attend to how *A Shining Affliction* is written, I am struck by how much psychology is enfolded within it. Yet Rogers never sacrifices her narrative line or its momentum. She never compromises her voice or distracts her readers from being fully engaged with those whose stories she artfully and sensitively tells.

4   Short Stories

. . . in order to write well you must first learn how to listen.
A. Alvarez, *The Writer's Voice*

Short stories have a long history, reaching back into the oral traditions of prehistory and across borders and centuries into the digital age. They have donned many guises, including the fables of Aesop, the character sketches of Chaucer, the Sufi teaching stories of Nasruddin, the macabre tales of Poe, and the nineteenth-century literary classics of Gogol, Chekhov, and de Maupassant. Short stories flourished in twentieth-century America with their publication in literary magazines by the nation's most talented writers. In the United States and elsewhere, they continue to reflect a rich diversity of voices, cultures, and forms.

One form that has been revived recently goes by several new names—sudden fiction, flash fiction, and the short short story. Defined by its length, it is about two pages or 750 words. Aesop, Chekhov, Kafka, Bradbury, Vonnegut, and Borges are some of its well-known practitioners.[1] As you might imagine, the elements of the short short story are stripped down to bare essentials. Teaching stories have a long tradition and may also be relatively short. In this chapter, we will look at two psychoanalysts who write in several genres. Leston Havens and Michael Eigen, a master of the short short form, write teaching stories in their own distinctive voice.

Michael Eigen's Prose

Eigen is a multivoiced writer. "To read him," Adam Phillips notes, "is to experience the moment-by-moment changes of heart that for him constitute the analytic encounter" (quoted in Eigen, 1992, back cover). In his introduction to *Rage* (2002), Eigen talks about his book as "a meditation on rage and pain and self" (p. 5). *Rage* is composed of fairly short stories of analytic sessions and short essays, each averaging fewer than seven pages. The book "works indirectly, informally, turning variations of rage over and over, considering them now from this angle, now from that. It is episodic, fragmentary, with inherent emotional rigor. The aim is

[1] Sometimes very specific distinctions are made between subgenres: Micro fiction is 400–750 words; flash fiction is 300–1000, sudden fiction, a little longer (Shapard & Thomas, 1986; Wikipedia, flash fiction).

gradual increment of experiencing. To experience rage rather than enact it opens places one could not have gotten to by blowing (oneself) up" (Eigen, 2002, p. 5).

The structural units in *Ecstasy* (2001) are even shorter, sometimes less than a page. They include flashes of ideas, questions, and short short stories—autobiographic, clinical, biblical, soul searching, and soul searing. The effect of so many different views of ecstasy and thoughts about the ecstatic core of psychoanalysis and life also builds incrementally. The book's " 'argument,' " Eigen (2001) explains, "is less rationalistic and linear, more a moment-to-moment showing of creative and destructive ecstasies at work" (p. vii).

Eigen calls himself a psychoanalytic mystic. "Mysticisms," he (1998) notes, "reflect the variable intensity of emotional life" (p. 22). In his introduction to *Emotional Storm* (2005), he writes, "My portrayals are concerned with letting feeling storms speak, letting them have their say, seeing where they lead. The kind of 'read' I hope for, the kind of writing I do, is a kind of 'training' or invitation to stay with experience without pressing the eject button too quickly" (pp. 9–10).

Each of the formal choices Eigen makes about how he writes reflects his sense of the self as "variable" and "a community of voices" (Eigen, 1992, p. xviii), each of which is welcomed in analysis. His writing celebrates subjectivity and emphasizes the experiencing of emotions and attitudes in all their intensity and variety. This view is consonant with his view of therapy, which embraces all of our human capacities—for rages, ecstasies, and emotional storms:

> One of therapy's blessings is to promote the freedom to allow all sorts of psychic productions to swim into view, so that we become a little less afraid of ourselves. Not only does therapy let us see more of ourselves, but it does so from many different angles. In time, we begin to transcend any given vision. We are more than the sum of the thoughts, images, feelings, and actions that we produce. We do not possess immunity from our attitudes, beliefs, and frailties. But we discover that home is not identical with anything we can pin down. (Eigen, 1992, p. 2)

A Short Short Clinical Story

I read the following untitled passage from Eigen's *Ecstasy* (2001) as a short short story, a teaching story that is only 406 words:

> A man once consulted me because he feared he would die without finding himself. He had heart disease and had just come out of the hospital in the wake of a heart attack. He was in big trouble at work. He was a counselor in a college and had seduced young men. One of these episodes blew up, and his job was threatened. His most recent heart failure followed. Explosion = explosion.

> I became paranoid when he told me he wanted me to write a letter to his college, saying he was in treatment dealing with his problem. I imagined he was hitting on me. He came to see me to get this letter, to keep his job. His rap about finding himself was a cover, a come-on. He would seduce me with the promise of psychoanalysis, the way he seduced young men with the promise of life.

Yet he came. He worked. He dug deeper. He raced time. Psychoanalysis in fast motion. Through layers of history, layers of psyche, the heart and soul of his life and being. Therapy ecstasies, self-knowledge ecstasies replaced ecstasies with young men. There was no time for both in those final months. Fear of losing his job was not the only spur. Time itself was the driving force: now or never.

There were moments when he had a sense of being at rest, perhaps not Plotinus's rest, not divine union, but perhaps not entirely removed from it either. More like Bion's sense of at-onement with self. He felt at peace with himself and his life. For the first time, he felt truly honest, as honest as his "taint" (his word) let him be. It is difficult to say what he meant by "taint" but it includes a disposition to deceive, a twist no amount of honesty can undo. Nevertheless, honesty grows, puts pressure on the twist of self, increasing hunger for truth the more impossible the latter seems to be. Something true comes through the taint, in spite of the latter, and makes contact with the true being of the Other. For the first time, he felt heard, seen, appreciated, accepted, loved—as he was, as much himself as he could be. I felt deeply moved being let in to such intimate chambers. We thanked each other.

One day he reported a dream of a black cat disappearing into a basement window. He died later that day walking into a subway. (Eigen, 2001, p. 14)

Reading as a writer, what do you notice about the way this short narrative is constructed? Do you want to respond before I ask a set of more focused questions?

Eigen does not present an immediate scene but writes a narrative summary so skillfully that he conveys a sense of immediacy. How does he do that? Which details stand out for you? In such a short piece, how does Eigen express his quality of engagement with his patient, who is not even given a name? What makes his choice not to name him effective? I was struck by how little Eigen actually tells us about his patient. By virtue of their brevity, short short stories are stripped down. Which narrative techniques does Eigen forgo? How does the brevity of this genre serve him?

What could be a more essential stripping-down process than death? Eigen's patient had no time to lose. His life is a short form, making Eigen's choice of the form of a short short story fitting. Let's take a closer look at how he executes that choice. The first paragraph, written as a narrative summary, establishes the situation of his patient's treatment—his existential crisis, his work crisis, and his health crisis. These links are symbolically expressed as an equation: mathematics as plot. What could be more concise? Like a poem's end line, the last line of a paragraph packs a punch. The patient's situation is doubly explosive. The equation's concision and compression are also symbolic of the press of time, the patient's fate.

In the second paragraph, Eigen, who feels seduced by his patient, brings his paranoid feelings alive with the charged slang that echoes his patient's unsettling seductions of young men. We discover this rub as Eigen does, not in the beginning of the story but in the midst of the action. Eigen's retelling enacts his discovery and gives us a sense of being in process with them. Although the story is told from the perspective of the past, it feels like we are learning what happens as it unfolds.

The third paragraph, with its cadence, repetitions, and imperative "now or never," picks up the pace, enacting the accelerating movement of the analysis running against the clock. The first four short sentences create a sensation of speed. Each one is no more than three or four syllables and propels the reader quickly forward, enacting "psychoanalysis in fast motion." In the fourth paragraph, the tempo slows, and the plot seems to move toward resolution. Eigen's patient begins to feel at peace. The narrative opens out from the immediacy of Eigen's feelings (in the second paragraph) and the compression of the treatment cycle (in the third paragraph) to his use of Plotinus's and Bion's ideas.

The fourth paragraph is the longest. Eigen introduces a particularizing detail (Stein, 1995), which also functions as an "authenticating detail," the one that makes a true story feel real (Gardner, 1991, p. 23). I am referring to his patient's *taint*. The word stands out and is echoed in the sounds that follow. I hear hard, sharp sounds in "a *d*isposition to *d*eceive, a *t*wist no amount of honesty can undo. . . . *p*uts *p*ressure on the *t*wist of self. . . . something *t*rue comes through the *t*aint . . ." (emphasis added). This taint is also a complication, but "honesty" and a "hunger for truth" grow. One resolution leads to another. "Something true comes through . . ."—recognition, appreciation, acceptance, legitimate intimacy, and love.

In the final paragraph, we learn that Eigen's patient disappears like the dream cat, the harbinger of death. The story is complete, like Eigen's work with his patient. It has a beginning, middle, and end. But Eigen's work is cut off, cut short. In another sense, the short short story is incomplete. How could it not be? It is pared down to the bone. So much is left out. There is no "descriptive, pictorial touch," (James quoted in Miller, 1972, p. 171), no dialogue, few details.

Boundary violations are all too familiar. We don't even need the patient's name. We have been here before. Baxter (1986) observes, "In the abruptly short-short story, familiar material takes the place of detail. . . . We've seen that before. We know where we are. Don't give us the details; we don't need them" (p. 229). Gornick (2001) explains, "Every work of literature has both a situation and a story. The situation is the context or circumstance, sometimes the plot; the story is the emotional experience that preoccupies the writer: the insight, the wisdom, the thing one has come to say" (p. 13). In writing specifically about the short short story, Baxter (1986) offers the equivalent for the short short of Gornick's idea of "the story": "What we need is surprise, a quick turning of the wrist toward texture, or wisdom, something suddenly broken or quickly repaired" (p. 229).

The turn toward texture in Eigen's piece, as I see it, is the taint that colors the patient's honesty. The insight is that "the honesty . . . puts pressure on the twist of self, increasing hunger for truth." This may be what Eigen has come to say. He and his wayward patient, he and this everyman, are deeply moved by their intimacy. Each comes to appreciate the other, the work they have done together, and what each has come through in the process.

"In *Ecstasy*," Eigen (2001) writes, "I portray the psychoanalytic heart beating through a range of experiences significant for who we are; pleasures and pains—threatening to sink the soul—culminate in faith and openness" (p. vii). For me, Eigen's piece has the quality of a parable. Before he dies, the man with a taint discovers he is capable of "at-onement" and real intimacy. I read this piece as a teaching story, a story of reclamation, of a psychoanalytic heartbeat.

Exercise 4.1

Short Short Stories

Narratives come in different shapes and sizes. Even when you open an anthology of sudden fiction, flash fiction, or short short stories, you'll find as many variations as there are examples. The proliferation of names is just one sign of this subgenre's variety. Dybek (1986) notes that "the short prose piece so frequently inhabits a No-Man's Land between prose and poetry, narrative and lyric, story and fable, joke and meditation, fragment and whole, that one of its identifying characteristics has been its protean shapes" (p. 241). Eigen's piece serves as one model, but you could also write a short short as an "*étude*" (Targan, 1986, p. 248), a reverie, immediate scene, or scrap of experiencing.

a. One way to start the process of writing a short short story is to think of a kernel of interaction around which a story might grow and begin with that. Emphasize only one or two aspects of a short story, e.g., character, situation, surprise, a dollop of wisdom, the clash of emotions. Write no more than two pages.
b. In keeping with the protean shapes sudden fiction takes and the multiplicity of voices you and our patients bring to therapy, write *several* short short stories, each reflecting a different angle of vision on your clinical work. With several stories, imagine the effect building incrementally, expressing the moment-by-moment variety, intensity, and range of emotions. Your "portrayals," like Eigen's, "may be concerned with letting feeling storms speak, letting them have their say, seeing where they lead" (Eigen, 2005, p. 9).

Wary of Trespass

How might a psychotherapist—in this case a psychiatrist and psychoanalyst who had been teaching for forty years—narrate stories and write essays about his clinical work when he is exquisitely sensitive to psychological trespass? "I can walk on your land if I secure your permission and practice respect of its contents. These simple rules do not now obtain between minds," writes Leston Havens (1994) in the opening paragraph of *Learning to Be Human*. "The result is: Human beings are trespassed on, their spirits hurt or crushed, many oblivious. And the intruders go their way unchecked" (p. 7).

Havens' book is composed of paragraph-long reflections separated by mandalas, "so the reader will not be hurried nor a strong continuity expected or imposed.

I want reading this book to illustrate its message—to be treated humanly is to find a time and a space of one's own" (Havens, 1994, p. 4). As you read his third paragraph, imagine Havens talking about a certain kind of narrative voice as a drunk driver.

⁂

A physical analogue for psychological trespass is the drunk driver: someone of clouded perspective propelling a dangerous instrument. The most common psychological instances are convictions of rightness driving powerful opinions. Convictions of rightness denote a clouded perspective whenever those convictions address areas for which only opinion and uncertainty are appropriate. Such areas include almost all of what people say about each other. Powerful opinions are essentially conventional opinions—that is, views backed by strong traditions with large bodies of often frantic adherents. (Havens, 1994, p. 7)

Havens respects "subjective spaces and times," which provide protection against "acts of aggression which are personally directed, as when *I* tell *you*" (Havens, 1994, p. 8). Such aggressive acts may also be perpetrated on the page when the dynamics that Havens describes come into play in a narrator's tone or through doctrinaire adherence to a particular theory that devalues other approaches. Havens is a pluralist, who appreciates the contributions of different schools of psychiatry, because no individual school is all inclusive (Havens, 1987).

In the clinical encounter, the analyst may protect against acts of aggression, including "the innumerable traps we put out for the capture of others" (Havens, 1993, p. 64). In the story we are about to examine, Havens (1993) writes,

My own traps were typically bait for drawing conclusions, posing questions or enticements to reveal, the results of which might give me that precious sense of knowing who the patient really is, to counter the troubling confusion that any honest study of human nature always meets. I had to mind my own business, lest the compelling need to dispel suspense and identify the enemy make her a prisoner of my ideas. (p. 64)

For Havens (1993), the therapist's provision of safety is paramount. The goal is the patient's *"coming to life,"* by which he means "something that has had many names: the emergence of a real person, self-possession, psychological being, selfhood, soul" (p. 2).

In paragraphs five and six of *Learning to Be Human* (1994), Havens differentiates between transgression and respect for subjective space. I invite you to notice the quality of this writer's respectful, reflective consciousness, here in essay form. Later you will see how he weaves this sensitivity into his clinical narratives.

Notice too how he presents complex ideas simply. How would you characterize his voice?

✳

Psychological trespass is easiest to see with young people whose space is treated as a common ground into which I can push my ideas of what a person must be, thin, quiet, married, above all "nice."

✳

Or I can sense your individuality and your promise, hold it for a moment in my contact with you, treasure it. (Havens, 1994, p. 9)

By contrast, the energy of Eigen's short short story is taut, intense, compressed, mirroring his subject. As I read Eigen, I find it difficult to take a deep breath and I imagine him leaning forward, attuned to his patient's urgent intensities that pulse through his prose. I sense Havens sitting back, allowing his patient and readers to take their time while he pauses here and there to let them reflect. In writing about Havens' prose, I want my sentences to unfold as his do, extending themselves to reveal thought in process. If Eigen sprints, Havens ambles. Havens' language is simple, everyday. His syntax lays his ideas out, one after another, for his readers' consideration and use. He lets us in on his thinking as it appears to evolve phrase by phrase. Notice, for example in the previous two quotations, how a simple sequence—"thin, quiet, married, above all 'nice'"—provides elaboration as if ideas simply tumble out to move the sentence along. Havens, like Winnicott, eschews jargon. He employs humor and understatement and writes economically, creating potential space in which his readers can think for themselves. Havens' voice is conversational and respectful but can also rise up to defend the self.

His short story "Some Gestures" (quoted in part below) opens with a paragraph that has the feel of an essay but the economy, balance, and deftness of poetry. It moves into a clinical narrative while maintaining qualities of a personal essay throughout. Havens employs a reflective narrative voice that keeps the focus on the analyst's internal process, reminding me of Henry James's use of a center of consciousness, the mind through which the story is told. For James, "actions by themselves are generally of limited interest; they become interesting only when they are reflected in an engaged consciousness" (quoted in Miller, 1972, p. 234). Characters are of interest for James in proportion to what they feel: "This is the fact I have ever found rather terribly the point—that the figures in any picture, the agents in any drama, are interesting only in proportion as they feel their respective situations" (quoted in Miller, 1972, p. 235).

Havens' consciousness is fully engaged and finely attuned to all the nuances in the analytic setting. His patient is quiet, depressed, and suicidal. In the excerpt quoted below, notice how he reveals the play of his mind. His prose reflects different narrative moves from those that Rogers and Eigen make. What do you notice and what do you hear? Here's the first paragraph of "Some Gestures" (1993):

> If the self is elusive, the connection between selves is even more so. Sealed within our perspectives, we catch a glimpse of life and resolve to change our ways. The resolutions pile up, the careful lists and careless hopes, but little happens. Or, better, any change we experience simply happens, apart from the resolutions and hopes. Sometimes these changes seem the result of attitudes we take toward one another, often expressed in gestures and movements, such as the mixture of concern and irony I felt toward the woman with the chestnut hair. I believe it was this way with the quiet woman in the episode about to be recounted. (p. 59)

Havens begins with the conditional "if," trying his ideas out one way, then another. "Sometimes," "simply happens, apart from," and "seem" qualify the nature of events. "I believe" underscores the subjective nature of what can be known. The words *essay* and *assay* come from the same old French *essai*, meaning "an attempt or trial." Havens turns his thoughts over, offering them up, proposing a way we may "catch a glimpse of life" and attempt to make meaning. A quality of ease permeates his cadences, putting his readers at ease and conveying a sense that Havens is at ease himself.

Havens' second paragraph is all narrative:

> One day she awoke, went to work, and around noon remembered that all morning she had not wanted to die. She told me it was the only morning in memory that she had not wanted to die. I was as surprised as she was, for the opposite reason. She came upon hope, and I came upon her despair. (Havens, 1993, p. 59)

This passage is actually a narrative summary, concise but not rushed, poetic in its simplicity, and more complex than it first appears. Has the quiet woman come upon a change that "simply happens apart from the resolutions and hopes?" So it seems. One experience follows another. We have narrative sequence but not causality and then, in the last sentence, meaning, which is quite different for Havens and his patient. Did Havens' coming upon her despair surprise you? I was surprised despite his warning. I didn't expect that sentence to take the turn it did even though it made perfect sense once I shifted my perspective. The surprise I felt mirrors the surprise Havens and his patient each experience in their own way. While the sentences are simply constructed, they are able to convey and enact a process of discovery. Did you notice that only a slight separation exists between Havens as an experiencing self and a narrating self? Although he uses the past tense (there's the separation), we experience the story as it unfolds.

Here are his next two paragraphs:

> I didn't think I knew her at all until she made a gesture the third time we met. Until then I don't remember ever feeling more at sea. She said almost nothing, was polite and friendly, greeting and parting, didn't treat me so much as a piece of furniture as another piece of furniture, like herself. I in my sixties, she in her fifties, we sat around, like the chairs and tables, inclined a little this way or that, until the gesture.

> It came out very gradually, like the opening of a flower. At first I imagined it was one of those obscure greetings young people make to each other: passwords in a secret society. Then it seemed odd, the way some people smile at nothing in particular. Finally, I thought she was taking her time. She had sat for a while; perhaps now she was starting to look around. She never tried to socialize, to conventionalize our meetings. She just let them develop. It seemed I had passed whatever test she set for the safety of our relationship. I had let her alone. That might be why she made the gesture. (Havens, 1993, pp. 59–60)

Would you recognize these paragraphs as Havens' if you read them out of context? Can you see the same rhetorical patterns and quality of mind that you have seen before? Havens is an unassuming presence on the page and in his consulting room: modest, natural, plainspoken, genuine. He is willing to feel his way along as the clinical situation evolves. He is inclined to be what his patient needs him to be even if it is only another piece of furniture. He waits patiently, respecting his patient's timing. He notices her slightest inclination. Havens' analytic sensibility comes through his narrative voice. Both are gentle, respectful, reflective, perceptive, and exquisitely sensitive.

In the next paragraph, Havens addresses his readers directly. We learn more about how his respect for his patient translates into an unobtrusive response and how he sees his narrative and those of others as limited:

> The reader of these pages may already have been frustrated by a lack of defining details that round out a story or anchor it in some fact. Or you may have sensed these are not stories, with beginnings, middles, and ends, because all such stories must be imposed on lives about which a great many stories can be told. Nor are any facts final, except for some story chosen as the best one. This was true of the quiet woman. Previous therapists had told different stories about her, and new facts, including the fact of her creative imagination, were always coming to light. The point is that I did not want to impose a story or pick one out. I wanted to see if there was a useful attitude I could take in

the happier, slight deflection of a life that had its own momentum. (Havens, 1993, p. 60)

The simple elegance of Havens' narrative voice used in service of exposition is evident in the paragraph above as it is in the next one.

> I wanted to make our relationship work. The way it worked, or didn't work, would be the only reliable knowledge I could ever have about her. Everything else would be secondhand; even her reports about herself could only be partial, for we are all partly strangers to ourselves. From long experience I have concluded that making a relationship work can be carried out into the world to make life work for the individual so treated. Such a treatment is less a curing than a learning to live, and less a learning to live than the making of a few corrections to habitual movements in order to encourage purposes often already in place. It is like the treatment of the body—most of the body works well, but here and there something needs to be done. (Havens, 1993, pp. 60–61)

Havens does not use technical terms or employ the discourse of the paradigmatic. Doing so could feel like violations of his narrative sensibility. He makes other choices as well. He doesn't use dialogue, and we only get a few hints about what he or his patient says. The drama, if you could call it that, is not easily visualized. Very little is even described as happening.

Toward the end of his story, Havens (1993) writes, "So we too sat around together. A stranger looking on would wonder what we were doing. Not much was said; there were no revelations, unless the growing safety she felt can be called that" (p. 71). What is interesting, as Henry James would say, is what Havens feels, how he processes experience. Notice how he crafts his teaching story to let us see what can't be easily seen:

> Her gesture, my attitude. She had relaxed, turned her face more toward me, creating the merest impression that could have been a figment tossed up by my hoping imagination. So I did nothing, lest I presume. Then she spoke, or rather whispered. This tall, strong-faced person appeared suddenly smaller, hidden. She said she felt far away. Again I didn't make much of this because, if she felt far away, I may have been too close and responding quickly might put me closer. I wanted her to find a comfortable distance, a good space in which we could get along. (Havens, 1993, p. 61)

Havens often strips his prose of the connective tissue between words—"Her gesture, my attitude"—but he doesn't create the same kind of bare-bones effect that Eigen does as Eigen and his patient race against time. Havens, as suits his work with this patient, takes time to qualify what he says—"she spoke, or rather whispered"—and deepen a comment—"appeared suddenly smaller, hidden." He reveals his own process but doesn't encumber his reflections with theory. Notice how he describes and elaborates a subtle movement that may be felt but barely seen while introducing an analogy to writing:

> My first response was little more than a slight movement toward her, immediately checked by a fear of intruding. It reminded me of how I feel when I start to write. There is an eagerness to begin before anything specific has occurred to me. I reach fearfully. Then I draw back, knowing how futile this is, and I wait. I keep my general subject in mind, but I have to wait. If significant and natural words are to happen, they just have to come up from the countless impressions germinating inside. The response I await gathers from within and announces itself by being unexpected. Previous, partial movements will be flicked aside just because they are expected, because they are platitudes. But with the unexpected one must hurry to catch up. (Havens, 1993, p. 61)

When Havens follows his associations to explain his subtle movement toward his patient, his prose becomes more energized. There is much to say. Even the activity of waiting for words and ideas is heightened. The unexpected "announces itself." One must "hurry to catch up."

In the next paragraph, Havens brings us back to that "unexpected inner movement" and the feeling and insight it created. Our understanding deepens. Underneath his words, we now have another narrative of Havens' writing process to draw on for understanding what can't be seen:

> The unexpected inner movement created in me was a feeling of the patient's fragility; she was desperately in need of honor and protection, but the natural right to claim such things had quite disappeared from her mind. I felt she won't ask for anything; to demand is at the opposite end of her universe, and I can't demand for her because that is so remote. My gestures felt both toward her and away, honoring and shying all at once. It was a feeling of impossibility corresponding to the conflicting impulses that occurred to me. (Havens, 1993, p. 62)

As you will see in the paragraphs below, the more deeply Havens explores his sense of his patient's inner dynamics, the more animated and political his language becomes. I feel his energy surge. Quiet states, as you are discovering with Rogers and Havens, may be very effectively described, explored, and explained through analogous narratives of much more active, even fraught, states.

> To be rightless in a world where the concept of rights, if not the reality, is widely proclaimed, to be without free thought, much less free speech, in a world resonant with a cacophony of protesting voices—is that possible? Yes, because a vast space separates public rights and expression from the inner world that is so often silent and faceless. What is assumed, heralded, legalized, can vanish inwardly toward an unbending sovereignty in which every

thought and action is controlled. She had said she felt far away. I responded, if one can call my timid movement a response. But we were not engaged, barely present, groping in the dark.

Imagine living with a watchful tyrant who is not just nearby but within your own mental space, in fact occupying more of the space than you do, so that feeling far away means you have been pushed to the periphery of your own existence. Worse, you are awed and self-reproachful, to the point of identifying with and even revering the power. Many such powers are remorselessly critical, and as insiders they are privy to any protesting thought. The result is a level of control unimaginable in the most tyrannical police state.

How can the patient be freed? The answer lies in a similar vulnerability of the police state. Recently we have watched one such state after another collapse, states once thought invincible. Their vast, intrusive, torturing machinery began to fall away once they lost the faith of the people. Ironically, the strength of the tyrant was found to be in the tyrannized themselves, their belief and reverence. Let these erode, the power erodes.

So it is within. The quiet woman could be freed as soon as she lost her loyalty to the inner ruler, and she could do this by finding a new loyalty. Hence the importance of my attitude. I had to gain her trust; not her obedience, which would be a fresh tyranny, but her trust, something freely given, perhaps her first free act and tested bit by bit to the point of self-possession.

But how was I to be with her? (Havens, 1993, pp. 62–63)

How does Havens describe this state of being he needs to embody? With a story:

I remember a story a friend tells of a mother watching her child paint. The child says, "Don't look at me that way." "What way?" "As if you were proud of me." The pride in the mother's glance falls on the child like an act of possession: how can she be free to do what she wishes? Maybe she hates painting; in any case she would not want to have to paint. My trustworthiness, too, must be established through successive acts of liberation, as much from me as from the inner tyrant. . . . (Havens, 1993, p. 63)

We will leave Havens' story here, a third of the way into its fourteen pages. A summary of how it ends cannot do it justice, because the way Havens writes is integral to what he says.

Exercise 4.2

A Gesture, Attitude, Sensibility

a. To germinate ideas for this exercise, think of a patient's gesture, fleeting expression, or subtle affective shift that could easily be missed and describe it as Havens might.
b. Think about the Havensesque aspects of your clinical sensibility. In what ways, for example, are you wary of trespass? How might such a sensibility show up in a session and on the page? Write about an episode of your clinical work that reveals your Havensesque qualities.

5   The Evocative Mode

> . . . the associative process also sets the self into subsequent deep internal
> imaginings, that is, back into the visual-sensorial-affective orders, more charac-
> teristic of life in the maternal order. Emerging from such reveries into speech the
> analysand renews language with unconscious depth.
>
> Christopher Bollas, *The Mystery of Things*

In the evocative mode, meaning reverberates. Evocative language propels readers into memories, associations, affects, and self states, into their own "internal
imaginings" (Bollas, 1999, p. 183). These are among the soundings that may be
evoked by writing that stirs us, creating undercurrents and overtones as its vibra-
tions move through the resonant chambers of our body, mind, and heart. To evoke
means to call out or summon forth. Evocation works by invitation and suggestion
and was first associated with religious practices and magic spells, with conjuring
spirits whose powers could be solicited but not compelled (Bollas, 1987, p. 240).

Following in Freud's footsteps, Loewald (1980) writes of the magical power of
evocative language:

> When we think of the magical-evocational aspects of language, we are con-
> cerned with the *power* of words. We are dealing then with words, not insofar
> as they refer to or are linked with things, but as embodying and summoning
> things and experiences, as bringing them to life. The relation of reference or
> signification, from this perspective, is merely a pale reflection, a faint echo, a
> highly derivative form of that original power of words to conjure up things.
> (p. 220)

The evocative thrives on connotation and association and may reach as far
back as our earliest bonds. The etymological root of evoke is the Medieval Latin
vōx, voice. Incantations were chanted or sung; the Latin *incantare* means to sing
in or upon. In utero, the infant first experiences its mother's voice as vibration
and sound in a sensorial sea. Postpartum, language is undifferentiated in the
evocative infant-mother field that Loewald (1980) calls "a primordial density"
(p. 186). Before words become separate and semantic, language is tone, cadence,

intonation, and affect. Before language is distinguished as propositional, it is laid down as music with the mother's heartbeat and the sounds and rhythms of her body and its surround.

Evocative writers working in both poetry and prose often draw on what T. S. Eliot calls the auditory imagination—" 'the feeling for syllable and rhythm, penetrating far below the conscious levels of thought and feeling, invigorating every word; sinking to the most primitive and forgotten, returning to the origin and bringing something back', fusing 'the most ancient and the most civilized mentality' " (Eliot quoted in Heaney, 2002, p. 81). Heaney (2002) notes that the auditory imagination reaches into these primordial layers and other rich deposits—into "the cultural depth charges latent in certain words and rhythms. . . the energies beating in and between words that the poet brings into half-deliberate play;. . . the relationship between the word as pure vocable, as articulate noise, and the word as etymological occurrence, as symptom of human history, memory and attachments" (p. 81).

Language risks becoming impoverished, Loewald (1980) writes, when it moves too far from "experiential meaning" or is cut off from the wellsprings of the evocative, unconscious, and sensory richness of experience as primal density. Language is most powerful, Loewald (1980) believes, when it

> is an interweaving of primary and secondary process by virtue of which language functions as a transitional mode encompassing both. It ties together human beings and self and object world, and it binds abstract thought with the bodily concreteness and power of life. In the word primary and secondary process are reconciled. (pp. 203–204)

And no more so than in the incantational voice of the evocative mode.

Conjuring Evocative Object Worlds and Self Experience

Whether an evocative object is something outside the self that evokes (or transforms) an inner state or is something that arises from within, it has what Bollas (2009) calls "experience potential" to provide "textures of 'self experience'" (p. 87). Let's see how Sue Grand (2003) uses evocative objects to convey textures of self experience:

> When Rosa came to me, I felt I already knew her. Our memories were drawn from the same landscape. Postwar Brooklyn, the row houses of Brownsville. Stickball in the streets. Delicatessen floors covered with sawdust, barrels full with pickles floating in their own brine. Grocers selling homemade pasta. The smells of mandelbrot, hot bread, sweet cannoli. Prices were always negotiable for a well-told story. And in Brooklyn there were stories. In Russian and Polish and Yiddish. In Italian and broken-English. The streets were rich with gossip, with the exchange of food and solace and unwanted advice. Couples courted and quarreled and scolded their children. Children ran free in a new

world. Everything was loud and public and impassioned. Voices quieted by nightfall, erupting again as dawn struck the street.

Inside the row houses was a dimmer universe. There were yellowed pictures, silver candlesticks salvaged from the old country. Old things, sacred objects, heavy with grief. There were wall-to-wall carpets, furniture sealed in clear plastic, pristine rooms that could not be entered. To be impoverished and to labor, to acquire a home, and at last to buy furniture. To seal that furniture in plastic for all perpetuity: this was discipline and hope and fatigue and sadness. It was a mimicry of America and a reverence for America, a longing for assimilation and a dread of dislocation. Outside, on the street, children were simply children. But within these interiors, the full weight of history was fixed on their backs. Expansive bodies shrank in upon themselves. Children moved with caution and sobriety through dark hallways, through the narrow confines of parental memory. At every opportunity, they fled to the streets. In spring, in summer, in fall. Then winter came, and ice would descend on Brooklyn. Exuberance would be pressed into dim quarters. (pp. 313–314)

Enlisting the auditory imagination, Grand calls vivid scenes to life with sensory details, resonant images, and incantational lists. Her evocation of this Brooklyn neighborhood stirs my own internal imaginings, drawing me into Rosa's world while simultaneously pulling me back into the evocative object worlds in which I grew up. Grand's passage illuminates the multiple meanings of the phrase "the evocative object world" as Bollas uses it (1987, 2009) to describe relationships with significant others as well as with the environments in which we live and the things and ideas we use to express ourselves.

Did you happen to notice the contrast between Grand's first and second paragraphs? In addition to their thematic differences, the sentences in the second paragraph are more complex, introduce weightier ideas, shift cadences, articulate paradoxes, and express sadder, more intense affects foreshadowing what is to come. We could read these paragraphs and the next two as short short stories or prose poems—rich in their compression and carefully wrought. The form, cadence, and sequencing of Grand's sentences work like poetic elements that shape momentum, punctuate ideas, and create resonance.

As you read the next paragraph, I invite you to notice what words and sentences stand out for you and why.

When I met Rosa, I knew she was from Brooklyn. I recognized her by the way she told a story: straight shooting, quick witted, dark humored, and absurd. She would have us roaring with laughter while pain sat upon our chests. Impassioned by the truth and resolute in her intentions, she looked back into the past and forward into the future. She seized life amidst dark places; she retrieved knowledge from obscurity. She could change the endings before she had even finished telling her stories. She had that kind of discipline and mobility and courage. She suffered. But she always did the right thing. From the first, she looked me in the eye and registered me as human. There would always be something simple and warm and authentic between us, a basic human decency and a basic human trust. It would take her years to offer that kindness to herself. She hated her body. She was depressed. She was always alone. She was not really lonely but coveted her isolation. There was a dread of invasion, an exhaustion at the prospect of any intimate contact. (pp. 314–315)

Grand portrays her patient as a straight shooter who is quick on the draw. Her prose also moves rapidly. Her phrases are often balanced, and when their symmetry is altered, expectation is disturbed. The two shortest sentences, "She suffered" and "She was depressed," poignantly punctuate the longer ones. They bring me up short and I take notice. The sentence that immediately follows "She suffered" has more structural elements in it: "But she always did the right thing." The next sentence is even more grammatically complex: "From the first, she looked me in the eye and registered me as human." The next one extends itself even further, playing on different patterns of repetition: "There would always be something simple and warm and authentic between us, a basic human decency and a basic human trust."

Each of these sentences adds content, subtly builds in grammatically complexity, structures the paragraph, and uses cadence to heighten the effect of the revelation that comes in the next sentence: "It would take her years to offer that kindness to herself." This sentence stills me. Responding to the musicality of the whole sequence, I pause to take this sentence in and bear the weight of its pronouncement. What follows is pivotal: "She hated her body." This short sentence and the next two—"She was depressed. She was always alone."—strike my ear like hammer blows. The next two sentences spread out again, the last one farther than the one before, each piling on another consequence, another body blow to the traumas Rosa has already suffered.

When listening to how these sentences create effects in language, I am reminded of Ciardi's (1959) *How Does a Poem Mean?* How does the poem, he asks, perform itself? Evocative prose is pictorial, sensorial, and sometimes incantational. At the implicit level, where language is music before it is content, evocative prose may also enact and perform its meaning in its cadences, sounds, crescendos, hesitations, stuttering, and stops. When the experience that is conjured is about dissonance, deadness, and self-hatred, how might you expect Grand's sentences to flow?

In the next passage, Grand poignantly makes use of her portraits of Rosa's world to craft a paragraph that performs Rosa's disjunctive self:

She lived the changing seasons of Brownsville. Professional life was the summer street: at work, she was sharp and real and really herself. Bold and independent, confident, risk taking, she was hard driving and hard working, ethical and generous in her business encounters. There were "work friends." But evenings and weekends found her in a wintry row house. There was deadness and panic, and an episodic blankness that transpired without memory. A desire to drink, and a struggle to avoid drinking. And a body she never looked at or allowed to be seen. She despised her orifices, her curves, and the places she thought she lacked curves. To Rosa, her body was nothing but a conglomerate of deformities: small breasts, sagging belly, fat hips, legs, arms. Attractive, she moved with grace, but she could not feel herself moving. For me, there was an appealing quickness to her physicality; I thought her shape made interesting shifts between the angular and the round. I was arrested by the immediacy of her eyes. Face, body, mind: I responded to her as an evocative whole. But, to Rosa, her body was in pieces, loosely linked fragments united by blunt hatred. She ate compulsively and vomited; she gained and lost weight. She joked about aspiring to anorexia. (p. 315)

To my ear, the cadences of the first two sentences in this paragraph, those in the middle, and the last three are direct, energetic, balanced, and easy on the ear. But these qualities are not sustained. The third sentence sputters: "Bold and independent, confident, risk taking, she was hard driving and hard working, ethical and generous in her business encounters." The sentence that follows—"There were 'work friends.' "—seems to hang in midair. After that, the cadences return to balanced rhythms only to be altered again, slipping into ordinary prose before resuming the more even rhythms of the final three sentences.

I. A. Richards "called rhythm a 'texture of expectations, satisfactions, disappointments, surprisals, which the sequence of syllables brings about' " (Richards quoted in Alvarez, 2005, p. 53). Whether Grand's sputtering segments are intentional or not, her paragraph effectively enacts the disturbances it describes. Continuity and balance cannot be maintained. At the beginning of her analysis, Rosa does not experience herself as "an evocative whole."

A More Personal Evocation

In *The Hero in the Mirror: From Fear to Fortitude*, Grand (2010) employs a much more conversational voice to evoke the same Brownsville immigrant world. While her autobiographical "stories involve fictionalized identities and events" (p. 11), she nevertheless captures the emotional and cultural truths of growing up in the fifties and sixties, the granddaughter of Russian Jewish immigrants.

In my family, stories were always losing their beginnings and endings. If you ever got to the middle, suddenly, the details would change. This left my family untroubled; they scoffed at anyone who was too preoccupied with the facts. If you listened long enough, you might emerge with some approximation of the "truth." They would have made excellent critical theorists and terrible accountants. Commentary, context, interpretation, and elaboration: These were the important features of a story. Sometimes I thought they were writing their own Talmud. Or an epic novel with subplots. Wherever a story took off, it inevitably went somewhere else. What mattered was political, historical, cultural, and familial coloration. Nothing could be understood without reference to something else. With this Russian Jewish family, there was *always* something else. If you asked a question, there were passionate responses, but there was never a simple answer. Whatever question you thought you were asking, it led back to the complexities of courage.

God forbid you asked for directions. They were immigrants, and they were preoccupied with departure and arrival. If you asked how to get to somewhere in Brooklyn, 5 relatives gave you 10 routes, and every landmark digressed into familial details. You turned left where Great Aunt Tessie once lived, with her first husband. No, someone would say, she lived there after he died. He didn't die, someone would claim, it's a scandal, he left her for someone else, and she had three children. "No, she didn't, one of them was a niece that she took in. Remember Tessie's sister, she died, it must have been cancer. So Tessie took little Esther in." "Well, she wasn't too bright, Tessie, she should have known he was a womanizer." Eventually, the digression would return to the problem at hand. By now, they needed a reminder: *Where are you trying to get to?* Well, if you're driving through Flatbush, you probably should turn right. If you turned right, you encountered Great Uncle Max, and you heard about the early twentieth century in Russia: pogroms, conscription, emigration to America. When I looked at Uncle Max, I saw a shriveled little man who spoke broken English. Apparently, he was young once, and he walked across Russia and made it to America. "No, he didn't." "Tell her, Max." "Well," he would say, "not exactly. . . " but he never got to finish. There was a stage whisper from the kitchen, "*Ach.* It's a *bubbameiseh.*"* (p. 11)

---

* An old wives' tale.

Grand's affectionate portrait of her family is seasoned with humor. Her voice is casual and immediate; her depiction, detailed and interpretive. It is easy to imagine such a scene and look in as through a window into a culture. If you write about the evocative object world in which you grew up, are you likely to adopt a more literary voice like Grand's first example or a more informal one like her second? You might want to give both a try in the exercises that follow.

Exercise 5.1

Conjuring Your Evocative Object World

a. Take a few moments to imagine the neighborhood(s) in which you grew up, your childhood home(s), or that of your grandparents.
b. Pick one or two of these settings and conjure a world of self experiencing, writing several short evocative paragraphs that are rich in vivid, sensory details.

Exercise 5.2

Conjuring Your Patient's Evocative Object World

Register in your mind's eye and your auditory imagination the evocative object world(s) of one of your patients. Pick one or two settings from his or her childhood, young adulthood, or later life and conjure up that world (or worlds) of experiencing by writing several short evocative paragraphs full of sensory-rich detail.

Textures of Experiencing

Sharon Manning evokes place and family in this writing exercise:

My Father Is a River

> For years I have dreamed of rivers. Walking along them, in them, through them. Sometimes flooded and sometimes empty and littered with artifacts. I am looking for something. Something important, but small enough to carry with me in my pocket.
>
> In one such dream, a man I loved stood with me on the banks of the Charles River at the place where Abbott Street ends. I tell him, "I grew up here. I played here as a child. This land was formed by this river. Deposits of clay along the banks cause some basements to flood. You must always check before you lay your foundations. This river is called the Charles. My father's name is Charles, and his father, my grandfather, is also named Charles. I come from this River. My father is a river. This is what you need to know." (Manning, Writing Exercise, 2013)

Exercise 5.3

Textures of Experiencing

a. Write a paragraph or two to evoke textures of experiencing, including dreams and reveries. Let Manning be your guide.
b. Try writing the same kind of piece from the perspective of one of your patients.

A Modern Incantation

In a passage Mitchell (2000) cites as exemplifying "the magical-evocational" power of words that Loewald describes, Loewald (1980) calls up the body's instinctual life via incantation. What do you notice about how he does it?

Triebe, instincts, were—much more than scientists, doctors, ministers, judges ("the educated circles") wanted to admit or know—what made the human world go around, what drove people to act and think and feel the way they do, in excess as well as in self-constriction, inhibition, and fear, in their daily lives in the family and with others, and in their civilized and professional occupations and preoccupations as well. They dominated their love life and influenced their behavior with children and authorities. They made people sick and made them mad. They drove people to perversion and crimes, made them into hypocrites and liars as well as into fanatics for truth and other virtues, or into prissy, bigoted, prejudiced, or anxious creatures. And their sexual needs, preoccupations, and inhibitions turned out to be at the root of much of all of this. Rational, civilized, measured, "good" behavior, the noble and kind deeds and thoughts and feelings so highly valued were much of the time postures and gestures, self-denials, rationalizations, distortions and hideouts—a thin surface mask covering and embellishing the true life and the real power of the instincts.

The life of the body, of bodily needs and habits and functions, kisses and sensations, caresses and punishments, tics and gait and movements, facial expression, the penis and the vagina and the tongue and arms and hands and feet and legs and hair, pain and pleasure, physical excitement and lassitude, violence and bliss—all this is the body in the context of human life. (Loewald, 1980, p. 125)

In their proliferation of words and phrases, Loewald's sentences enact the unceasing flow of instincts. Even the word *instincts* is presented in two languages, and the collective noun *educated circles* by itself wouldn't do. Four iterations are produced instead. Loewald's first sentence ends with a surfeit of phrases that branch out in seemingly unstoppable subordinated constructions, enacting the constant pulse of instincts coursing through us. The structure of the first paragraph's last sentence works the same way. I read Loewald's iterative structure as a version of the incantational. His second paragraph is more obviously incantatory as he calls forth the body's life noun by noun. By the time you arrive at the last sentence, the assertion he makes about the influence of the body's instinctual life is remarkably persuasive even though an argument has never been made.

Michael Eigen's Incantatory Voice

Eigen is a master of the contemporary incantational voice in psychoanalytic prose, which he often uses to evoke multiplicity, possibility, and the associative richness of a word or idea. In the opening paragraphs of *Emotional Storm* (2005), he evocatively elaborates his title metaphor:

Emotional storm—a highly charged expression with many meanings and dimensions. A colorful term, mixing dark, light, danger, thrill, richness.

Stormy night, stormy feelings. If there are such things as primal words, words that unify opposites, slide through contrasting realities, 'storm' must be one of them.

Many years ago, I was taught that mind uses properties of physical things to express itself, its states, its feelings: first, perception of the outside world, then emotional use of what is perceived. One experiences a physical storm, then uses storm to express feelings: first outer, then inner. As if inner is some kind of analogical tail.

But what if psychic storms come first or howling storms of infancy do not distinguish between soma and emotion? The baby has a bad feeling and kicks or waves, trembles with fear, fury, tightening in the face of pain. The baby screams, a scream one feels. It pierces, rushes through one, strikes a direct hit. Most adults respond with care, but some respond with rage and try to close their ears and hide until the screaming stops. One way or another, disturbance is passed along and demands attention. Such screaming storms. I believe the scream of infancy never stops. It is part of our beings all life long. We never stop hearing, if only in whispers, a screaming self. A storm with infinite faces. (Eigen, 2005, p. 1)

Eigen's sentences are a play in contrasts. The first three lack the subject-verb-object structure—"the essential chunk of syntax" that Voigt (2009) calls "the fundamental" (p. 10). Meaning is concentrated by dropping words out and turning sentences into verbal equations. Meaning is also expanded through multiple descriptors that suggest the iterative nature of experience and knowing. Eigen does not write "an emotional storm is" but instead uses two predicate nominative phrases—"highly charged expression" and "a colorful term"—without a linking verb. Not one but five contrasting qualities—"dark, light, danger, thrill, richness"—characterize environmental and emotional storms.

Employing the logic of metaphor, Eigen borrows what we know about one kind of storm to describe another, but he doesn't spell these relationships out. He evokes them instead by incanting "stormy night, stormy feelings." In contrast, the last sentence of this paragraph has a full complement of grammatical parts and lays out the logic of his thinking more incrementally. The meaning of primal words is also elaborated in the doubling of descriptors—"words that unify opposites, slide through contrasting realities"—to suggest that complex shadings of experience cannot be adequately contained in a single phrase.

Before I move on to Eigen's third paragraph, can you identify the patterns of iteration, elaboration, compression, and contrast in his second paragraph?

In his third paragraph, Eigen turns around the order he has established ("first outer, then inner") and responds to the question "what if?" with a narrative sequence. Once again verbs, adjectives, and descriptive phrases abound to elaborate meaning and enact the unfolding nature of the meaning-making process and the bounty and diversity of life. By the time Eigen writes "a storm with infinite faces," its incantational force carries with it a "spectrum of meanings" (Eigen, 2009, p. 2) that Eigen has summoned up.

Exercise 5.4

Contemporary Incantations

a. Pick a subject that lends itself to the exercise of your incantational voice and write several paragraphs that demonstrate the power of words to summons things. Let Grand, Loewald, and Eigen be your guides.

b. If a subject does not readily come to mind, you might improvise one from the evocative titles of some of Eigen's books: *Damaged Bonds; Psychic Deadness; Toxic Nourishment; The Sensitive Self; Rage; The Psychotic Core; Lust; Feeling Matters; Emotional Storm; Ecstasy*; and *The Psychoanalytic Mystic.*

Evocative Terms

Evocative terms like D. W. Winnicott's *potential space*, Christopher Bollas' *unthought known*, Donnel Stern's *unformulated experience*, and Barbara Pizer's *relational (k)not* are metaphors that extend meaning by bridging from the known to the new. Evocative terms stir our associations and contain clusters of ideas that make up the concepts they name. Like poems, evocative terms may be difficult to translate, which is part of their appeal. They are themselves potential spaces in which meaning is realized in an interactive process of engagement with their originator's ideas, clinical examples, and our own elaborations. While the denotation of an evocative term may be expressed fairly concisely, something may be lost in translation. Connotation exceeds denotation. The metaphoric nature of an evocative term may help it elude reification and makes the concept's complexity more explicit, reminding us that its meaning is not to be too narrowly confined.

As suggestive as they are, the metaphors that inform evocative terms do not supply enough explanatory power by themselves. That comes with the work you do with them. You need to define evocative terms, differentiate them from other terms and concepts when necessary, and show your readers how they work. In the abstract to her paper "When the Crunch is a (K)not, A Crimp in Relational Dialogue," Barbara Pizer (2003) describes her evocative term concisely (it can be done) as a point of departure, not a final destination:

> . . . a relational (k)not negates truly intersubjective dialogue by shutting down the spaces, between and within persons, for mentalization, reflective functioning, genuine affect, and negotiation.
>
> In treatment, relational (k)nots appear as repetitions that—unlike Russell's "crunch," with its intensities of crisis—coerce states of noninvolvement between patient and analyst. Persistent relational notting produces a crisis of mutual *detachment.* (p. 171)

Over the course of her paper, Pizer introduces Russell's (2006/1975) concept of a crunch and distinguishes it from her concept of a relational (k)not. She presents her theory of how relational (k)nots develop; elaborates her definition; cites Laing; and presents four brief examples and one extended clinical example to explicate the meaning of her new concept. If you read her paper, you will see how she focuses on different facets of relational (k)notting in each example, developing her concept incrementally over the course of her entire paper (see also my pp. 190–193).

The Resonance of History

Some terms, like Freud's repetition compulsion, may be evocative because of their history and import while others, like Bollas' unthought known, may be evocative because they surprise and delight us with their originality. One person's historically resonant term may be another person's jargon, a drag on contemporary prose. I have never been fond of the word cathexis and doubt that I would use it except in reference to its historical context, but I would hate to retire a word like countertransference even though our views of the phenomenon have changed. Using the word countertransference with new meaning allows me to stay connected to its history even as I push beyond the confines of earlier definitions. When you use a term that has spanned the years, crossed disciplines, or found its way into different analytic conversations, it will be crucial for you to clarify its meaning, distinguishing it from other applications (pp. 184–188).

Exercise 5.5

Evocative Terms

a. Make a list of evocative terms. Book titles are a great source.
b. Create a list of concepts that would be well served by having a more evocative name and propose one.
c. As you go through your day, jot down ideas for evocative concepts and give them evocative names. Just having that intention may heighten your awareness and stimulate your creativity.
d. Take any one of the evocative concepts you have identified and illustrate what it means by presenting an immediate scene that also gives your readers access to your internal experience. You will find several examples in Pizer's (2003) paper "When the Crunch Is a (K)not."

---

6   The Enactive Mode

I cannot have as much confidence in my ability to tell the reader what has hap-
pened as I have in my ability to do something to the reader that I have had done to
me. I have had an emotional experience; I feel confident in my ability to recreate
that emotional experience, but not to represent it.

Wilfred Bion, *Cogitations*

We meet the enactive mode in the sonorous words we call onomatopoeias, such as
sizzle, buzz, thud, and whack, which enact or perform their meaning in the sounds
they make. Think of Russell's (2006/1975) crunch and Pizer's (2003) relational
(k)not. Poet Mary Oliver (1994) notes that "words have not only a definition and
possibly a connotation, but also the *felt* quality of their own kind of sound" (p. 22).
She asks us to consider the difference between rock and stone:

> Both use the vowel *o* (short in *rock*, long in *stone*), both words are of one syl-
> lable, and the similarity ends. *Stone* has a mute near the beginning of
> the word that then is softened by a vowel. *Rock* ends with the mute *k*. That *k*
> "suddenly stops the breath." There is a seed of silence at the edge of the sound.
> Brief though it is, it is definite, and cannot be denied, and it feels very different
> from the—*one* ending of *stone*. In my mind's eye I see the weather-softened
> roundness of stone, the juts and angled edges of rock. (p. 24)

Meaning is also enacted in the music that sequences of words make. A sentence,
Frost (1995) proposes, is "a sound in itself on which other sounds called words may
be strung" (p. 675). Gass (2009/1996) takes us on an amazing ride in a single-sentence
paragraph in which he describes and performs "the music of prose":

> For prose has a pace; it is dotted with stops and pauses, frequent rests; inflec-
> tions rise and fall like a low range of hills; certain tones are prolonged; there
> are patterns of stress and harmonious measures; there is a proper method
> of pronunciation, even if it is rarely observed; alliteration will trouble the
> tongue, consonance ease its sounds out, so that any mouth making that music
> will feel its performance even to the back of the teeth and to the glottal's

stop; mellifluousness is not impossible, and harshness is easy; drum roll and clangor can be confidently called for—lisp, slur, and growl; so there will be a syllabic beat in imitation of the heart, while rhyme will recall a word we passed perhaps too indifferently; vowels will open and consonants close like blooming plants; repetitive schemes will act as refrains, and there will be phrases—little motifs—to return to, like the tonic; clauses will be balanced by other clauses the way a waiter carries trays; parallel lines will neverthe-less meet in their common subject; clots of concepts will dissolve and then recombine, so we shall find endless variations on the same theme; a central idea, along with its many modifications, like soloist and chorus, will take their turns until, suddenly, all sing at once the same sound. (p. 314)

Your sentences don't have to be as "exuberantly baroque" (Kirsch, 2012, p. 13) as Gass' to enact their meaning. Although sentences, for Gass, are "the basic building blocks of prose," "the show words put on," and "an occasion for a new display of virtuosity," as Kirsch (2012) observes, "sometimes fireworks are called for, sometimes a match" (p. 13).

Do you remember the third paragraph of Eigen's excerpt that I characterized as a psychoanalytic heartbeat (pp. 32–35)? The sensuous properties of his shorter sentences simulate the accelerated pulse of an analysis racing against the clock. Likewise, the aural qualities of Grand's prose enact Rosa's disjunctive self (my pp. 46–49) while the structure and quiet cadences of Havens' sentences in the first para-graph of *A Safe Place* (1996) enact the feeling of being safely held (my pp. 99–100). Written in a colloquial voice, the opening paragraphs of Barbara Pizer's (2007) lyric narrative "Maintaining Analytic Liveliness" enact the analyst's experience of noticing and forgetting what Aaren tells her about the spelling of his name (my pp. 87–89). These writers do not set off fireworks for the enactive potential of their prose "to do something to the reader" that was done to them (Bion, 1992b, p. 219).

Writing in the enactive mode does more than invite, suggest, or call on the reader's imagination as evocative prose does. It often scoops us up and carries us along. Sometimes it compels engagement up close and experiential. Like poetry, enactive prose "is inseparable from its performance of itself" (Ciardi, 1959, p. 668). Writing in the enactive mode catches readers up in *living an experience* even before it is thought (Piaget in Bruner et al., 1967, p. 17). The enactive mode is one of the ways we learn from experience. Infants take the world in by mouth-ing and grasping. The enactive mode, which is our first mode of representation, lays the foundation for procedural knowledge and is followed developmentally but is not eclipsed by the iconic and symbolic modes (Bruner, 1966).

Enacting Trauma

Paul Williams' (2013) *Scum* is a striking example of writing in the enactive mode that catches readers up in experiencing the mind-shattering effects of trauma:

Summer came went as it does what was left of it spent in The Woods no lon-ger alone boys turned up some to play others to shoot sparrows blue tits heat frogs in milk bottles until they swelled up and burst scanned them all talked to no-one hid in bushes avoid the ones who killed the animals protest against cruelty rose in his throat finding no voice turned away feelings squashed. Hated a small refined cat the woman called mother bought dismissed it tormented frightened it it hated back didn't feel like a sick dance he did to it what she did to him what boys did to animals what he did to himself.

Birthday eleven unnoticed grammar school signaled the end of The Woods eight years refuge no sadness dampness settled into him as if left out in the rain though the summer sun still shone couldn't move didn't want to sit for long periods cast down less vigilant not noticing not caring. A ghost can prevent detection but the energy to keep the security camera running ran out paid the price.

"Gerrout yer fuckin' l'il wanker."

Animal killers kicked beat drove him out of The Woods requiring he check before entering something not done before retraced at dawn trails hideouts before the summer melted the main pond the fallen log dugout Europe South American darkest Asia China bulrush pond ditch imprinted branded on his body if he could pacing back forth touch each in turn. The most intense memories save the violence are of The Woods colours textures smells heat cold sunshine stillness dignity of ancient trees alive in him today groups of tall peaceful adults not complaining of comings and goings creaking their familiar welcome standing by him whispering contentment with any game, any time, including when tired eyes closed their rustling goodbye never harsh a reminder they would be there waiting. Things went wrong in The Woods but not enough to destroy the tie not even at the final goodbye he had to leave they knew. (pp. 1–2)

In *Scum*, "the life of the boy and the life of the sentences" are inextricable (Ogden quoted in Williams, 2013, back cover). That's how enactive writing works. *Scum* is difficult to read, understand, and bear, because it enacts the fragmenting effects of experiencing the incomprehensible and unbearable. Trauma disrupts, disorients, fractures. Grammar does not hold. "Thinking flounders, language does not stick, emotion becomes an arch enemy" (Williams, 2013, p. vii).

I discovered *Scum* was easier to understand when I inserted line breaks within sentences and paused briefly after each. See if your experience of reading and your ability to make sense of things change when you pause after each slash:

Summer came/ went/ as it does/ what was left of it spent in The Woods/ no longer alone/ boys turned up/ some to play/ others to shoot sparrows blue tits/ heat frogs in milk bottles until they swelled up and burst/ scanned them all/ talked to no-one/ hid in bushes/ avoid the ones who killed the animals/ protest against cruelty rose in his throat/ finding no voice/ turned away feelings/ squashed. Hated a small refined cat the woman called mother bought/ dismissed it/ tormented frightened it/ it hated back/ didn't feel like a sick dance/ he did to it what she did to him/ what boys did to animals/ what he did to himself./

Birthday eleven unnoticed/ grammar school signaled the end of The Woods/ eight years refuge/ no sadness/ dampness settled into him as if left out in the rain though the summer sun still shone/ couldn't move/ didn't want to sit for long periods/ cast down/ less vigilant/ not noticing/ not caring./ A ghost can prevent detection but the energy to keep the security camera running ran out/ paid the price. (pp. 1–2; slashes added)

In Williams' enactive prose, I catch only rare glimpses of narrative coherence. Sentences that are organized in complete clauses are all the more poignant by virtue of their being scarce. I find only three in the paragraph above.

In *The Fifth Principle* (2010), Williams writes about the first eight years of his life and his mind's "efforts to prevail in oppressive circumstances" (p. 9). But "the mind in question, insofar as it resembles other minds, will speak to the reader in ways that are recognizable, though some of the things that are written about may be unfamiliar" (Williams, 2010, p. 9). As you will see, the forms of Williams' sentences in *The Fifth Principle* are no less moving for being written in grammatically familiar patterns of the narrative mode:

> Ghosts are meant to be invisible. I became a ghost because everything I said or did was wrong, and I could not bear the shame of it. No retreat was far enough. I was made of the same stuff as my mother and father. They hated themselves, each other, their children and their lives, so it was inevitable that I would feel that there wasn't a shred of goodness in me for others to recognize. I needed to conceal the disgrace that I had failed as a child. My shame could not be exposed under any circumstance. When a fox is run to ground, to be dug out by beaters' spades in order to let the hounds in, it is a fate beyond contemplation. (Williams, 2010, p. 55)

Williams' narrative is retrospective: His narrating self looks back on his younger, experiencing self. They are separated not only by years but also by the development of his mind. The closing image is excruciatingly painful and hard to escape, yet it works as evocative rather than enactive prose. The reader's empathy and imagination transform the words and image on the page to produce their powerful effects; the words themselves do not create an experience to be lived in the kinesthetics of a voiced reading as they do in the enactive mode.

In a Patient's Mind

In the enactive opening of "Mental Interference," Bollas (1999) replicates the thought patterns of an obsessional patient:

> Helmut lies in bed. It is eight-thirty in the morning and although he has slept at times throughout the night, his mind has been racing. It is hard to remember

what exactly he had been thinking about. He could recall pondering a conversation with his brother who had told him with earnest affection that he should start up in business as an ice cream vendor. He had replayed this conversation many times. He had imagined applying for a license, looking for a van, reading up on the production which should be so simple, but well. . . he just did not know. He could see his elder brother's love and exasperation, a face that haunted him. But where would he go to find a van? Where do they make them? What would his friends think of him sitting in the van? Perhaps he should hire somebody to do that side of the business. . . . He found himself thinking of the colours of the van. White with a blue line around it? Blue with a white line? Did that fit in with the customer's association with ice cream? Maybe it would be red with white lettering. What should it say? What would he call the ice cream company? Helmut's Ices? The Flavour Van? The Ice Cream Van?

What would people think? He imagined countless types of people all responding differently to the name. Increasingly exhausted by these considerations, he thought to himself that maybe the ice cream business was not for him. What did he know about it? Nothing. Nothing at all. . . .

The night wore on. (pp. 88–89)

Exercise 6.1
In a Patient's Mind

a. Following Bollas' lead and writing in the enactive mode, take your readers into the mind of one of your patients.
b. Bollas uses the third person pronoun *he*. You may want to try this exercise by writing it once with a third-person pronoun and again using the first person *I*, writing in your patient's voice.

In the Analyst's Mind

The quality of Havens' respect for his patients, the analytic process, and his readers is enacted in the way he writes "Some Gestures" (my pp. 37–42). As you may remember, his voice and analytic sensibility are both soft spoken, reflective, and exquisitely sensitive. His sentences unfold graciously, showing us how his unhurried mind considers this and that and giving us space to do so ourselves. He avoids jargon, addresses his readers directly, and offers ideas as thoughtful comments rather than revered theory: "Or you may have sensed that these are not stories, with beginnings, middles, and ends, because all such stories must be imposed on lives about which a great many stories can be told" (Havens, 1993, p. 60).

Barbara Pizer's (2005b) prose also enacts her state of mind when she experiences the turmoil of Julian's anger as they are caught up in an enactment (my pp. 3–5).

In the session after she lends him one of her papers, he tells her he thought her "being a person crossed the line" (Pizer, 2005b, p. 27). She instantly remembers wriggling under a fence into forbidden territory at her grandmother's farm and getting stung unmercifully by yellow jackets. The childhood trauma she recreates on the page not only reveals her immediate associations but also enacts the surprise attack and stinging shame of the clinical moment as Julian aims his transference-biting accusations at her. That's what makes this passage enactive. Her childhood experience enacts her helpless, wordless terror she can show us but can't show Julian while under his relentless attack. By interpolating segments of the earlier drama with those of the present moment, each narrative plays off the affective intensity of the other, heightens suspense, and reveals what can't otherwise be seen.

Writing Silence, Enacting Chaos

In a daring experimental manuscript that enacts the disorienting experience of the analysis of a silent patient, Jade McGleughlin (2001) pulls readers into their shared chaos, asking her readers to "listen as if in a dream" (prologue, a later version). Echoing Bion (1992b), McGleughlin writes about the difficulty of representing this analysis:

> I cannot simply describe the disorientation I experience as Sarah's analyst. I cannot represent what felt like a necessary undoing, my sinking into a passionate world in which nothing I knew about myself, about myself in relation, about my self as an analyst held true. But I can try to recapture it. . . . Drift with me as I did, untethered and unmoored. Both Sarah and I start to emerge somewhere in the middle of these words. This treatment is—no, was—a kind of ongoing hysteria. Not just Sarah's, mine. I think a kind of madness was required. (prologue, a later version)

McGleughlin begins the first section, "Version I, September," with a narrative summary. Notice how she subtly shifts verb tenses and brings her experience alive:

> My patient Sarah and I have just reached the other side of a terrible impasse that has threatened to destroy the analysis. Spring and summer have been marked by profound silence, unendurable pain and constant chaos. Sarah has felt that it is too painful to come to sessions, sometimes too painful to speak by phone. Each day threatens to be the last day. The analysis is under constant assault. There is only enactment.
>
> My summer vacation has brought some reprieve and needed space for both of us. We speak once a week by phone and each conversation slowly restores some equanimity. A chance encounter during my vacation reminds Sarah of the pleasure of my company. She comes back into the office in September after months of physical absence or psychic retreat and we are both giddy with the pleasure of each other's company.

This is why I am giddy. To feel a small window open, to be standing with her in that frame. . . .

This new feeling of our pleasure makes her ill. She is literally sick. Being in my presence makes her tense, sometimes in actual pain between her ribs. It's a sharp specific pain in her back. She can't breathe when she has it. She is breathless. When she leaves my office, she can get sick; nausea, diarrhea, explosive expulsion. . . .

I think of Dora and what cannot be spoken between us. A hysterical symptom. A conversion. She cannot know about her desire. Or her destruction. She has no place to house it. No way to know about the feelings between us, no way to tolerate them in a linguistic or affective register. (pp. 2–3)

Linear time organizes this opening sequence and loosely organizes each of the paper's three main sections, but it's an order that cannot hold. McGleughlin tells their story not once but three times. Her text is a fluid mix of narrative, poetry, fantasy, associations, countertransference feelings, bits of self-analysis, reflection, dialogues with theory, and dreams. We never hear the voice of this silent patient. Instead, we are left to experience what runs through the analyst's mind and our own:

My mind wanders. My mother has noticed my effort toward her and rumples my hair. (This never happened.) Maybe if I can catch her attention just long enough . . .

I can't help my mother, I know that, but I will die trying. This dogged misplaced persistence, my own failure to mourn, is what I am up against in myself. It has allowed this work to go on, and I am sure (am I sure?) it stops it.

Omnipotence. It's the curative fantasy.[1] I can make her better.

Heroic rescue some might say. I am not so sure. I think of the conditions for loving.

I spin tops, I shoot marbles, I slay dragons, I steer boats clear of lobster pots.

Oh, I know how to stop on roller skates, to be at the bottom of hills, the end of movies, or scripts, the line between where I take off and the close of your eyelid, the slowing of your grin.

For a brief moment we have lived in perfect pitch. In wonderment, our senses opened, the world pulsing with life. . . .

And then it's over. Thud. (pp. 4–5)

---

[1] [A.] Ornstein's idea of the curative fantasy.

McGleughlin's way of writing enacts her mind's roving movements and fluid associations. The music of her prose tells a story. Lyrical moments end with a thud. We don't know what will come next, because McGleughlin doesn't pretend to. The music of McGleughlin's prose is broken and edgy. Fragments, bits, borrowings, confusions enact what does not cohere. Even footnotes are incomplete. The text is still in process, like the analysis, one among many drafts, rough, intense, full of incongruities, gaps, questions.

McGleughlin ends "Version 1 (Again), September, 2001" with these reflections on her writing process:

> And when my text is barely coherent, in fragments, nonlinear, I have meant for you to wonder who is subject, who object, who patient, whose pain. These are some of the analytic questions informing this piece, this treatment. The writing disrupts the notion of the patient as the object of inquiry and the analyst as knowing subject. (p. 17)

In "Version 3," the reader can discern more details of Sarah's history and analysis but will experience little relief from "the analyst's necessary vertigo" (McGleughlin, 2011). Despite the writer's use of the past tense, time is not well delineated. Although analytic separations and reunions are marked, the narrative is cyclical, evoking the timelessness of primary process. What kind of music do you hear?

> We would wear each other tight against our chests, seeping into each other, in pieces broken up in one, then the other. This is what it felt like. She'd die. She insists on our separateness. *Up against that dry barren harsh geography of near death. Pieces and parts. Her missing. My mess. How I followed the disappeared. How I followed her following her disappeared. Did I lead? I have my own "dead mother."* [2]

> Followed found entered became that split-off part of the self that desperately needs understanding but is not available because she has/I have located it in the other and it is years before she will/I will get here. [3]

> I had imagined the paper would begin more like this.

> I first met Sarah inside my living room on my couch. She had come into the wrong part of my house. My office occupies my first floor and my house the second and third. I had given the usual directions. Many years. No mistakes. Deep blue door on the right. Door's open. Enter right into the waiting room. Sit down. I'll come get you.

---

[2] Green, The Dead Mother
[3] Betty Joseph's concept In The Difficult To Reach Patient

And I had left the other door on the left unlocked. Up a flight of stairs into a cathedral ceiling room deep colored, hundred photographs lining every mantel and shelf, my partner and I, the children, our family and friends, toys strewn about, books, colors, dramatic art. Beauty and chaos, some order, lots of life.

When I found her, she sat across the room under the sharp-eyed stare of my two Birman kitty cats facing her down across the living room. Haughty, possessive, suspicious. Sumptuous, voluptuous, beautiful. Inviting and refusing closeness and touch. She was sitting very still. Sweat pouring from her. Rivulets, small rivers.[4] (Why have I gone on about the dryness?)

Travelers at least have a choice. Those who set sail know that things will not be the same as at home. Explorers are prepared. But for us, who travel along the blood vessels, who come to cities of the interior by chance, there is no preparation.[5]

She was sweating. Overwhelmed shocked. She told me right off, I am a stranger in a strange land. *Passion is not so much an emotion as a destiny.*[6]

This is how we began. My heart was pounding. I swept my eyes over what she would see. I tried to imagine how she would see it. And I felt her terror enter me. How I would feel I had invaded her, taken her over, shocked her into frozen wordless dread.

I didn't feel just then intruded on. I noted that but it didn't seem important. It wasn't how I felt. Only how she was inside me from the start. And how that scared her. How I had to protect her from that knowing. And how that fails us. Whom do I protect? But *I* know the meaning of a house. I've read Freud. She was inside my whole being, my body, my heart pushing her in and out. Pounding surf, unsteady shoreline. Fragile dune.

Oh, she would hate the drama of these large unsteady words. The sudden drawing of light taking note to what she would rather have unnamed. The mismatch of my language, affect, movement. I tried to still. I thought right then, move slowly, as I tumbled up my stair from my office, already having waited during the 15 long minutes of my previous patient hour with her in my house. I was always waiting for her, to reach her, to tell her, she was in the wrong place. (pp. 17–18)

---

[4] [Jeanette Winterson] The Passion
[5] The Passion
[6] The Passion pg 68

A few paragraphs later, McGleughlin explains why she writes this way:

> I can't write it in another way. Because it came to me in fragments. Each fragment reminds me and reminds me of our fragmentation. We didn't have our own words. In truth we started without words, finally with poems. *The gaps are what we have.* (p. 19)

Even McGleughlin's title enacts the fluidity of the analytic field and her multiple attempts to put its meaning into words:

> Titles or fragments
> Letter to A Patient or
> Love letter to a Patient or
> On processing the Counter transference or
> Life in the First year or
> Conversations between the Contemporary Kleinians, post-Cartesian thinkers
>   and the Relationalists or
> When Kleinian theory holds me but self psychology holds the patient or
> The demand for intersubjectivity before the birth of the patient's self and the
>   problems that follow or
> How poetry always leads theory or
> The undoing of a psychoanalyst or
> The way you changed me or
> The passion (p. 1)

When another patient eludes McGleughlin (2013), her writing enacts her patient slipping away:

> I am disoriented from the start and don't even know how to address her. She doesn't want me to say her name. She seems slightly out of all her names, slightly out of the frame, like the lipstick of my favorite schizophrenic. I think it's not quite on her lips. Too bright, just slightly fuzzy. An old woman smoking from two mouths at once. But the pink pink colored outside the lines is on right. Tight. That's the funny thing, the rub. Or the stick. That's there too. The fag, the smoke. The pathos, doubled. The doublings of loss. Then and now? The doubleness of death—first her father, then, essentially, her mother. It's worse than being cross-eyed.
>   She's ephemeral, ethereal. Just past my grasp. Every time I think I see her, she's gone. She is, there is, something always moving, sliding away. (p. 1)

McGleughlin's prose moves quickly. One phrase or clause slides easily into the next, qualifying what was just said and moving on. Notice the doubling of phrases in the last sentence. The second phrase of each pair steers the reader in a slightly different direction than the first. Look at how many references McGleughlin makes to doubling and how many times the structure of her prose enacts a double take with a difference. Things aren't exactly the same from one take to the next—for example, from one pink mouth to another; from "rub" to "stick"; "then and now?"; the loss of the patient's father, then her mother; "ephemeral" to "ethereal"; "she is" to "there is"; "always moving" to "sliding away."

I imagine McGleughlin didn't consciously try to write this way but instead let her voice express her feelings and let her feelings find their own form as Eigen does in his enactive and incantational prose (personal communication). That's how enactive writing often emerges. Although McGleughlin intended to write "A Letter to A Patient . . . " in an experimental mode (as Dimen, 2001, and Sweetnam, 2001, do in their experiments in clinical writing), enactive prose is more often an emergent property of a writer's surrendering to the remembered experience. Revisions can then heighten the desired effects.

Exercise 6.2

Writing Silence, Enacting Turbulence

a. Imagine writing in an experience-near way about one of your most challenging patients. How does it feel to be with this patient?

b. Write from a "felt sense" (Gendlin, 1981/1978; my pp. 248–249) of your experience to draw your readers in and let them experience what you experience. Let your feelings find their own forms, and you may discover that your prose performs its meaning.

Enacting Ideas

When Loewald (1980) writes about instincts, his sentences enact their flow with a profusion of iterative, subordinate structures (my pp. 51–52). When Ogden (2001b) writes about "the frontier of dreaming," that metaphoric space between the preconscious and unconscious from which much of our creativity arises, his sentence enacts the generativity of that creative frontier:

> That frontier is the "place" where dreaming and reverie experience occur; where playing and creativity of every sort are born; where wit and charm germinate before they find their way (as if out of nowhere) into a conversation, a poem, a gesture, or a facial expression; where symptomatic compromise formations are generated and timelessly go on haunting us and sapping vitality from us as they provide order and illusion of safety at the cost of freedom. (p. 7)

In the eloquent unfolding of a single sentence, Ogden's incantational voice sounds through a series of evocative dependent clauses. Ogden demonstrates here (and elsewhere) how the enactive may be enfolded within the paradigmatic. His prose, as Loewald's, elaborates an idea, the currency of the paradigmatic, but the means by which it does so are evocative and enactive.

Ogden's writing often illustrates the "forms of generative interplay of style and content, of writing and reader" (Ogden, 2001a, p. 307) that he admires in Winnicott's prose. What do you notice about Ogden's next passage?

The frontier of dreaming, as I am conceiving it, is a psychological field of force over-brimming with freeing, taming, ordering, turning-back-on-itself, impregnating, "versifying" impulses. The versifying impulse is the impulse toward symbolic expression generated not only by the unceasing striving of the unconscious for conscious expression, but also by the phenomenon of "consciousness run[ning] to meet it [the unconscious] on all occasions" (Andreas-Salomé 1916, p. 42). For instance, we feel somehow cut off from ourselves when for a period of time we are unable to remember our dreams, or find ourselves unmoved by music, poetry, painting, humor, lively conversations, or any of the other sorts of creative expression that once held the power to touch us deeply. But I am less concerned at this point with the product of the creative act that emanates from conversation at the frontier of dreaming (e.g. the dream, the poem, the drawing) than with the experience of the impulse toward symbolic expression. The moment prior to speaking or drawing or dreaming is not a moment of affectless waiting; it is a moment alive with the desire, the impulse, the need to give voice to the inarticulate. It is a form of aliveness not found in speech itself, for once the words have been spoken (the dream dreamt, the line drawn), the impulse toward symbolic expression has been spent and, in a sense, killed. The frontier of dreaming is crackling with the impulse toward symbolic expression. It is a space "utterly empty, utterly a source" (Heaney 1987, p. 290), a place where the moment of creativity is sustained as "an imminence . . . never fulfilled" (Borges 1981, p. 39), a place where "all nominative cases must be replaced by the case indicating direction, the dative" (Mandelstam 1933, p. 284). (Ogden, 2001b, pp. 8–9)

Like the frontier of dreaming, Ogden's language is "crackling with the impulse toward symbolic expression." The paragraph's first sentence summons no fewer than six modifiers to describe the noun impulses, and the source of the last three ("turning-back-on-itself," "impregnating," and " 'versifying' ") is Ogden's own creative impulse, his play with the word conversation that animates the second paragraph of *Conversations at the Frontier of Dreaming* (my pp. 218–219). As Ogden (2001b) clarifies that his interest is not in "the product of the creative act" but in the process that is emergent in the prior moment, his descriptors multiply again. It is a "moment prior to speaking or drawing or dreaming" that is "alive with the desire, the impulse, the need to give voice to the inarticulate." As the paragraph reaches its climactic end, Ogden creates another series of three descriptions, each from a different creative source; each one consisting of two musical phrases that create a chord (Ogden, 1997, pp. 4–5); each in its own voice yet speaking through Ogden as one.

Reading with Ogden

Ogden's (2012) close readings of Winnicott and Searles, among other analytic writers (Freud, Isaacs, Fairbairn, Bion, and Loewald), show us how the enactive mode operates in clinical prose, although to date he has not used the term enactive (or the verbs enact or perform*)* to describe it. His choice of words is different from mine although their meaning is the same: He writes about what language does and the effects it creates. For Winnicott—and for Ogden—language is not "a means to an end: a means by which analytic data and ideas are conveyed to readers as telephones and telephone lines transport the voice in the form of electrical impulses and sound waves" (Ogden, 2001a, pp. 320–321). Instead, "meaning is *in* language and the effects created by it. We listen *to* language, not through it" (Ogden, 1997, p. 201). "Winnicott, for the most part, does not use language to arrive at conclusions; rather, he uses language"—as Ogden does—"to create experiences in reading that are inseparable from the ideas he is presenting—or, more accurately, the ideas he is playing with" (Ogden, 2001a, p. 299).

In "Reading Winnicott" (2001a), Ogden identifies more than two dozen examples in which "the life of the writing is critical to, and inseparable from, the life of the ideas" (p. 300) in "Primitive Emotional Development" (1945). To show you how Ogden reads the enactive dimension of Winnicott's prose, I quote three (out of four) paragraphs of his analysis of just one of Winnicott's sentences, which begins the excerpt below.

> There are long stretches of time in a normal infant's life in which a baby does not mind whether he is in many bits or one whole being, or whether he lives in his mother's face or in his own body, provided that from time to time he comes together and feels something.

This sentence is distinctive, not only for the originality of the ideas it develops, but also for the way in which its syntax participates in a sensory way to the creation of those ideas. The sentence is constructed of many (I count ten) groups of words that are read with very brief pauses between them (for instance, a pause after the words "time," "life," "mind," and so on). The sentence not only states, but brings to life in its own audible structure, the experience of living in bits ("for a long time"), in a meandering sort of way before coming together (for a moment) in its final two bits: "he comes together" and "feels something." The voice, syntax, and rhythm, and carefully chosen words and expressions that constitute this sentence—working together as they do with the ideas being developed—create an experience in reading that is as distinctively Winnicott as the opening paragraph of *The Sound and the Fury* is distinctively William Faulkner, or as the opening sentence of *The Portrait of a Lady* is uniquely Henry James.

The reader of the sentence being discussed is not moved to question how Winnicott can possibly know what an infant feels. . . . Rather the reader is inclined to suspend disbelief for a time and enter into the experience of reading (with Winnicott) and to allow himself to be carried by the music of the language and ideas. The reader lives an experience in the act of reading that is something like that of the imagined infant, who does not mind whether he is in many bits (experiencing a floating feeling that accompanies nonlinear thinking) or one whole being (experiencing a "momentary stay against confusion" [Frost, 1939, p. 777]). Winnicott's writing, like a guide "who only has at heart your getting lost" (Frost, 1947, p. 341), ensures that we will never get it right in any final way, and we do not mind.

Subliminally, the pun on "mind" allows the clause "a baby does not mind whether he is in many bits or one whole being" to concentrate into itself different overlapping meanings. The baby "does not mind" because the mother is there "minding" him (taking care of him). And he "does not mind" in that he feels no pressure to be "minded"—that is, to create premature, defensive mindedness which is disconnected from bodily experience. In punning, the writing itself deftly and unselfconsciously creates just such an experience of the pleasure of not minding, of not having to know, of not having to pin down meaning—and instead simply enjoying the liveliness of a fine experience in the medium of language and ideas. (pp. 308–310)

Ogden has published more about writers and clinical writing (see references) than any other analytic writer I know. As he demonstrates in "Reading Winnicott," he does so with literary sensitivity, psychoanalytic savvy, and originality. His contributions to understanding and appreciating clinical writing permeate and inspire my work. The enactive dimension of a text emerges for Ogden (2009) as an indication of its quality: "When the writing is good, the author creates in the experience of reading something like the phenomenon that he is discussing" (p. 52). In the enactive mode, readers are recruited, carried along, and caused to experience something the analyst has experienced. They are moved not primarily by what the prose conjures up in their imagination as they are by evocative prose but by how language kinesthetically enacts or performs its meaning, creating an experience to be lived by readers as well as thought.

"The Medium Is the Message"

Freud and Jung were original, prolific, and creative writers whose beliefs about the psyche developed along different lines that contributed to the rupture of their friendship.

Whether considering their theories, clinical techniques, or authorial voices, one would not mistake one for the other, yet both wrote enactive prose, generating a tradition of enactive writing in our field and spawning a critical discussion about it (re Freud: Brooks, 1992/1984; Derrida, 1978; Mahony, 1984, 1987/1981; Morris, 1992, 1993; Ogden, 2002; re Jung: Gardner, 2013; Rowland, 2005). Both experiment with literary form (Mahony, 1987; Ogden, 2005b; Rowland, 2005) and often present their thoughts as they unfold in the process of writing (Ogden, 2002; Rowland, 2005).

Jung is famous for circumambulating a subject, and Mahony (1986) characterizes Freud's style in the case of the Rat Man as "ambitious (Latin *ambulare*, to walk)" (p. 200). Jung and Freud both demonstrate new ways of thinking (Ogden, 2002; Rowland, 2005) and leave traces of unconscious processes in their texts (Derrida, 1978; Mahony, 1986, 1987; Morris, 1993; Rowland, 2005). For Mahony

(1984), much of the "vitality" of Freud's writing resides in its "embody[ing] the quintessential psychoanalytic experience of ongoingness or processiveness" (p. 854); "not a thought, but a mind thinking, or in Pascal's words, *la peinture de la pensée*" [thinking thought] (p. 854).

Ogden (2002) notes how Freud would often

> make no attempt to cover his tracks, for example, his false starts, his uncertainties, his reversals of thinking (often done mid-sentence), his shelving of compelling ideas for the time being because they seemed to him too speculative or lacking adequate clinical foundation. The legacy that Freud left was not simply a set of ideas, but, as important, and inseparable from those ideas, a new way of thinking about human experience that gave rise to nothing less than a new form of human subjectivity. (p. 767)

In detailed close readings in *Jung as a Writer*, Susan Rowland (2005) demonstrates the numerous ways Jung "is not just describing the creativity of the psyche, his words also enact and perform it" (p. 2). Jung thought his writing about psychology "was only truly valid if it retained a trace of the spontaneity that he believed to be integral to psychic functioning" (Rowland, 2005, p. 2). The use of contradictory metaphors, for example, posed no problems for him. In one paragraph of "The Structure and Dynamics of the Psyche" (1949), he writes, "If it were possible to personify the unconscious, we might think of it as a collective human being . . . having at his command a human experience of one or two million years, practically immortal." In the next paragraph: "The collective unconscious, moreover, seems to be not a person, but something like an unceasing stream or perhaps an ocean of images and figures which drift into consciousness in our dreams or in abnormal states of mind" (quoted in Rowland, 2005, p. 1). Such contradictions remind me of Whitman's "Songs of Myself": "Do I contradict myself? Very well then I contradict myself,/ (I am large, I contain multitudes.)" (Section 51) and Freud's belief that "the laws of logic—above all, the law of contradiction—do not hold" for unconscious process (Freud, 1933, p. 104). Jung's contradictions enact the limits of rationality and the polytheistic structure of the psyche (Hillman, 1977).

"Jung believed *and wrote as though he believed* that the thinking and discriminating mind—conventionally used to produce non-fiction argument—was situated within a sea of unconscious creativity" (Rowland, 2005, p. 1). Jung's prose draws on rational arguments while it also "appeal[s] to more than rational understanding" (Rowland, 2005, p. 2). Although Jung's style of writing has not escaped criticism, his "textual creativity provides new ways of being at home in modernity, by writing the psyche *whole*" (Rowland, 2005, first unnumbered page).

Deconstructionist critics argue "that a text—not unlike DNA with its double helix—can have intertwined, opposite 'discourses'—strands of narrative, threads of meaning" (Murfin, 1992, p. 189). This intertwining resists privileging one strand over another. According to J. Hillis Miller, the project of deconstructionism is "not a dismantling of the structure of a text, but a demonstration that it has already dismantled itself. Its apparently solid ground is no rock but thin air" ("Stevens' Rock" 341) (quoted in Murfin, 1992, pp. 179–180). When Jacques Derrida (1978), the French philosopher whose name is synonymous with deconstructionism, reads the second (*fort/da*) chapter of Freud's *Beyond the Pleasure Principle*, he notices that

> something repeats itself, and this process of repetition must be identified not only in the content (the examples, the materials described and analyzed) but also in Freud's very writing, in the "steps" taken by his text, in what it does as well as in what it says, in its "acts" as much as in its "objects." What obviously repeats itself in this chapter is the movement of the speculator [Freud] to reject, set aside, make disappear (*fort*), defer everything that seems to call the PP [pleasure principle] into question. He notes that it is not enough, that he must postpone the question. Then he summons back the hypothesis of something beyond the pleasure principle only to dismiss it again. The hypothesis returns only like something that has not really returned but has merely passed into the ghost of its presence. (pp. 114–115)

Had Freud been privy to Derrida's analysis, do you think he would have revised his text? This hypothetical question points to a difference between unintentionally created rhetorical enactments that an author would retain once discovered and those he would not. Mahony (1986) detects the latter kind of enactments in Freud's case of the Rat Man, when for example, he "did not sufficiently trace the ratlines, the symbolic lineage, of his patient's symptoms back to his childhood. In this and other ways, isolation is analytically [and rhetorically] enacted as well as described, inscribed in Freud's very text, with the result that the text is a mixture of literary failure and overwhelming achievement" (p. 179).

Even if you don't intend to write in the enactive mode, you may want to look for its traces in your text. Is your "medium the message" (to paraphrase McLuhan, 1994/1964) that you want to convey or does your style of writing subvert or confuse your efforts? I see an important difference between writing that is confusing and writing that is well crafted to create an experience of confusion. Writers who are perceived as confused or confusing trip themselves and their readers up. They not only miss an opportunity to make effective use of the enactive mode, but they may be discounted by readers they confuse.

Exercise 6.3

"The Medium Is the Message"

a. Name a fundamental belief or new idea you have about the psyche and/or psychotherapy.
b. Imagine how you might write in a way that enacts your belief in the form your writing takes. How, for example, might you enact multiple

self states or a kaleidoscope of self/other configurations in the aesthetics of your prose? How might your prose enact the psyche's creativity and spontaneity? How, like Ogden, might you reflect the generativity at the frontier of dreaming in the sounds and syntax of your sentences (my pp. 67–68)? Like Havens, you might recreate prosodically the feeling of safety that is needed for healing to occur (my pp. 99–100).

c. Write a paragraph or more that enacts one of your core beliefs or a new idea you have about psychotherapy. Even if you start with the intention to write enactive prose, you may have more success if you surrender to the experience of writing without thinking too much about technique.

7 Lyric Narratives

In psychoanalysis we try to find our way to new experience. That is the main thing. Only when we have freed ourselves to experience something new can we think about it in a directed, ordered, effortful way. . . . What matters is the freedom to allow new experience, which requires a commitment to uncertainty and curiosity, a commitment to taking your hand off the tiller, to not knowing where new experience is going to go.

Donnel Stern, "Narrative Writing and Soulful Metaphors: Commentary on Paper by Barbara Pizer"

The Lyric Narrative Mode

A lyric narrative is an evocative narrative that exemplifies the qualities Bruner associates with a literary story—one that "means more than it says" (Bruner, 1986, p. 26) and is "open to multiple interpretations," is "somewhat uncertain" and "undetermined" (Bruner, 1990, pp. 53, 54). I call these narratives lyric, because they feature not only what happens in our consulting room but also "the music of what happens" (Heaney, 1998; quoted in Ogden, 2005a, p. 16) in the lyric present (Culler, 2001). They stir our emotions as music does and sing to us as we are moved and carried on "the wings of our experiencing" (Pizer, 2007).

Whether lyric narratives are read as texts or heard as presentations, that is, whether they are taken in by eye or ear, they seem to me to be experienced as voiced or spoken even if they are seen and read. Sentences that create the illusion of being spoken and heard may seem more effervescent than those on the printed page. They go by like the fleeting present moment (Stern, 2004). Words in this context "are not separate items, open to time-free contemplation; they are crests or troughs in a stream, parts of a wave pattern" (Richards, 1947, p. 203).

A lyric narrative incorporates many narrative elements. It tells a clinical story with a beginning, middle, and end, but its end may only mark a moment in an ongoing process, and the clinical story does not highlight retrospective knowledge. Unlike other narratives such as memoirs, a lyric narrative does not "assemble the puzzle of what happened in the light of subsequent realization" (Birkerts, 2008, p. 8). A traditional narrative structure as a "syntax of a certain way of speaking our understanding of the world" is not fundamental to its structure (Brooks, 1992, p. 7).

The century in which psychoanalysis was born revered history and "conceived certain kinds of knowledge and truth to be inherently narrative, understandable (and expoundable) only by way of sequence, in temporal unfolding" (Brooks, 1992, pp. xi–xii). With the loss of religious certainties in the nineteenth century, "the plotting of the individual or social or institutional life story takes on new urgency when one no longer can look to a sacred masterplot that organizes and explains the world" (Brooks, 1992, p. 6). Brooks (1992) notes how the nineteenth century became obsessed with "questions of origin, evolution, progress, genealogy . . . [and] historical narrative [emerged] as par excellence the necessary mode of explanation and understanding" (pp. 6–7).

Psychoanalytic writers employing the lyric narrative mode still honor the influence of the past on personality and the clinical exchange, but as writers, they focus on present experiencing, on recreating a succession of present moments, and on the possibilities and limitations of present knowledge. Interpretations of clinical experience are more tentative than certain. Meaning is provisional, subjective, mutable, and primarily experiential—for writer and reader alike.

With close affinities to the evocative and enactive modes, lyric narratives often incorporate them as they propel their readers into experiencing a dynamic, nonlinear, evocative present. Culler (2001) explains that "the fundamental characteristic of the lyric [poem] . . . is not the description and interpretation of a past event but the performance of an event in the lyric present" (p. xi). Vendler (1995) notes that the lyric poem has "the appearance of spontaneity . . . the look of casual utterance . . . of immediate outspokenness. . . . the look of encounter, of naked circumstance" (p. 4). She continues: "It is generally thought that the lyric is the genre of 'here' and 'now'" (p. 5) and that it has "a structure which enacts the experience represented" (p. 6). Each of these associations suits the lyric narrative as a mode of clinical prose that invites—and sometimes compels—its readers to experience what the analyst experiences *as the analysis unfolds*.

A lyric narrative, like psychoanalysis, lends itself to being experienced in a receptive state. In "Passion, Responsibility, and 'Wild Geese': Creating a Context for the Absence of Conscious Intentions," Barbara Pizer (2005a) asks her readers not to consciously steer a course through its pages or make an effort to ponder its meaning while taking it in. Instead, as Donnel Stern (2005) writes, reading it requires "me to take my hand off the tiller and let the writing wash over me. Rather than penetrating it or pinning it down or getting a fix on it, I need to allow this kind of writing to do whatever it will do to me" (p. 86). Stern continues:

> You have to let the writing have its way with you right off the bat, and then, later on, you can wonder about what you might have taken from it. What has found its way into your mind? This kind of reading requires commitment. . . . It's the commitment to freedom of thought, an insistence on allowing whatever will arise by itself in experience. It's a commitment to the unbidden. (p. 86)

We can, of course, read any text associatively and be surprised by what may arise unbidden in our listening/reading experience. I am suggesting something else: that a lyric narrative is constructed and guides readers to participate in listening or reading in a way that parallels our experience of poetry, psychoanalysis, and life itself. That is, experiencing comes first, comes before understanding, interpretation, and articulating meaning. Given the writer's commitment to demonstrating how experience precedes comprehension, reflection, and the creation of meaning, the aesthetic of the lyric narrative reflects this commitment and is fundamentally different from that of the narrative and paradigmatic modes.

A Note on This Chapter

I will quote substantial portions of Barbara Pizer's (2005a) "Passion, Responsibility, and 'Wild Geese,' " so you may begin to immerse yourself in the experience of reading before reflecting on what you've read. Talking about a specific lyric narrative in detail before inviting you to experience its effects violates the raison d'être of this distinctive mode.

To date, I have not discovered another psychoanalytic author who has written what I call a lyric narrative. Yet Pizer's examples will help us discern the potential of this experimental form to enact in its aesthetic a more contemporary Weltanschauung and "to move intersubjective experience from the consulting room into the space between clinical author and reader" (as one reader of this chapter put it). "Like lyric poetry, lyric narratives seek not only to convey a therapeutic experience to the reader, but also to recreate [or evoke] in the reader the actual feelings of that experience" (as another reader noted).

Barbara Pizer's "Passion, Responsibility, and 'Wild Geese' " as Lyric Narrative

Pizer (2005a) begins "Passion, Responsibility, and 'Wild Geese' " by quoting Stephen Mitchell (2000) and inviting her readers to surrender to the experience of her paper as Mitchell invites his analysands to surrender to the experience of analysis without preconceptions:

> Stephen Mitchell (2000), in differentiating role responsibilities in the mutual but asymmetrical relationship between analyst and patient, writes, "It is the analysand's job, in some very important ways, to be irresponsible. That is, we ask analysands to surrender to their experience, to show up and discover what they find themselves feeling and thinking. We ask analysands to renounce all other conscious intents. As we all know, this is not easy to do" (p. 131). It is in this context that I ask you to surrender to the experience of this paper—to go along with me without dwelling too much on the content until we're done, and then we can look back to see what meaning may be found. (p. 58)

Immediately after extending this invitation, Pizer tells us about her relationship to poetry. Her description of the process of writing a poem carries a metamessage:

> Going in and coming out, the thing has a tone to it, a music that I discover before I know where and how my words are traveling. I seem to be carried

along by the tone of a developing idea or image, and it is the tone that dictates the rhythm and shape of the written lines. If I feel surprise and the surprise brings pleasure, I begin to work on honing the progression of thoughts. (p. 58)

The work of creating a poem continues: "A kind of dialogue takes place between myself and the lines that have been set down. What exactly have I evoked?" (p. 58). Receptivity to process precedes reflection and meaning making; form evolves. Tone and music arrive first. Whatever emotional tones may be struck, the poet, and by analogy the reader, is carried along by the music of what is happening.

Pizer tells her readers that she may sometimes read a poem to a patient:

> These are times when it seems that a particular poem, more than an interpretation of my own, will best interrupt a familiar ritual or provide by its surprise an unexpected opening, a play space, a soothing, or a saying of something difficult to hear but not unbearably humiliating, because it is spoken without the actual speaker in the room and is spoken in some metaphor that can first be dealt with in the darkness and protected privacy of a quiet listener's soul. (p. 59)

Pizer's paper works on many levels. In describing "how poetry infuses her way of thinking, feeling, and writing, and her way of working analytically," she introduces her concept of the nonanalytic third—"the analyst's personal, intimate and substantially abiding relationship to some body of experience unrelated to *materia psychoanalytica*" (p. 57). A nonanalytic third is

> unique to each analyst [and] constitutes a source of enrichment, texture, and dimensionality as well as personally compelling metaphors that the analyst may offer to the patient as other-than-me substance and a placeholder for cultivating the potential in the discourse of analytic potential space, in addition to serving as a facilitator and comfort for transition when the analyst must recognize and promote the necessary ending of an intimate analytic relationship. (p. 57)

Lyric narratives do conceptual work. Pizer's ideas about how poetry functions as a nonanalytic third constitutes one level of this work. Her relationship with her patient constitutes another. Mitchell's (2000) notion that an analysand might approach analysis with the "absence of conscious intents" and Pizer's way of using her own feelings to help a patient do that constitute a third. If you read Pizer's paper in its entirety, you will recognize how these levels are interwoven.

Before introducing Sam to her readers, Pizer picks up Mitchell's idea that analysands start treatment by pursuing their own goals—as Mitchell (2000) writes, of

> getting "better" quickly, avoiding trouble, taking care of the analyst, and so on. So we work with them on articulating their conscious intentions and discovering what would make it safe enough *not* to pursue them. *We are trying*

to create a context in which the absence of conscious intentions will allow feelings to emerge, feelings like love and hate [p. 131; emphasis added]. (quoted in Pizer, 2005a, p. 60)

In contrast to the analysand's job " 'in some very important ways, to be irresponsible,' " (Mitchell quoted in Pizer, 2005a, p. 58), our job is "to employ our own emergent feelings in trying to facilitate those conditions wherein the patient can open to unattended passions, with the goal of getting to know those feelings and the part they play in making, breaking, or masking a life" (Pizer, 2005a, p. 60). Pizer's paper shows us how she follows this credo.

In her next paragraph, Pizer introduces Sam:

> For my patient Sam, the very notion of irresponsibility triggers trouble, unhappiness, and deep remorse. More than 30 years ago, in one of the confusing off-again cycles of a long-term, passionate, on-again, off-again college love affair, Sam was suddenly struck and then smitten by an elegant and popular new woman on campus. He was just finishing graduate school when she became pregnant with his child. The idea of keeping the baby seems not to have been considered much—least of all when I inquire about it in the treatment. When I ask him how he felt about the abortion, he describes a brief moment in the hospital when his Amy was wheeled back from the operating room, her face as white as the sheet that covered her, white as a sheet with the stain of her blood on its edge. How did he feel? He fainted dead away. How did he feel? He tells me that a few days later, he proposed to her. (pp. 60–61)

With deft strokes, Pizer creates this portrait of Sam as a young man. Cadence, repetition, and craft play their part in creating it, yet the overall effect is one of apparent spontaneity. In the last four sentences, Pizer gives her readers what they need to understand something about Sam's affective and relational competence. Sam can only tell Pizer what he did, not what he felt, leaving clues to his feelings in externalized details and omissions. Pizer gives us the evidence she had—and no more—and lets us draw our own inferences.

In a footnote referenced in this passage, Pizer explains that she may use the present tense when describing past events "in an attempt to locate the reader more fully in the 'present' moment of each clinical event no matter when it occurred. The implicit nonlinearity of time is intentional and consistent with my wish to invite the reader (as Mitchell asks analysands) to surrender to experience, to approach a state of 'absence of conscious intentions' " (p. 60).

In the next paragraph, Pizer employs backstory and narrative summary, yet she creates a sense of immediacy with her use of the present tense:

> I see Sam first in a couples context. It is the early 1970s. Amy complains that Sam is critical and controlling, righteous, and disdainful. Sam, a tall, broadshouldered man with a boyish air, does strike me as controlling. In contrast to Amy's bright, conversational ease, Sam appears more wary, more deliberate

in his choice of words. "Amy falls apart over strong emotions," Sam explains, "and she is sexually passive. And I feel jealous that she concerns herself with everybody else's needs but mine." Amy counters with a detailed rationale of her own, and in my presence the two of them manage to transform angry disappointments into formal conversation. Such conversations continue week after week, until finally one day Sam breaks the intellectual standoff with an ardent plea for them to make a baby. When she agrees, they terminate the treatment. (p. 61)

Pizer is skilled at presenting just enough material to move the story along but not too much to weigh it down. Too much detail can crowd readers out, leaving little room for the play of their imagination.

Here is Pizer's next well-pruned, affect-centered paragraph:

In 1991, 17 years after I first saw him, Sam shows up again, alone. He wants some insight into why he works so hard to "fill in" for others and yet receives so little in return. As for his marriage, he is happy to report a few significant changes: two beautiful children, Allison and Robin, and he and Amy have "great sex." But their day-to-day relationship remains the same—"cordial" at best—and he notes within him a somewhat frightening and unrequited hunger for hugs. (p. 61)

In her next paragraph, Pizer maintains her distinctive conversational voice while building even more complexity into her story:

According to Sam, Amy is not totally truthful in certain areas of their conversation; furthermore, she has a particular way of overriding him when it comes to the kids. A detailed inquiry reveals, however, that he too has certain secrets from Amy, holds back with her, primarily around his fantasy life. Although he describes these fantasies as sexual, when ultimately he spins them out for me I hear a yearning for intimate connection that must be paid for by prowess. Being a good guy and a responsible citizen becomes a predominant theme. In the weeks that follow, I have a sense of Sam's deep yearning for intimacy and passion and his fear of it as well. When I suggest that keeping his intense fantasy life to himself will surely not promote the intimacy he yearns for with his wife, he gives me two clear reasons for his silence. In the first place, Amy wants no part of his expressiveness. Instead of feeling empathy for his response, say, to an intrusion by a neighbor or to his mother's repeated interruptions, she considers him rude. Her focus is on everybody else's comfort. "Second," he says, "if I tell her something, I'll never know what happens to it, where she stores it, what she makes of it." Perhaps for emphasis, he reiterates, "Don't forget, Barbara, Amy wants me to lighten up." Looking over at the sturdy gangle of his body, slouched hopelessly across my couch, I somehow want to laugh at the sadness of all of this. "Amy doesn't talk to me about intimate things," he says. (pp. 61–62)

In this paragraph, Pizer draws together what she learns over time, creates an immediate scene, prepares her readers for what she senses, and captures Sam's language and feel of things. We learn what Pizer's detailed inquiry adds to Sam's report and gain more access to her thoughts. This layering of perspectives suggests that life is experienced by each of us from different, partial, changing vantage points.

In the next paragraph, Pizer maintains the ambience of an immediate scene even though she tucks in narrative summary and offers a glimpse of what's to come (prospection):

> I will have one year to work with Sam before he disappears for another six. The more I think that I understand what's going on, the more I don't. For one thing, I cannot comprehend the depth of warmth that he evokes in me. I am more accustomed to an unwelcome clutch of tension and effort when interacting with a man like Sam who maintains such vigilant control over what goes in and what comes out. But somehow I sense that Sam wants me to know, to find the person he keeps hostage, to recognize the wordless struggle taking place within him despite his massive efforts to contain it. I sense a history of both love and pain. (p. 62)

Pizer's openness to not knowing—"The more I think that I understand what's going on, the more I don't"—sits side by side with what she intuits. This mix of uncertainty and intuition permeates Pizer's way of working analytically, being in the world, and writing in the lyric narrative mode.

Now we will jump ahead several pages to keep our focus on this paper as a lyric narrative. Two months after Sam returns six years later, he decides to try analysis. One morning he wakes up " 'thinking of Julia's body, and . . . this image of a gushing fire hydrant' " (p. 69). He gives his analyst "his Freudian interpretation" (p. 69). Pizer counters:

> "Could well be," I say, "but you never know. Could be you're trying to put out a fire. Could be that you feel critical again, and angry because you think Amy is more interested in her daughter than in you. Could be that you're trying to flush away or flush out the thought that Amy doesn't love you anymore, because you're so bad; so . . . undeserving." Sam lets loose a disdainful grunt. I can tell that I will lose him momentarily. "Sam," I hear myself insisting, "a fire hydrant can be something more than just a penis."
>
> "What do you mean, 'just?' " he jokes. (p. 69)

Sam's "disdainful grunt" and Pizer's sense of losing him momentarily hint at the possible collapse of reflective space. In response, Pizer asks Sam if she can read him Oliver's poem "Wild Geese." Earlier, Pizer prepared us for such an intervention. After she reads the poem, she tells us:

> I do not know Sam's initial response to the poem, because he is silent for a long time. When he speaks, he talks about carefree high school days. He talks

about the passion and despair he experienced throughout the crazy-on again, off-again relationship with the woman he knew before Amy. He talks, as he tends to do these days when feeling vulnerable, about his fantasies—particularly about Liza. (p. 70)

Sam then finds words to tell his analyst what brings him back into treatment, what happens when he runs into Liza in Paris and they dine together, what makes him cry that night, keeps him up, and makes him wonder if he is losing his mind.

As you read what happens next, notice how Pizer continues her story:

The day after he heard "Wild Geese," Sam came in with a question. "Do you have a supervisor?" he asked. "Why?" I queried, hoping to cover the feeling of a sudden blow to the stomach. "Because," he said to me, "I'm very worried that if I tell you how upset I was after hearing that poem, you'll retreat and I don't want you to." Throughout this session, Sam talks about how the poem "shook him up." What does this mean? He finds himself "tearing up" in the car, "just tearing up over nothing in particular." Now I remember his slip from the day before. He is talking about the image of the fire hydrant. He means to say that it is "exploding" with water, but it comes out "exposing." I think again about his question: "Do you have a supervisor?"

Between the two of us, who actually had been exposed? What elicited my frightful shame? Was it Sam's rubbing my face in outrageous analytic behavior? Was it the shocking freedom or power I heard in his tone? Or all of the above? In retrospect, I believe it was the first time I experienced between us, in the room, the raw presence of anger, shame, freedom, and desire. "Do you have a supervisor?" Had I made a terrible mistake? Shamed him by surprise? Was Sam handing over his internal supervisor and asking me to handle it myself? Could we ever know the many meanings of his unparked response to my reading "Wild Geese" to him? Because my repeated probing never produced contradicting material from Sam, we must remain content with his insistent, and perhaps one-sided, view that he feared somebody would stop me from working with him in the way I did, that when he let me know how truly painful it felt to open up to feeling, I would turn "responsible." Or somebody else would "intervene."

Over the next months, we recognize that something has opened between us. We are both aware, also, that our poem is no more than a place marker, a way station shared along an uncharted course toward a destination that cannot be predicted until we get closer—if we ever do. And we can note together—between the seemingly endless tedium of days on days—small arrivals and crossings over dangerous terrain. So it goes. (pp. 70–71)

As this passage demonstrates, a lyric narrative is carefully crafted to recreate what happens in the unscripted present, in the conversations Pizer has with her patient and herself. Her experience-near prose conveys a sense of being in process, of her entertaining multiple possibilities without narrowing them down to a certain few. Pizer explains that her paper is "constructed in the hope of coming closer to *reexperiencing*—rather than merely weighing from some analytic distance—the unfolding case of Sam and me" (p. 73; emphasis added).

The aesthetic of the lyric narrative is isomorphic with poetry, the analytic process, and life itself. In all three, "the medium is the message" (McLuhan, 1994/1964): "Going in and coming out, the thing has a tone to it, a music that I discover before I know where and how my words [and their meanings] are traveling" (Pizer, 2005a, p. 58). Each of these forms of experience shows us how we "are *caught up* in meaning, before . . . [we] actually experience meaning reflectively" (Johnson, 2007, p. 79). Meaning catches us up before we catch up with it.

That's why Sam was "shook up" when he opened himself up to experiencing Pizer reading Oliver's poem. That's why he finds himself " 'tearing up' in the car, 'just tearing up over nothing in particular' " after he opens the door to his feelings, feelings that fall into words. That's why Pizer feels Sam's accusation "Do you have a supervisor?" first as a body blow, then as the sting of shame. Meaning is often implicit, embodied, relational. Whose shame? "Between the two of us, who actually had been exposed?" Pizer asks. Does one have to choose? There are two participants here, each with a history of vulnerabilities and exposures. In this analytic field, exposure is a relational act.

Meaning in the lyric present is open and undetermined—not settled, final, definitive. In the way she tells her story, Pizer shows us that meaning is implicit and emergent. Even though she tucks the phrase "in retrospect" into the second paragraph above, she captures only a small part of their process from that perspective. The meaning of their sharing Oliver's poem is not completely knowable in the present; it unfolds over time and may never be completely known. Pizer does not land on one meaning of the question Sam asks about her having a supervisor or one meaning of the shame it elicits in her.

Let's look more closely at the last paragraph I just quoted. What do you notice about the way it is written? What does its form imply, especially about a lyric narrative's epistemology?

Every major part (and sometimes more than one part) of each sentence points to the limitations of what we can know, predict, or achieve. "*Something* has opened" between these analytic partners (emphasis added), but what that is, is not yet clear. The shared poem stands in for something, but what that something is and what it means are not yet clear. What is shared is called a "way station," but the way is "uncharted," and the destination is not in sight and may never be. Days follow days in a "seemingly endless tedium." Only "small arrivals and crossings" can be marked, modest approaches and transitions "over dangerous terrain." "So it goes." The process continues with the same measure of indeterminacy, which implies both limitation and possibility. Knowing is always in process and open to possibility while at the same time it is always limited by where we are, who we are with, and by what has not yet arrived (or been allowed) into our experience (Stern, 1997, 2010).

Pizer (2005a) also makes these points more explicitly, in declarative statements, which can be accommodated in a narrative mode:

> Just as I believe that stories about people are never neat or complete, the ideas and themes that have unfolded thus far in this writing—also not

complete—have a history and a future I cannot claim. We all must be aware that ideas become unique as they are discovered, lived, and used by the people who receive them (see Levenson, 1983; Stern, 1997). (p. 72)

The sharing of Oliver's poem seems to have prepared Pizer and her patient for the shocking intrusion of another nonanalytic third—the 9/11 attacks. When stranded in Paris, Sam emails his analyst, and Pizer incorporates their correspondence into her paper to track the intimacy that spans an ocean. The presentation version of her paper ended with their email exchange and Sam's dream of a "cheerful baby," who knows his own name, the name Pizer's patient is given in her paper. But the dreamer doesn't know who the baby's mother is. How apt that the last paragraph of this lyric narrative's first ending is a yet-to-be interpreted dream, a potential space like a poem, that is open to multiple meanings.

When Pizer's story ended here, some listeners and readers apparently were left wondering what happened next "when Sam came home from Paris. How did he look back on our e-mail correspondence? What was its effect on the treatment? What conclusions, they asked me, do I draw from these rather unconventional exchanges between us, and where do they fit in the overall frame of the work, as I perceive and present it?" (Pizer, 2005a, p. 79).

Curiosity was not their only response. "Some of those who asked these questions also felt moved by the paper without knowing why or have commented that they didn't know what to say about it after they finished reading it" (Pizer, 2005a, p. 79). Pizer wrote a new conclusion for her published paper, creating a coda in which she steps out of the lyric narrative mode and moves between the narrative and paradigmatic modes. If you read her new conclusion, I think you will be struck by how it differs from the main body of her paper and functions as a coda. This shift highlights the aesthetic of the lyric narrative. Let's take a look.

Pizer asks, "Could such an initial absence of speakable response [from her audience] be one purpose of the work as I have set it down?" (p. 80). Her answer is presented in the paradigmatic mode:

> Perhaps, in this case, the medium is the message. I'm asking us, *as analysts*, to go through once more what we ask our patients to do. The suspending of preconceptions, the surrendering to process, can be like listening to a new poem or a beloved piece of music; it takes a while to come back from experiencing its tones and nuances before finding the words to formulate an articulate response or ask a question. Maybe such an exercise makes for new learning about ourselves and our patients. (p. 80)

In the paradigmatic mode, sequence involves a progression of ideas and the development of an interpretation, hypothesis, or argument rather than the tracking of events through time or the opening up of the lyric present for readers to reexperience. We might infer ideas when presented with a narrative sequence, but we are explicitly presented with ideas in the paradigmatic mode (and in reflective commentaries woven into other modes).

In the next paragraphs of her new ending, Pizer shifts her attention to "some of the ideas I came with, and came to, in my work with Sam" (p. 80). Here's an example:

> As a young man, Sam experienced untenable rage behind a closed door. Face-to-face with an intrusive, penetrating maternal presence, Sam built himself an internal firewall that equipped him to create the appearance of open access while maintaining vigilant control over what came in and what went out. If things got really bad, he could withdraw with no one knowing it, and when they got worse, he could always disappear . . . however, not without cost to him of a more genuine spontaneity and the intimacy he claimed to yearn for most. So I believe that my offering the potential of poetry into analytic discourse allowed him to experience an other voice between us—indirect and multimodal, the primitive and essential prosody of a communicating process whose particular meanings he could find on his own if he chose to. That experience, I believe, contained the possibility of transforming in him a historical and calcified habit of shutting down at the threat of impending intrusiveness and shock, thereby permitting me, at times, to overcome my own historical and transferential tendency to feel outrageous in my efforts to speak my mind or, as Sam might say, to "advocate for myself." The "Wild Geese" experience, I would like to believe, became a prosodic process that provided us a kind of unwitting procedural preparation (or thirdness) for dealing creatively with the reality of an unanticipated other. We somehow managed to speak, to even sing to one another from a great distance, during the shared terror of 9/11. (p. 81)

Notice how Pizer moves stepwise from interpretation and example up to the conceptual level and back down again, working the levels as I call it (my pp. 108–112). This work is characteristic of the paradigmatic mode. Incrementally, sometimes clause by clause, Pizer's first three sentences build an understanding of the dynamics of Sam's rage. That prepares us for her explanation of why she read "Wild Geese" and how poetry can function as "an other voice." The effects of a shared third are explained as Pizer moves back down to the level of interpretation and example. Imagine stacking her ideas according to their level of abstraction, with the most specific on the bottom. The last few are shown that way in figure 7.1.

Thirdness

a prosodic process

an unwitting procedural preparation

for dealing creatively with 9/11

We speak/sing to one another from a great distance.

Figure 7.1 Layout of a couple of Pizer's (2005a) ideas from "Passion, Responsibility, and 'Wild Geese'"

Pizer acknowledges that her work with Sam is still ongoing. She includes her verbatim notes from the first session after Sam's return from Paris. Here's how that narrative begins:

> I sit down to write immediately after he leaves, entitling the session in red— *"Naked and Potent"*: I can't remember how we began exactly; Sam just stood in front of me. I concentrated very hard on staying in contact and not hugging him. I felt glad to see him. He smiled. He gets on the couch, facing me, and recounts the story of his coming home. . . . (p. 81)

Three paragraphs later, Pizer marks the end of this narrative segment and shifts into the paradigmatic mode to consider the analytic work that remains: "Direct expressions of anger, for Sam as well as for me, will not come easily between us" (p. 82). A narrative example in service of the paradigmatic follows, including both transference and countertransference interpretations:

> Sam still parks some of my comments, and when I experience myself in a fusion of horizons with him, he is prone to imagining a sort of personal merger—that either I hold his agenda or I impose one of my own. At these times, I still feel powerless and prone to retreat in shame. I hope we can learn more about this unhelpful interaction together. (p. 83)

In the last paragraph of her published paper, Pizer returns to her idea of a nonanalytic third and the question of how she relates poetry to clinical practice: "Poetry has served Sam and me for a good while in our analytic endeavor, because it is compelling yet indirect and can be picked up, related to, played with, or put down at will. Yet, like love and hate experienced in the work between us, it too has a life span" (p. 83). An analyst's nonanalytic third, however, "accompanies her before the arrival and after the departure of a patient. And it is just such an enduring object that can be relied on during the ultimate and necessary ending of an intimate analytic partnership" (p. 83).

Pizer purposely lays more out in this paper than she draws together, inviting readers to make their own discoveries. Goldner (2005) observes that Pizer's reading of Oliver's poem becomes a transformational third and transformational object (Bollas, 1987) for both of them. A lyric narrative, like a literary narrative, "means more than it says" (Bruner, 1986, p. 26) and leaves much of the work of interpretation to its readers. Well-written papers in the paradigmatic mode lay their evidence and reasoning out. Sometimes the two modes sit side by side as they do when Pizer frames her lyric narrative with a coda in the paradigmatic mode or intersperses conceptual and theoretical commentaries between narrative segments. Yet each mode has a distinct aesthetic, draws on different principles of organizing experience or "worldmaking" (Goodman, 1978), and represents particular ways of knowing (Bruner, 1986).

A Lyric Narrative in a More Colloquial Voice

As Pizer (2005a) notes, a lyric narrative is written "in the hope of coming closer to *reexperiencing*—rather than merely weighing from some analytic distance" a clinical case as it unfolds (p. 73; emphasis added). As you read the opening of Pizer's (2007) "Maintaining Analytic Liveliness: 'The Fire and the Fuel' of Growth and Change," notice how she brings us into her experience with her patient and writes in a much more colloquial voice than we heard in "Passion, Responsibility, and 'Wild Geese' ":

> When a patient lets me know he's changed his first name, I don't say anything right away, but I take notice. Exactly where I take my notice remains unclear for a while. Of course I'm not saying very much about my own prescience or patience because, after all, it was Aaren who *gave me* the notice. Patients take their time to let you in on certain things, and that alone is not unusual either.
>
> But the point I want to make here is that even *after* Aaren told me about this name change (on the day I handed him his first bill), I didn't know how to think about it. Often I would just forget. Aaren Kahn was born and named Aaron Kahn. He still *is* Aaren Kahn. His secret is hidden in the spelling. Aaren spells himself with an "e"—Aaren Kahn—instead of the "o" he was born with—Aaron Kahn. Now if it was simply a matter of hiding his ethnicity, he could have worked on his last name instead; removed the "h," added an "e," and turned himself into Aaron Kane. But that wasn't the crux of what he decided to do. To my ear, and I imagine everybody else's, Aaren Kahn is still Aaron Kahn. So what's my story? (pp. 3–4)

What do you think Pizer is setting up in these first two paragraphs? She makes a very different opening move here than she does when she quotes Mitchell and explicitly invites her readers "to surrender to the experience" of her earlier paper (Pizer, 2005a, p. 58). Here she lets her story and voice pull us in. While the beginning of this lyric narrative draws on the conventions of storytelling, Pizer simultaneously destabilizes the certainties temporal sequence usually provides and points to the insufficiency of historical details. Her narrative does not begin at the beginning of Aaren's treatment but at some unspecified time early on. Details don't add up. Connections remain out of sight. A historical perspective does not yield significant meaning. Pizer emphasizes what it is like when things are left hanging or begin to fall apart.

Pizer's opening is also constructed to pique our curiosity about Aaren's name, drawing us into their story and creating the impetus for us to read on. In its initial sentences, this introduction enacts an important aspect of Pizer's experience of Aaren as she quietly takes notice of his name change but can't hold on to what she learns. We can follow this progression sentence by sentence even though we could miss it as easily as we could miss the spelling of Aaren's name. Although Pizer takes notice of that change, where she takes notice "remains unclear." She credits Aaren with giving her notice, shrugging off any claim to "prescience" or "patience." She acknowledges that Aaren takes his time letting her in on "certain things" and at the same time takes away any attribution of Aaren's behavior as unusual. Do you see how something is being subtracted with each sentence? "The medium is the message" (McLuhan, 1994/1964). But in case we missed the point, which is the point, that is, that something has gone missing, Pizer tells us that she didn't have a way to think about what she knows about Aaren's name, and then she forgets.

Here in a few deft strokes is her story of experiencing Aaren—noticing and forgetting—left for us to miss and discover in plain sight like the purloined letter. The enactment of her prose is another clue that we are in a lyric narrative, which, like the lyric poem of Vendler's (1995) description, has "a structure that enacts the experience represented" (p. 5), thus placing it in close proximity to, if not at times overlapping, the enactive mode. The lyric narrative is also closely related to the evocative mode, because its aesthetic is "affective-expressive" (Miner, 1990).

You may remember that Bion (1992b; my p. 57) said he has little confidence in his ability to represent in writing what happens in an analysis, but he feels he can "do something" to the reader that was "done" to him. He has "had an emotional experience," and he has confidence he can evoke that experience in his readers (Bion, 1992b, p. 43). The distinction between representation and evocation, which Bion makes, is fundamental to the study of poetics (Miner, 1990). Culler (2001) writes: "Whereas Aristotle's poetics is mimetic because of its base in drama (the representation of action), the various lyric-based poetics are, as Miner styles them, 'affective-expressive because they presume that a poet is moved by experience or observation to give expression in words and that that expression is the cause of moving the listener or reader' (24–25)" (p. xvi). The poetics of lyric narratives are affective-expressive, because they are constructed to move the listener/reader as the analyst is moved by the analytic experience as it unfolds.

What else do you notice that is in plain sight but could easily be missed in the opening of "Maintaining Analytic Liveliness"? What else does Pizer show us about how she works analytically? And how is the way she works analytically related to the way she writes?

Her prose plays on "the music of what happens" (Heaney, 1979, quoted in Ogden, 2005a)—or doesn't happen, on what emerges and then disappears. We can hear how she remains open to the analytic process as it unfolds with all its uncertainties, ambiguities, and limitations of present sight. In "Passion, Responsibility, and 'Wild Geese,'" Pizer (2005a) doesn't narrow down the possible meanings of reading Oliver's poem to her patient. She doesn't foreclose the meaning of Sam's question of whether she had a supervisor. Likewise in this paper, she does not rush to meaning with the information Aaren gives her. She stays open to possibilities with an absence of conscious intention. She stays open to being moved by her experience with Aaren, even to the point of blanking out.

I sense something else happening in her prose. Try this experiment: Holding the content of what Pizer says about Aaren aside, notice what is happening *in you* in response to her voice as you read. Take, for example, her phrases "remains unclear for a while"; "Of course I'm not saying very much"; "after all"; "that alone is not unusual"; "But the point I'm trying to make here"; "I didn't know how to think about it"; "Often I just forget"; "So what's my story?" To my ear, these off-hand comments suggest more than a casual attitude. To me, they convey someone who is at ease in the midst of not knowing, someone who is not holding herself out as an expert or getting ahead of her story, someone who doesn't have to impose order at the expense of narrowing potential meanings. I take Pizer in as someone who is unguarded and willing to let me in on whatever she is thinking. Her informality and openness put me at ease. I hear her voice as if she's speaking to me, and I am carried along by her cadences as she is carried along by her experience. I am also comfortable knowing only what she knows, comfortable even with her forgetting, because it doesn't ruffle her.

As you read the next few paragraphs, see if you experience any of these reading effects. Does hearing Pizer's more informal voice make the idea of your writing a lyric narrative seem more approachable? Thinking as a literary critic, can you imagine why this paper is written in such a colloquial voice? Here's the next passage:

> Maybe I should begin with a brief portrait of how I view this man: middle height, middle aged, a hidden sweetness somewhere, but nothing particular to say about his looks except in those sudden, open moments when he breaks into the most remarkable smile because of a pun he makes—original and ridiculously funny!
>
> And don't let me forget to tell you about this nonverbal quirk that I've grown so accustomed to I hardly notice when it's going on. You might call it a tick of some sort, or now that I come to think of it, a rhythmic ticking like a metronome. It's a syncopating gesture Aaren makes when he is working through an idea or trying to recapture some vague remembrance. His gaze goes out to nowhere while his right arm rises up away from his lap as if to draw attention to itself but not *him*self. With pointer and middle finger slightly crooked, the hand conducts a formulation back and forth to accompany whatever it might be that can or cannot yet be said.
>
> Aaren, father of three—Rachel, Benjamin, and Sarah—married a psychologist, which may account for the large store of quotes and facts he holds about analytic theorists and theories. Perhaps his extensive knowledge of psychology (along with other esoteric subjects) contributes to his success as a lawyer, but who knows. Maybe his hungering for every kind of information relates to his favorite Grandfather, who owned a grocery around the corner and held all the items of his varied inventory in his head by heart! Only Aaren's Bubbe let him handle the long-polled grocery grabber that he rode like a horse around the town in Bubbe's game of search and grab the Kellogg's Crunch. Or maybe Aaren's endless quest for intellectual erudition helps defend against depression over having dropped his natural musical gifts and the pursuit of a life-long wish to play his violin in a national orchestra.
>
> Not that he should change his profession or anything—after all, he and a group of friends have formed a little quartet, and they do play together when

they find the time. But I have said to Aaren on more than one occasion that I thought his giving up his dream of a musical career sits inside him like an ungrieved stone that puts a barrier between himself and feeling free with other people. Little did I know when we began together, the full extent of the inertial drag of loss on this man's living. But I am getting ahead of myself. (Pizer, 2007, pp. 4–5)

This excerpt is also marked by colloquial phrases that underscore the writer's conversational address to her listeners/readers, her focus on the lyric present, and her respect for what can't be known in present experiencing: "Maybe I should begin with"; "And don't let me forget to tell you about"; "You might call it . . . or not . . . come to think of it"; "perhaps . . . but who knows"; "But I am getting ahead of myself."

Notice how Pizer paints a portrait. A few nondescript details are followed by two particularizing details, the first of which speaks to an animating smile that suddenly breaks out when Aaren puns, and the other, a "nonverbal quirk," is associated with a metronome, which is described in more detail than Aaren's smile. One tension of Aaren's character is visually displayed, and the weight of the evidence goes to the nonverbal quirk that characterizes Aaren's self-absorption.

Lyric narratives, as I have said, do conceptual work. In the very next paragraph, Pizer (2007) does some of that work while still maintaining her conversational voice. This paragraph makes artful use of the story of Aaren's name:

Before going on about Aaren and me, I need to bring up some unavoidable truths about the telling. We need to keep reminding ourselves—or I do, anyway—that interactions in the consulting room unfold before we actually realize what is experienced within and between the two persons involved. We may be forming an impression that's attached to an idea, but there is nothing reliable to count on in the moment. *Experiencing* precedes whatever theoretical view we might have about what happened. Naturally, we can't avoid our preconceptions, nor should we try. But it helps me to bear in mind that whatever working assumption I pick up from the past necessarily narrows the field of present experiencing. That's just how it is. Anyway, when I do come around to putting my theory together with clinical narrative, or even the narrative with a theory in order to tell it to my colleagues, you have to know I am doing a kind of biased, backwards, job. However I might end up telling you my narrative, much of the story remains as silently out of sight as the story of Aaren Kahn, born Aaron Kahn, is Aaren Kahn. (p. 6)

Pizer uses her own words rather than quoting others, which she will do later when she brings Gendlin (1981) in by name and discusses how we create a dialogue between our "felt sense" and the words we use to approximate meaning (my pp. 248–249). Can you spot the markers of her colloquial voice? I would select "or I do, anyway"; "That's just how it is"; "Anyway, when I do come around"; and "a kind of biased, backwards, job."

In the next paragraphs, Pizer (2007) follows her "truths about the telling" with an example:

> For example, Aaren Kahn has come to my home office for over ten years, beginning in the summer of 1996. He soon became my first appointment of the morning. Always he arrives early and always with a book. On his days, initially, for some unthinkable reason, I have left the door between my office and the waiting room open—allowing Aaren the freedom to come in and sit on my couch to read before I arrive. Some place in my awareness I must have recognized the absolute necessity for Aaren to prepare himself in my space in this particular way before we could attempt to be with one another. Not that he hadn't *already told me* that he always carried a book around, a book chosen from the latest stack picked up at the library. *He told me* that waiting at the train station to go to work he reads, riding the train he reads, sitting on a stool in the department store while his youngest daughter, Sarah, shops, Aaren reads. He "has to do it," is all that he can say. I "knew" this to be a fact, but that is not the way I took it to heart.
>
> The reason I can grasp Aaren's need to sit in my space with a book before he can look up and return my greeting is because it happened in a process of awareness operating well ahead of my carrying it forward as an explicit bit of felt meaning. And I can refer to an aspect of it now because of that experience one morning when unmindful of the clock, I walked into my office fifteen minutes early. Surprised to see my patient reading in his place, I hastily excused myself and retreated. I felt "caught!" Can you imagine that, in my own office? Almost stealthily, I moved back into home quarters, biding my time until a few minutes before the appointed hour.
>
> In this moment, I'm not exactly sure why I feel so ashamed about leaving my door open and having backed off like that. For now I am content to simply mark the body sense and save the rest for exploring in my own time. I could too easily divert myself from the task at hand. I need to try and stay as closely as I can to one unfolding neighborhood of happenings between Aaren and me. (pp. 6–8)

Pizer is content to save a few things for exploring on her own and intentionally leaves things for her readers to explore themselves. The temptation to tie clinical threads up too neatly can be an occupational hazard in doing our work and especially when we write about it. Later on, Pizer elaborates this point:

> And if we simply overlay what we perceive is happening with what we think we know already, we contribute one more set of bricks to the firewall that separates us from vital growth and change in any relationship. Or, stated more explicitly, my experiencing in interaction with Aaren and all the tools at my disposal *must be felt within my body self as new* if I am to overcome the challenges in maintaining analytic liveliness in the face of all that threatens me with deadness and in my attempt to keep track of clinical momentum when it is stopped in the name of sheer survival. (p. 25)

This cautionary note suggests another reason for Pizer's colloquial voice. It doesn't lead with ideas or theory, from higher levels of abstraction, but rather moves from embodied experience, bottom up, to ideas. Pizer moves from heart, gut, hunch, and "felt sense" (Gendlin, 1981; my pp. 248–249) to meaning. Even when she brings in theory, she does so in a straightforward, grounded way, using her conversational voice, drawing on personal experience and countertransference insights, and introducing quotations of others as she narrates her own process of sorting things out.

Here's an example that includes a description of how felt sense works:

> Holding theoretical considerations while maintaining analytic liveliness may constitute a paradox that we have to deal with from the start. Speaking for myself, resonant theories serve as essential tools when I connect them with my current experiencing. I don't mean to say that my sense of an arrangement of particular character traits won't call to mind a theorist I've read. In the initial phases of being with Aaren, I might well have glanced over to my bookshelf at the faded, once-blue dust jacket of a book containing a collection of Harry Guntrip's papers about schizoid phenomena. I might even have paused to wonder about Aaren's insurance diagnosis and whether or not I'd ever put schizoid or avoidant personality on a form, because a metronome is not the music of experiencing.
>
> A resonant theory works the other way around. You've been sitting with a person for a period of time, and then something nags in you that is unfamiliar. You can't quite recognize the thing. But if you focus on the ambiguity, if you attend to it, refer to it within yourself, you get a kind of nonverbal sense. After a while you find a word or a phrase that may or may not match up with this sense, and you keep on going until you feel like you've got it. Often it is at this point that a resonant theory arrives in your head full blown; *it* connects to *you* like a sudden unexpected guest who puts the whole thing in perspective. (Pizer, 2007, p. 11)

Pizer's "Maintaining Analytic Liveliness" is an artful interweave of narrative summary, immediate scenes, self-reflections, and occasional use of concepts and theory. Yet none of the non-narrative elements by themselves or in combination overpowers the narrative flow or comes before the reader has a chance to inhabit the lyric present.

I have another hunch about Pizer's use of a more colloquial voice. In the beginning of his analysis, Aaren is unavailable for relationship—with his analyst or himself, prompting Pizer to ask, "How do we locate felt experiencing within ourselves when experiencing within the other is adamantly denied or when it is specifically requested that we do not know what we might know before the other finds it in himself?" (p. 25). Using such an unguarded voice in her writing is one way Pizer locates her experience for her readers and herself. In another paper, Pizer quotes Jonathan Foer's explanation of why he writes: "It's not that I want people to think I am smart, or even that I am a good writer. I write because I want to end my loneliness" (quoted in Solomon, 2005, p. 3). As Leo Gursky says in Nichole Krauss's (2006) novel *The History of Love*, "I wanted to describe the world because to live in an undescribed world was too lonely" (p. 7).

As I continue to think about Pizer's voice, an association to the vernacular tradition in American literature clamors for attention. The vernacular tradition begins in early American humor and often plays on the contrast between the vernacular speech and wisdom of the country bumpkin and the so-called sophistication of the city slicker. From there, it stretches out through Huckleberry Finn and Will Rogers to Holden Caulfield and beyond. I also think of the softly lined face of the sage Leston Havens as he interviews a psychotic patient in front of an audience of interns and hospital staff. Havens' body language is as soft and rumpled as his face, calming the other by joining in his or her dis-ease. Havens creates a safe place and close alliance, sitting as an unobtrusive presence and empathic witness alongside the person he sees as a fellow human being. Havens is able to put his interviewee at ease in part because he presents himself in such a plainspoken, vernacular style.

Tanner (1965) writes, "A new vision clearly requires a new style to transmit it. For language, as Eric Auerbach so brilliantly demonstrated in his book *Mimesis*, reflects a particular attitude toward reality, a certain way of world-watching: style *is* vision. It concentrates on certain aspects of reality and omits, ignores and neglects others. It determines focus and distributes emphases" (p. 12). The aesthetic of a lyric narrative conveys a vision of the way we work as analysts, our attitudes, and certain ways of "world-watching" and "worldmaking" (Goodman, 1978), present moment by present moment. "Style *is* vision," and a writer's voice speaks more than words.

Exercise 7.1

Beginning Your Lyric Narrative

If the examples of Pizer's lyric narratives are enough of an impetus for you to start writing one of your own, please begin. If you'd like a few more prompts, read on.

a. Be a narrative sleuth. Look at another writer's clinical narrative that is not written in the lyric narrative mode and mark all the evidence that the writer/narrator relies on retrospective knowledge to construct meaning.

b. Rewrite a portion of the other writer's narrative as a lyric narrative even if you have to make up material to bring the uncertainties of the present moment alive.

c. Pick a clinical moment in a narrative you have already written and write it up as a lyric narrative. Use dialogue, the present tense, interior monologue. Suggest more tentative understanding than certainty, even confusion if you felt it, as befits being in the lyric present rather than looking back on it with the wisdom of hindsight.

8 The Paradigmatic Mode

The imaginative application of the paradigmatic mode leads to good theory, tight analysis, logical proof, sound argument, and empirical discovery guided by reasoned hypothesis. But the paradigmatic "imagination" (or intuition) is not the same as the imagination of the novelist or poet. Rather, it is the ability to see possible formal connections before one is able to prove them in any formal way.

Jerome Bruner, *Actual Minds, Possible Worlds*

Ideas are the currency of the paradigmatic mode. I think of them as having attributes such as texture, weight, tension, resonance, intrigue, direction, edge, shape, and complexity. In the paradigmatic mode, ideas may be presented straight up (pp. 154–155) or infused with passion and significance. Here are several examples:

All our stories are about what happens to our wishes. (Phillips, 1998, p. xiii)

Psychopathology represents the scar tissue of the injury to the capacity to feel. (Russell, 1998, p. 34)

When at work, we bumble, stumble, and get lost. We know we are into mixes of not yet knowing (our dumb spots), of not being free to know because of acquired biases and preference for theory and technique (our hard spots), and of having lost, for reasons of intrapsychic conflict, our hold on what we know or thought we knew (our blind spots). (McLaughlin, 2005, p. 188)

In everyday usage, motivation is the answer to the questions "What do I want to do?" and "Why do I want to do it?". . . In our view, motivation involves a complex intersubjective process from which affects, intentions, and goals unfold. Motives are not simply givens; they emerge and are cocreated and constructed in the developing individual embedded in a web of relationships with other individuals. (Lichtenberg, Lachmann, & Fosshage, 2011, p. xiii)

A central contention of this paper is that enactive knowing develops and changes by processes that are intrinsic to this system of representation and that do not rely on translation of procedures into reflective (symbolized) knowledge. This is not to contend that translating enactive knowledge into words may not be an important therapeutic tool or developmental step; it is to contend that development does not proceed only or primarily by moving from procedural coding to symbolic coding (or from primary to secondary process or from preverbal to verbal forms to thought). Procedural forms of representation are not infantile but are intrinsic to human cognition at all ages and underlie many forms of skilled action, including intimate social interaction. (Lyons-Ruth, 1999, p. 579)

There is a surprising variation in the stated goals of psychoanalysis from the differing schools. A Kleinian might say that the aim is to return projectively identified parts of the self to the individual, a Kohutian that it is to alter pathological self-object relations and replace them with generative self-object relations, an ego psychologist that it means enlarging the conflict-free sphere of the ego, and a Lacanian that it is to bring the patient into a position to comprehend the truth of his desire. Each of these aims refers to a complex theoretical system and to clinical practice waiting in the wings. (Bollas, 1999, p. 61)

Have psychoanalysts become dinosaurs, fighting a losing battle against extinction as their ecological niche disappears? I think not, but survival of psychoanalysis depends on analysts believing in what they have to offer in this brave new world and acting resourcefully to expand the niches in which they make their contributions. (Altman, 2010, p. xvi)

Although these examples are quite diverse, each presents ideas their authors believe are worth our attention. The word *idea* is derived from the Greek verb *to see, idein*, and is associated with the look of something, a pattern, image, notion, appearance, conception, or form. Ideas express ways of organizing and naming experience. Arguments, in the broadest sense of the word, are ways to persuade others of your point of view (Lunsford, Ruszkiewicz, & Walters, 2010). Let's see what these examples demonstrate about presenting ideas in the paradigmatic mode.

Phillips' (1998) sentence creates an intriguing beginning that could go in any number of directions. I wonder how he will treat his subject given his reference to stories, a word that is rich in overtones. I find his sentence elegant in its simplicity and nod in assent, but such a statement, like a promise, awaits fulfillment. How will it be illustrated, explicated, or played out?

To express his resonant idea, Russell (1998) uses a layered image that implies a narrative. His sentence is declarative, suggestive of the paradigmatic mode. Yet what stays with me is his condensed, evocative metaphor that contains a story. Scar tissue protects. It's the body's way of healing. Metaphorically, it closes off the wound and is a marker of trauma that is mostly hidden. If you rub your finger over a scar, you won't experience feeling on the surface. It's numb. Russell's sentence demonstrates that writing in the paradigmatic mode can be infused with evocative imagery and contain implicit narratives.

McLaughlin (2005) uses accessible language when he defines dumb spots, hard spots, and blind spots. In just two sentences, he sorts, names, and describes phenomena we probably have all experienced. The work of the paradigmatic does not have to be hard work or a slog to get through to be of value. However, self-evident ideas will not hold your readers' interest or be worthy of publication (my pp. 158, 194–195).

Lichtenberg, Lachmann, and Fosshage (2011) open their book with a straight-forward definition of motivation and then add complexity to it. Notice how their ideas unfold progressively with each of their word clusters. Here is one way to mark that progression:

> Motivation involves a complex intersubjective process.
> Affects, intentions, and goals unfold from motivations.
> Motives are not simply givens.
> Motivations emerge.
> Motivations are cocreated and constructed in the developing individual.
> The developing individual is embedded in a web of relationships with other individuals. (Adapted from Lichtenberg, Lachmann, & Fosshage, 2011, p. xiii)

When these authors introduce more complexity to their definition, they do so in a clear, concise way. This passage functions as exposition, a form of the paradigmatic mode.

Ideas in the paradigmatic mode may also be presented with edge, or emphatically, as Lyons-Ruth (1999) demonstrates in her paper that draws on attachment theory, infant research, cognitive neuroscience, and dynamic systems theory. She makes a number of distinctions: between enactive knowing and symbolized knowledge; what she is contending and what she isn't; procedural and symbolic coding; primary and secondary processes; and preverbal and verbal forms of thinking. When authors make such distinctions at the same level of abstraction, they contribute to a paper's conceptual clarity (pp. 184–188). Lyons-Ruth adds emphasis to what she proposes by drawing clear boundaries so she can stake out her claim (my pp. 216–217) and simultaneously defend against misunderstanding. Her paper combines two functions of the paradigmatic: exposition and argument.

Bollas' (1999) distinctions create a clear, concise, and elegant statement about the distinctive aims of four psychoanalytic schools. He writes for knowledgeable readers who would understand the technical terms he uses and appreciate his finesse in using them. Bollas demonstrates that technically informed writing in the paradigmatic mode may be executed with literary style.

Altman's (2010) question catches my attention. Even though he denies that analysts are fighting a losing battle against extinction, the terms in which he casts his question raise the stakes. He goes on to argue "that psychoanalysis has developed as an exclusionary discourse. Classism, racism, and ethnocentrism embedded in our theory are manifest, at the level of practice, by the exclusion of nonmainstream members of our society as 'nonanalysable'" (p. xix). Altman proposes that it is time to carry psychoanalysis beyond its usual boundaries, so it becomes more inclusive in theory and practice. His prose demonstrates that arguments and advocacy can work together in the paradigmatic mode.

Underneath the diversity of these examples lies a common structure of a paradigm as a shared model that succeeds in "solving a few problems that the group of practitioners has come to recognize as acute" (Kuhn, 1970, p. 23; also p. 175). The problems our clinical papers attempt to solve may not always be acute, but papers written in the paradigmatic mode often take on the problem-solving or clarifying tasks of "normal science" (Kuhn, 1970)—to define, differentiate, puzzle out, explicate, demonstrate, compare, evaluate, document, report, review, apply, hypothesize, and synthesize. And they use conceptual structures to do that. When significant anomalies are discovered that can't be accounted for by a community's commonly held beliefs, new paradigms need to be created.

Toulmin, Rieke, and Janik (1979) make a similar distinction between "arguments that scientists put forward *within*, or as *applications of*, theories whose credentials they are not challenging" and "arguments by which scientists seek to challenge the credentials of current ideas and put forward alternatives or refinements in their place" (p. 247). The first kind of argument "presuppose[s] that current ideas [and paradigms] are sound, relevant, and applicable to the phenomena under consideration and use them as a source of reliable warrants" (p. 247), statements that legitimize the link between a claim and its supporting evidence (Toulmin, 2003, p. 91; my pp. 207–209). The second kind of argument "challenge[s] the credentials of current ideas" and thus calls into question "the soundness, relevance, and applicability of the corresponding warrants" (Toulmin, Rieke, & Janik, 1979, p. 247). The paradigmatic mode may be used for both kinds of arguments, but in paradigm-changing arguments, you need to do more work at the theoretical level since you can't take the usual warrants or previously held theories for granted.

Exercise 8.1

The Currency of the Paradigmatic

List several ideas that influence your work as a psychotherapist. Rather than pick ideas that are self-evident, select ones that are more controversial or debatable. Write a few sentences about each. Use the examples from the beginning of this chapter as models.

Exercise 8.2

Just the Idea

Do you have an idea or two on the back burner waiting to be fired up? Try writing each out as briefly as you can, resisting the temptation to elaborate or support it with evidence or reasoning.

Exercise 8.3

Another Way to an Idea

One of the best ways to find an idea is to ask a question or articulate a problem you haven't solved. In this exercise, ask a question or state a problem you would like to explore. You may have more than one.

Exercise 8.4

Go for It!

Write a brief answer to the question(s) or problem(s) you just identified in exercise 8.3. You don't have to back anything up, so you might as well be daring. Feel free to play with the currency of ideas without having to tally their cash value.

Exercise 8.5

Teaching Points

Looking at what you wrote for the first four exercises in this chapter, notice if you start to tell a story. If so, can you extract your main teaching points from it and cast them in the paradigmatic mode?

Exercise 8.6

Paradigm-Affirming and Paradigm-Challenging Ideas

Notice if the ideas you identify in the previous exercises in this chapter affirm, apply, modify, challenge, or upset current paradigms.

Moving Matters

When therapists write about principles guiding their work, their language is often moving and their prose may be enactive even though they are writing in the paradigmatic mode. The opening paragraph of Havens' (1996/1989) *A Safe Place: Laying the Groundwork of Psychotherapy* is a perfect example:

The work of psychological healing begins in a safe place, to be compared with the best of hospital experience or, from an earlier time, church sanctuary. The psychological safe place permits the individual to make spontaneous, forceful gestures and, at the same time, represents a community that both allows the gestures and is valued for its own sake. It stands at the crossroads of society and solitude, at the intersection of those often divergent and equally necessary paths leading to ourselves and to what we need for ourselves—others. In this safe place, created by doctor and patient, we can learn our inhibitions, false alliances, community-denying demands, and why we despair of anything better; and still more important, experience these bits of sickness within a deft association that provides tolerance and hope. Finally, this little community serves as a preliminary, general model for those eventual, particular lives we search for outside it. (p. vii)

I find the direct, active structure of Havens' sentences reassuring and feel safely held by his words and their arrangement, which enact their meaning—to create a safe place for meaning making. When phrases are added to the basic subject-verb-object sequence that Voigt (2009) calls "the fundamental," that sequence retains its prominence. The structure of the fundamental is then repeated from sentence to sentence. Meaning unfolds in a straightforward manner with confidence and ease. You can follow its elaboration phrase by phrase. There are no sudden turns but rather a steady accretion of significance. Havens' compelling images call up my own associations. His echoes of Winnicott add even more resonance for me, because I share Winnicott's values. Havens speaks softly, without flourishes. His resonant words, like pebbles dropped in still waters, send ripples radiating out in all directions as they find their depth.

As evocative and enactive as this passage is, Havens writes paradigmatic prose. This excerpt is organized conceptually. Its ideas, rather than a narrative, are primary even though his writing has the feel of a story being told. There aren't any actors, any narrative agents to propel a plot. Its subject is an idea, the safe place in which psychological healing may occur. As Norton (2009) puts it, "In exposition, the 'protagonist' is an idea and the 'plot' a series of supporting arguments through which the idea must pass, like a classic hero whose journey is marked by tests of strength and wit" (p. 95).

Toward the end of her introduction to *The Unsayable: The Hidden Language of Trauma*, Rogers (2007) evocatively states her purpose. She incorporates questions, employs metaphoric language, and stirs her readers' associations:

This book reveals specific aspects of my work toward one end: to write history where silence reigned, where silence was broken by an undeciphered cry that went unheard. When all the traces of history have been erased and the body itself is inscribed with an unknown language, how does a child begin to speak? How is it possible to listen so that the child comes to know something vital, and speaking freely becomes possible, so that living inside one's own body is no longer a nightmare? These are the questions that would guide my listening. (p. xiv)

In the next quotation Gerson (2009) evokes the therapist's role as a witness to trauma. Listen to the music of his prose (Gass, 2009) and notice the imagery he employs:

> What then can exist between the scream and the silence [of massive trauma like genocide]? We hope first that there is an engaged witness—an other that stands beside the event and the self and who cares to listen; an other who is able to contain that which is heard and is capable of imagining the unbearable; an other who is in a position to confirm both our external and our psychic realities and, thereby, to help us integrate and live within all realms of our experience. This is the presence that lives in the gap, absorbs absence, and transforms our relation to loss. It is the active and attuned affective responsiveness of the witnessing other that constitutes a 'live third'—the presence that exists between the experience and its meaning, between the real and the symbolic, and through whom life gestates and into whom futures are born. (p. 1342)

As these three evocative writers demonstrate, writing in the paradigmatic mode presents "more than cool reason," draws on metaphor (Lakoff & Turner, 1989), appeals to our values, and engages our emotions, which is "a matter that no discussion of argument can ignore" (Booth, Colomb, & Williams, 1995, pp. 144–145). While we have tools to evaluate an argument, its emotional appeal and a writer's character are not measurable in the same ways. Yet "every argument depends on all three—*logos, pathos*, and *ethos*" (Booth, Colomb, & Williams, 1995, p. 145). Writing with a motive (chapter 11) and letting your prose sing will contribute to your paper's pathos. Your *ethos* as a writer will be conveyed through a number of elements, including your voice (chapter 10), your respect for your readers, and your ability to give readers enough data so they can understand your perspective and form their own.

Exercise 8.7

Moving Matters

Pick an idea about some aspect of your clinical work that you find moving and write one or more paragraphs in the paradigmatic mode to convey the meaning this idea has for you. I invite you to experiment with the use of metaphors to add resonance. Let Russell, Havens, Rogers, and Gerson inspire you.

The Narrative and Paradigmatic Modes

While teaching two concurrent seminars, Jerome Bruner (1986) developed his ideas about the narrative and paradigmatic modes as "two modes of thought" with their own "distinctive ways of ordering experience" (p. 11). I didn't know this material when I was teaching writing at the college level, but it complemented the way I taught. You'll soon see why.

At the New School for Social Research, Bruner's students were primarily psychologists; his class at the New York Institute for the Humanities was composed of writers, critics, and editors (Bruner, 1986). While both groups had similar interests in psychological and literary issues, each class approached the same texts differently. "One group, the psychologists, was dedicated to working 'top-down,' the other to working 'bottom-up'" (Bruner, 1986, p. 9). The psychologists privileged concepts and theory, leading Bruner to conceptualize the paradigmatic mode. The particulars of the text were useful to them only in so far as they supported or disproved ideas or theory at higher levels of abstraction. Bruner (1986) writes:

> Armed with an hypothesis, the top-down partisan swoops on this text and that, searching for instances (and less often counter-instances) of what he hopes will be a right "explanation." In skilled and dispassionate hands, it is a powerful way to work. It is the way of the linguist, the social scientist, and of science generally, but it instills habits of work that always risk producing results that are insensitive to the contexts in which they were dug up. (p. 10)

The more literary types privileged the particulars of the text, the currency of the narrative mode. They were partisans of a bottom-up approach:

> Their approach is focused on a particular piece of work: a story, a novel, a poem, even a line. They take it as their morsel of reality and explore it to reconstruct or deconstruct it. . . . the[ir] effort is to read a text for its meanings, and by doing so to elucidate the art of its author. They do not forswear the guidance of psychoanalytic theory or of Jakobsonian poetics or even of the philosophy of language in pursuing their quest. But their quest is not to prove or disprove a theory, but to explore the world of a particular literary work. (Bruner, 1986, p. 10)

Let's imagine a clinical narrative as the object of attention in Bruner's two seminars. How do you think each group would approach it? I think the poets and playwrights would listen carefully to the dialogue, look at what distinguishes particular clinical moments, discuss aspects of the writer's craft, and explore layers of meaning, the resonance of metaphors, ambiguities, and affects. If they were psychologically savvy, they might talk about transference dynamics, for example, or put details of the narrative into a more conceptual context, but their primary allegiance would be to the uniqueness of the patient and the therapeutic process, the multiple meanings and resonances of each analytic couple's story, and the character and quality of the writer's prose.

The psychologists, on the other hand, would appreciate the patient's narrative primarily for what it teaches them about human development, trauma, psychotherapy, etc. Its value would be in its use as an illustration of an idea, concept, or theory. The psychologists would build up from the details of the individual case through higher levels of generalization in order to make an argument or identify principles. Their allegiance would be to ideas, the currency of the paradigmatic.

Clinical papers (as distinct from research studies and theoretical papers) usually create interweaves of narrative details and ideas (chapter 9). If the primary thrust of a paper is through its narrative details, it is likely to be written in a narrative mode and organized temporally (chapter 12). Writing in the paradigmatic mode is organized conceptually and emphasizes the links the author makes between clinical material, interpretations, concepts, and theory (chapter 13). A narrative paper may also reach into higher levels of abstraction (e.g., interpretations and concepts) just as a paper in the paradigmatic mode will unfold through the dynamic path of its arguments, which are usually supported by narrative examples. In most papers, either a temporal movement or a conceptual structure takes precedent. Journal articles in our field are usually written in the paradigmatic mode and rely on narrative details for illustration. They may incorporate evocative or enactive passages, but their primary allegiance is usually to ideas and establishing connections between them rather than to the particulars of the clinical narrative and its temporal unfolding.

From Story to Interpretation

When I taught expository writing at the college level, I used the blackboard as a visual aid to help students understand the difference between retelling a story and developing an interpretation of it. Some students were challenged to make that shift when writing their first college papers just as new clinical writers are often challenged to lift ideas out of case histories, develop concepts about their clinical work, and shift into the paradigmatic mode.

I asked my students to think of narrative details as the data or rhetorical evidence in which they would ground their ideas. To illustrate, I drew several clusters of Xs along the bottom of the blackboard to represent details or narrative sequences. As our discussion of the text got underway, I would draw other clusters of Xs a little higher up but not always directly above the first ones. What I was demonstrating with the second tier of Xs is that writers who are interpreting narratives have to extract meaning from the story, because a plot summary doesn't do the trick. Narrative details often have multiple meanings, and interpretations usually take into account clusters of phenomena. As we talked about Milkman in Morrison's *Song of Solomon*, the blackboard filled with groups of Xs representing narrative details, characters, and ideas at the same and different levels of complexity. At the end of our discussion, what we had represented schematically on the blackboard was an organized network of narrative details, interpretations, and arguments about Morrison's novel that could define the intellectual field of a paper.

Once the intellectual field has been established, you still have a lot of work to do. For example, you need to develop strategies to capture your readers' attention, create momentum, organize your ideas, illustrate them, incorporate sources if appropriate, and bring your paper to its conclusion. Writers I have worked with find it helpful to think of the process of developing the intellectual field of their paper as a first step that is separate from deciding how they will organize what's there and guide readers through it.

Waelder's Levels of Abstraction

In reference to Freudian psychoanalysis, Waelder (1962) distinguishes six levels of abstraction, starting with the least abstract, which includes "data" and its "configurations" that the analyst observes "under the conditions of the analytic situation" directly or indirectly through "derivatives." He calls this "*the level of observation*" (p. 620). "These data [of observation] are then made the subject of interpretation regarding their interconnections and their relationships with other behavior or conscious content. This is the *level of clinical interpretation*" (p. 620). At the next level up, generalizations "leading to statements regarding a particular type such as, e.g., a sex, an age group, a psychopathological symptom, a mental or emotional disease, a character type. . . and the like [constitute]. . . the *level of clinical generalization*" (p. 620). According to Waelder, the levels of observation and interpretation are "indispensible, not only for the practice of psychoanalysis but for any degree of understanding it. Clinical generalizations follow at close range" (p. 620).

Waelder names the next tier up the "*level of clinical theory*" and identifies it with Freudian concepts such as "repression, defense, return of the repressed, regression" (p. 620). This level is "necessary too, though perhaps not in the same degree" as the first three (p. 620). Waelder observes that the distinction between theory and metapsychology, which constitutes the next higher level, is not clear cut, because metapsychological concepts are also concepts, just more abstract. Waelder lists "cathexis, psychic energy, Eros, [and the] death instinct" (p. 620) as examples of the "*level of metapsychology*." At the top of his schema, he identifies "*the level of Freud's philosophy*," which "was, in the main, the philosophy of positivism, and a faith in the possibility of human betterment through Reason" (p. 620).

A Contemporary Model of the Levels of Abstraction

Figure 8.1 presents a contemporary adaptation of Waelder's levels of abstraction that I created to help writers visualize ways to abstract ideas from the narratives of their clinical work and conceptualize them at different levels of complexity. As you will see, this model is a useful tool for developing, analyzing, and evaluating the structure of an argument or a paper. Thinking in conceptual terms and theoretical models (chapter 13) is one way of worldmaking (Goodman, 1978), one way we divide qualitative experience into graspable units. Conceptual structures rise above the ground like a jungle gym, allowing us to gain different perspectives on our clinical experience. But the higher we go, the further removed we are from specific examples and particular details of our clinical work and the more general, abstract, or speculative our thinking becomes. At the highest level of philosophy and epistemology, we think about thinking and how we know. Let me walk you through my model (figure 8.1) and then we'll put it to use.

Philosophy   Epistemology

Psychoanalytic Tradition or School of Psychotherapy

Metapsychology   Body/Brain/Mind

Theories

Concepts

Clinical Generalizations

Interpretations/Explanations

Narrative Details, Scenes, Selected Clinical Phenomena

Figure 8.1 Levels of Abstraction. Adapted by Suzi Naiburg from Waelder (1962).

The Analytic Field

My model includes a three-dimensional schematization of the analytic field, a concept that Waelder does not employ. I think of the analytic field as a cocreated, interpersonal and intersubjective dynamic system in which conscious, noncon-scious, and unconscious elements are in constant circulation within and between participants. From a Jungian perspective, the analytic field also includes arche-types as form-giving potentials, as image schemas that reflect the human mind's propensity for patterning and self-organization (Knox, 2003, 2004). While the analytic couple consciously and unconsciously contributes to the creation of the field and the constellation of archetypes, the field also influences each participant and their interactions (Stern, 1997).

I do not think of the field as a level of abstraction but have suggested its pres-ence with lighter, curved lines to imply that it is multidimensional and nonlinear, the (back)ground or surround from which experience arises and is discriminated. If the field becomes the focus of a writer's attention, it may be treated as a phe-nomenon on the FIRST LEVEL OF ABSTRACTION or brought into play at higher levels depending on how it is used (e.g., as an explanatory model rather than a phenomenon experienced through its effects).

Because the meaning of the concept of an analytic field is not the same across continents and theoretical orientations, you may want to replace my definition with your own. You will find similarities and important differences, for example, among the field theories of Jung (Cambray, 2011), Sullivan, the Barangers, Don-nel Stern, Bion, and Ferro and Civitarese (see *Psychoanalytic Dialogues, vol. 23*, numbers 5 and 6).

A Quick Tour of My Levels of Abstraction

All the levels of abstractions are represented in ascending order with the most experience near at the bottom. Some of my distinctions and vocabulary differ from Waelder's, because they reflect a more contemporary psychoanalytic orientation. The levels of abstraction are open ended, so the template can be used by those of different persuasions. But they're not completely theory free, because I call atten-tion to the analytic field and a need to address the relationship of body, brain, and mind while leaving definitions and the nature of that relationship up to you.

Thinking in narrative terms, what you select to form your FIRST LEVEL OF ABSTRACTION (represented by Xs clustered at the bottom of my blackboard) may be specific clinical moments, scenes, and episodes of your clinical work as well as flashbacks, associations, dreams, and reveries. Both dimensions of the narrative landscape (Bruner, 1990) will be represented here: what's happening and your experience of what's happening.

Phenomena on the FIRST LEVEL OF ABSTRACTION are carved out of larger wholes and are clustered and connected in meaningful ways to render their significance more apparent. Sometimes called clinical facts, such phenomena are nevertheless subjective, context and theory dependent, provisional. We might think of them as presenting "a transient depiction, of a perceived moment—a freeze frame—in an epigenetic process" (Gardner, 1994, p. 936). What you present along the FIRST

LEVEL OF ABSTRACTION are the specifics that become the basis for interpretations, ideas, concepts, and theories at higher levels. As I see it, what you present at each level of abstraction provides the grounding for what you present on the next level up.

As you engage in your clinical work and reflect on it after a session, you may make interpretations to your patient and yourself, draw inferences, and entertain hypotheses and hunches. Let's call these small "i" interpretations. I see them as part of the analytic field whether you explicitly communicate them to your patient or not (Symington, 1983). They influence the field and may also have an existence outside of it, often finding their place at the level of INTERPRETATIONS/EXPLANATIONS, where the significance of your narrative details (on the FIRST LEVEL OF ABSTRACTION) begins to take more articulated shape.

CLINICAL GENERALIZATIONS, CONCEPTS, AND THEORIES are stacked above INTERPRETATIONS/EXPLANATIONS, but the relative heights of each level and the separations between them are not absolute. They are context and user dependent. Such differences, however, will not affect how we put this model to use.

Above THEORIES at the level of METAPSYCHOLOGY, I have added BODY/BRAIN/MIND to signal that new information from the neurosciences is having an influence on clinical theory and practice. I want to underscore that how you understand these relationships (however you do) is an aspect of metapsychology.

PSYCHOANALYTIC TRADITION OR SCHOOL OF PSYCHOTHERAPY is the next level up. Like a system of concepts we call a theory, a system of theories we call a tradition or school influences how we hear and see what happens in our consulting rooms, where we place our attention, and what we write about. One reviewer of my manuscript noted that "you can tell reading clinical material whether you are reading a Kleinian or an Interpersonalist, for example, from what aspects of the clinical work are emphasized (and this is so even if not one word of theory is presented in a given clinical description)." Thus we would expect a measure of coherence between what is presented at different levels of abstraction as the influence of a particular school (or schools) works its way through. Borrowing too freely from different theoretical perspectives, however, may create a hodgepodge and leave your readers believing you haven't grasped the implications of what you are doing unless you explicitly acknowledge that you're shifting theoretical frames.

I have included EPISTEMOLOGY with PHILOSOPHY at the highest level of abstraction even though these influences are often implicit in our written work and may be assumed based on one's allegiance to a psychoanalytic tradition or school.

Filling in this template with your ideas may make it easier for you to see how your ideas are situated in the context of other ideas at the same and different levels of abstraction. In the paradigmatic mode, clinical writers work the levels by making links vertically between ideas on different levels of abstraction and/or by drawing distinctions laterally between ideas at the same level of abstraction (chapter 13). By contrast, narrative papers do their work primarily along the FIRST LEVEL OF ABSTRACTION. They are organized temporally rather than conceptually. Often clinical narratives incorporate reflective, interpretative material and evocative and/or enactive passages as you see in Rogers' *A Shining Affliction*, but the trajectory of narrative writing remains primarily horizontal or temporal.

Analyzing the Structure of an Argument

To see how you can use the levels of abstraction to analyze the structure of a writer's ideas, we'll turn to the beginning of Stephen Mitchell's (1988) "Penelope's Loom: Psychopathology and the Analytic Process." Here are his opening two paragraphs:

> A twenty-year-old student, shortly after beginning analysis, recovers a memory of himself as a nine-year-old boy just back from a camping trip with his father. The latter is a fiercely independent man whose periodic trips out into the "mountain" provided him with continually sought relief from what he experienced as the suffocating degradation of his domestic captivity. This was the first time he allowed his son to join him. The trip had been enormously difficult for the eager and spunky boy, as his father eschewed any concessions to convenience or comfort, combining obsessive self-sufficiency with a taunting challenge to his son. The boy felt vast relief at having survived the trip without disappointing his father in any major way.
>
> Later in analysis he recalls speaking with his mother, an anxious, intrusive, overprotective woman, who had waited nervously for his return and then bathed him in effusive sympathy and solicitousness. Although he was unusually frightened of his mother's ministrations and therefore tended to avoid them, after the Spartan regime of life on the mountain, he was enjoying her interest and concern, telling her details of his trip which were bound to elicit even greater sympathy. In the midst of his account he became aware of his father's presence at the doorway and glanced up to catch a look of surprise and total disgust on the older man's face. Later in analysis he recalls the memory with a dizzying, sickening sense of self-loathing and isolation from both parents. (p. 271)

Mitchell immediately draws his readers in with a powerfully rendered portrait of his patient as a nine-year-old boy caught between impossible parents. He weaves interpretive material in so skillfully that his prose has the feel of a gripping story rather than a didactic presentation. His patient's memories, at the FIRST LEVEL OF ABSTRACTION, serve as the narrative evidence for the conceptual work that follows. Did you notice how these childhood stories are framed by another set of narrative markers? They are easy to miss, because the clinical material is so arresting. The patient's memory of his camping trip is recalled "shortly after the analysis began," the memory of his speaking with his mother is recalled "later in analysis," and the memory of his father's reaction is recalled still later with particularly strong feelings. Thus there are two stories that form the narrative or temporal axis of this paper: the patient's childhood memories and the history of their unfolding in an analysis that allows this patient to experience such disquieting feelings in the safety of a new relationship.

The opening sentence of Mitchell's next paragraph tells us how to read his patient's life narrative as an unfolding of strands of these early memories. In this paragraph and the next, Mitchell shifts from the narrative details of his patient's memories (on the FIRST LEVEL OF ABSTRACTION) to their interpretation (on the SECOND):

> This memory came to play a central role in deciphering and disentangling the strands of this analysand's life. He writes constantly, and his ambition is to be a poet. He works almost completely alone, as if on the mountain, yet with a constant longing for the products of his labors to be loved and taken into people's homes and treasured by them. When a longed-for success in the form of publication or positive critical reaction punctuates a period of dedicated effort, he immediately changes his style of composition. He dreads becoming a panderer for commercial success; the only way to keep his artistic process pure is to abandon immediately any work that gains the approval of others.
>
> His relationships with women are dominated by these same themes. He is drawn to women with deeply depressive longings and helps them in a very sensitive and compelling fashion. He sets them up in a life in which he is the desperately needed emotional center, then constructs realms of escape in which they can only long for but never get to him. There is an aching loneliness for him in these relationships, as he is perpetually struggling to design emotional attachments which, because of their cloying and suffocating quality, he needs always to escape. (p. 272)

Although Mitchell's writing continues to have the feel of a captivating story, the work he does here is interpretive and explanatory. His patient's memory reveals early relational dynamics that are unconsciously repeated in his work and social life, reflecting conflicting loyalties to each of his parents. Mitchell presents the patterns of his patient's adult behavior so we can see the parallels. He connects some but not all of the dots. For example, his patient's working alone "as if on the mountain" is an allusion to his father, which Mitchell draws. The patient's longing for his poems to be treasured is an allusion to the approval he didn't get from his father and got too easily from his mother, which is an interpretation Mitchell leaves for us to formulate. Mitchell also allows us to draw the connection between his patient's dread of pandering for approval and the self-loathing he felt as he remembered his father's disgust when he basked in his mother's attention.

I have placed the material in these two paragraphs on the SECOND LEVEL OF ABSTRACTION on the basis of how it functions in the structure of Mitchell's chapter. In the absence of these childhood memories, in another context, or in a different rhetorical argument, this material might fall on the FIRST LEVEL OF ABSTRACTION. But the point that Mitchell makes—"This memory came to play a central role in deciphering and disentangling the strands of this analysand's life"—announces a relationship between the interpretive material in these paragraphs (the SECOND LEVEL OF ABSTRACTION) and the earlier memory as narrative detail (on the FIRST LEVEL OF ABSTRACTION). It's that relationship that tips us off as to what's what—that Mitchell is dealing with *an idea* about this memory. The difference between whether you map something on the first or second level of abstraction has to do with how that material is used in an argument rather than the content of the material itself.

In the next two paragraphs, Mitchell (1988) introduces a story and image from Greek mythology that lend resonance to his idea that "the relational matrix within which each of us lives" is like "a tapestry woven on Penelope's loom" (p. 272). At the end of this passage and based on the work he does so gracefully, Mitchell moves to the level of theory, proposing an evocative and accessible definition of psychopathology by using the language of the image he has just employed. With each of these moves up the levels of abstraction—by drawing on Homer's narrative to explain a concept (the relational matrix) and theory (of psychopathology), he demonstrates how you can work the levels and write evocative prose in the paradigmatic mode:

> Homer in the *Odyssey* depicts Penelope, Odysseus's loyal wife, as besieged by suitors during his many years' absence. They urge her to abandon her missing husband, who has never returned from the battle of Troy, and marry one of them. She is not interested in entertaining this world of new possibilities and wants to wait for Odysseus's return. In order to keep her ardent suitors at bay, she tells them she cannot think of remarrying until she fulfills her obligations by weaving a shroud for Laertes, her father-in-law. She weaves during the daylight hours and, after the household has gone to sleep, unravels her work by torchlight. She spends years at her endless project, whose seeming futility belies its effective and poignant role in preserving her dedication and holding together her subjective world.
>
> One might regard the relational matrix within which each of us lives as a tapestry woven on Penelope's loom, a tapestry whose design is rich with interacting figures. Some represent images and metaphors around which one's self is experienced; some represent images and phantoms of others, whom one endlessly pursues, or escapes, in a complex choreography of movements, gestures, and arrangements woven together from fragments of experience and the cast of characters in one's early interpersonal world. Like Penelope, each of us weaves and unravels, constructing our relational world to maintain the same dramatic tensions, perpetuating—with many different people as vehicles—the same longings, suspense, revenge, surprises, and struggles. Like Penelope in the seeming purposiveness of her daytime labors, we experience our lives as directional and linear; we are trying to get somewhere, to do things, to define ourselves in some fashion. Yet, like Penelope, in her nighttime sabotage, we unconsciously counterbalance our efforts, complicate our intended goals, seek out and construct the very restraints and obstacles we struggle against. Psychopathology in its infinite variations reflects our unconscious commitment to stasis, to embeddedness in and deep loyalty to the familiar. (Mitchell, 1988, pp. 272–273)

Penelope's tapestry becomes a particularly effective image not only because it is pregnant with meaning but also because Mitchell carefully draws so many links between Penelope's story and the relational dynamics he uses it to portray. I think of these as vertical links, because they form connections between levels of abstraction. Establishing explicit and cogent links, or working the levels, creates your paper's integrity (chapter 13).

Laying Out the Structure of an Argument

In figure 8.2, you will see how I lay Mitchell's ideas out on the levels of abstraction. You may want to read this material both ways—starting at the bottom and working up (bottom up) and starting at the top and working down (top down).

Relational Psychoanalysis

A Theory of Psychopathology

"Psychopathology in its infinite variations reflects our unconscious commitment to stasis, to embeddedness in and deep loyalty to the familiar."

The Concept of the Relational Matrix

Like "a tapestry woven on Penelope's Loom . . . rich with interacting figures"

Image and Story of Penelope's Loom

"Like Penelope, each of us weaves and unravels, constructing our relational world to maintain the same dramatic tensions, perpetuating—with many different people as vehicles—the same longings, suspense, revenge, surprises, and struggles."

". . . like Penelope, in her nighttime sabotage, we unconsciously counterbalance our efforts, complicate our intended goals, seek out and construct the very restraints and obstacles we struggle against."

Patient's Relationships with Women

[Loyalty to father in relational matrix]   [Loyalty to mother in relational matrix]

"Constructs realms of escape"   "Drawn to women with depressive
                                            longings"; "helps them in a very
                                            sensitive and compelling fashion";
                                            "becomes the desperately needed
                                            emotional center"

"Aching loneliness"

Centrality of Childhood Memory in "Deciphering and Disentangling Strands of Analysand's Life"

"Writes constantly" "works almost completely alone as if on a mountain."	Longing for productions "to be loved and taken into people's homes and treasured by them"	"Dreads becoming a panderer for commercial success"
		"Immediately abandons any work that gains the approval of others"
Father's characteristics		Mother's characteristics

Memories

Memory of "Spartan" camping trip with father at 9 years	Memory of "enjoying" his "mother's interest and concern" when he tells her about the trip; father's presence in the doorway; his father's surprise and disgust	Recalls memory with "a dizzying, sickening sense of self-loathing and isolation from both parents"
Shortly after the analysis begins	Later in the analysis	Still later in the analysis

Figure 8.2 Layout of Mitchell's (1988) ideas from "Penelope's Loom: Psychopathology and the Analytic Process"

Laying your arguments out the way I've done with Mitchell's can help you differentiate what you think you've said from what's on the page. In one of my workshops, a writer discovered she had devoted so much attention to a comparative theoretical issue that it distracted from the work she wanted to do at the conceptual level. She realized she had been writing defensively and needed to restructure her argument and reorganize her paper to strike the balance and tone she wanted.

You can also use this template to develop ideas for a paper before you start drafting it. In exercise 8.9, I'll guide you through that process, but first I suggest you start with an exercise to reveal the structure of another writer's ideas.

Exercise 8.8

Analyzing Another Writer's Ideas

a. Find a passage in a clinical article that is clearly written and traverses more than one level of abstraction. Lay the writer's ideas out as I did with Mitchell's.

---

b. What do you notice after doing this? Do you see any gaps between the clinical material and its interpretation? Are concepts adequately grounded in interpretations and clinical details to appear to arise out of the clinical material rather than be imposed on it? Is the clinical material consistent with a particular approach(s) to psychotherapy? Which one(s)? What else do you notice about the way the author negotiates the levels of abstraction?

Exercise 8.9

Developing Your Ideas

I'll walk you through the steps of using the levels of abstraction to help you develop your ideas for a paper. I imagine you will start with selected clinical material and work bottom up.

a. Turn a large sheet of paper sideways to create more width. Jot down a few words at intervals along the bottom of the paper to indicate the selected clinical material you will use. Place your notes in chronological order with the earliest material to the left. Remember you are sketching in ideas to generate your intellectual field, not creating a map of how you will present this material to your readers.
b. Now work your way up through each level of abstraction that you think is relevant, placing notes at intervals as you move up from the bottom of the paper towards the top to indicate what you might want to say at the next level.
c. Go only as high up the levels of abstraction as you'd like to go for this particular paper. Don't try to be encyclopedic. That could be overwhelming for you and your readers, not to mention a lot of work.
d. When you're done, the layout of your notes may look somewhat similar to those in figure 8.2, but that will depend on what you want to say and how you interpret and employ the levels of abstraction in your own distinctive way.

Exercise 8.10

a. Look at what you've noted in exercise 8.9. Can you detect any gaps that need to be filled (chapter 13)?

b. Where would you locate the work of your paper, that area where you are doing your most significant work? At what level of abstraction? Do your notes reflect the focus and priorities you want to pursue? If not, make any necessary changes.

Chapters 12, 13, and 14 will pick up from here. Ideas drive the paradigmatic mode and call out for conceptual thinking. Yet papers in the paradigmatic mode don't have to follow the same format. Even in the paradigmatic mode, you may experiment with form and establish a distinctive voice.

9   Narrative Moves and Interweaves

*Even etymology warns that "to narrate" derives from both "telling" (*narrare*) and "knowing in some particular way" (*gnarus*)—the two tangled beyond sorting.*
Jerome Bruner, *Making Stories: Law, Literature, Life*

Psychoanalysis and history are distinctive disciplines that share important affinities. Both are narrative and interpretative arts that respect the influences of the past, seek to understand them, and put that understanding in service of the present. Narratives organize experience *through time*. They select some phenomena to order and interpret (White, 1981) and use these selections to create continuity and coherence. Exceptions and anomalies call out for explanation, and we respond with narratives that "forge links between the exceptional and the ordinary" (Bruner, 1990, p. 47).

Narratives beget ideas, and ideas may be presented as having a history. In this chapter, you will see how writers execute a variety of narrative moves and interweaves, propelling their ideas and stimulating the reader's while bringing narrative and conceptual knowing into close proximity.

Setting a Context

Clinical writers often set the concepts they use within a historical context by tracing continuities and/or discontinuities in the history of ideas. While some authors make the tracing of precedents their subject, as Ellenberger (1970) does in his seminal study, *The Discovery of the Unconscious: The History and Evolution of Dynamic Psychiatry*, clinical writers typically employ a few sentences, paragraphs, or pages to establish such contexts and put them to particular use. Many use Freud, Jung, or other progenitors as reference points to establish continuity, context, or contrast with their own ideas. They may also use them to borrow, align with, or set themselves up to challenge authority. Establishing historical antecedents can be effective if skillfully done, but if the precedents don't add significance or are merely obligatory, they are better left on the cutting room floor.

Gabbard and Westen (2003) begin "Rethinking Therapeutic Action" by identifying a need for clarification: Interpretation is no longer viewed "as the exclusive therapeutic arrow in the analyst's quiver," yet its role "remains unclear" (p. 823). To establish a context for a necessary rethinking of this concept, the authors identify two historical precedents:

> Loewald was of particular importance in the transition to a broader view of therapeutic action. In his seminal 1960 paper, he noted that the process of change is 'set in motion not simply by the technical skill of the analyst, but by the fact that the analyst makes himself available for the development of a new "object relationship" between the patient and the analyst . . .' (pp. 224–5). Strachey (1934) similarly foreshadowed more recent views in his classic paper on the mutative interpretation, in which he argued that the analyst as a new object is introjected into the patient's superego and thus modifies its harshness. (p. 823)

Shifting from a diachronic perspective to a synchronic one, Gabbard and Westen articulate three current trends that challenge the privileged position of interpretation in psychoanalysis: "(1) . . . the acknowledgement of multiple modes of therapeutic action; (2) the shift of emphasis from reconstruction to the here-and-now interactions between analyst and patient; and (3) the importance of negotiating the therapeutic climate" (pp. 823–824). As you might imagine, the next three sections of their paper elaborate these themes and do so in the same order in which they are presented in their introduction. Gabbard and Westen's use of Strachey and Loewald as reference points highlights both the time it took for change to occur and how much ideas about therapeutic action had changed.

In a similar way, Fosshage (2000) puts a Freud/Ferenczi controversy to specific use in "The Meanings of Touch in Psychoanalysis":

> Physical touch within psychoanalysis has been hotly debated beginning with Freud and Ferenczi. Ferenczi (1953) felt that nurturing touch could facilitate the analysis by helping a patient to tolerate pain that was characterologically defended against. Freud felt that physical contact would almost certainly lead to sexual enactments. In the heat of this controversy, Ferenczi's patient (Clara Thompson) boasted to one of Freud's patients that she was allowed to kiss "Papa Ferenczi" anytime she wished. Freud strongly objected, admonishing Ferenczi that this sort of behavior would inevitably lead to a downward spiral to full sexual engagement. Unfortunately Freud's and E. Jones's subsequent silencing of Ferenczi, now well-documented (Rachman, 1989), forced the issue of touch to go underground. (p. 21)

Fosshage not only establishes a historical context in which to situate his reappraisal but uses that context to underscore the need for his project.

Exercise 9.1

Setting a Historical Context

In a few lines, paragraphs, or pages, set a historical context for an idea you would like to write about. Think of this exercise as an application of intellectual history, cultural history, or psychoanalytic history to situate your idea in a larger context.

Personal Narratives

Another way to set a context for your ideas is to tell your readers how you discovered or developed them. On a practical level, this approach can help you get started. Did you stumble on something significant by chance? Were you trying to solve a problem? What's your story? In his introduction to *Forces of Destiny*, Bollas (1991/1987) explains what he noticed that led him to conceptualize the destiny drive. He begins by setting the stage:

> Psychoanalytic work is most intriguing. After years of a training analysis and the spirited if intense companionship of different supervisors, the psychoanalyst is at last delivered to his place of vocation, seated in that very particular chair, behind that even more special couch. To that place of employment the analyst brings his many acquired skills; he is equipped with cabinets of psychoanalytic models of the mind and theories of motivation and mental process, and yet, how strangely removed from obvious use these factors are when the analysand enters that space and takes up his position. It is such an amazingly complex phenomenon. Shall we ever truly understand it? I wonder. (p. 1)

The merest hint of what is in the analytic space ("that particular chair," "that even more special couch") invites readers to evoke the scene for themselves, filling it in with their associations and imagination. With cabinets of psychoanalytic models and theories "strangely removed from obvious use," readers may wonder what will be used instead. Bollas elicits our curiosity and imagination as his are elicited in his clinical work.

He continues:

> Years ago, a patient, Jerome. . . taught me a great deal about the analysand's use of the elements of psychoanalysis. He did so by changing his use of me, although it is very difficult to just say in what way I changed. He got me thinking about how an analysis can provide the patient with transference objects that seem to facilitate the analysand's spontaneous expression of unthought known elements of his own character. Jerome, like many analysands, used different elements of my own personality—factors he knew to be common

features of human personality—to exercise personality potentials of his own. Indeed he thrived on his uses of me by eliciting a variety of personality elements which seemed to nourish his own personal establishment.

This all took place alongside ordinary essential analytic work, and I noted it, but I could never quite make sense of it. It just seemed to happen, to be important, but not analysable, as his employment of me was natural and not the action of projective identifications aimed at installing anything of himself into me. Indeed the concept of his putting into me or of my containing a part of him just didn't apply. (pp. 1–2)

Although I find echoes of Winnicott in this passage, Bollas does not trace this lineage or present his ideas in the paradigmatic mode. Instead, he tells the story of what he learns from his patient's use of him. Bollas incorporates versions of the word "seems" three times and repeatedly notes what he did not know. Twice he casts aside two possible explanations. His use of the narrative mode rather than the paradigmatic facilitates an open-ended, experience-near perspective and process orientation.

The next paragraph begins with a "time tag" (Alberts, 2010), an indication of the narrative mode. Bollas' curiosity continues to propel his story:

Time passed and my wife gave birth to our son whom I helped to look after for half of each day from his birth. What struck me was how he was who he is from scratch. He seemed to be in possession of his own personality, his own very unique configuration in being (what I term an idiom) that has never really changed in itself. He has of course taken on much more and is as complex as the rest of us due to his life with his mother and myself, but the very core of him is as it was. But what is this idiom? How does one provide evidence for it? I have been mulling this over now for some time.

Who knows how recognitions come to one. One day, while at work with an analysand, I simply realized that one of my functions for him was to be of use for his idiom moves—private articulations of his personality potential—which could only be accomplished by eliciting different elements of my own personality. He used me well I thought. He presented a dream, indicated he wanted me just to mull it over, then suggested he wanted my associations, but not an interpretation. He also wanted an affective response and he picked a good quarrel with me. Later he drew upon my sense of humour, then my ability to recall the previous sessions and so on. I was impressed by how the uses of me seemed natural, if not conflict-free, then irrelevant to the conflict model of the self, and yet urgent. He was not engaged in a form of unconscious communication, either in narrative content or in the transference—countertransference paradigm. In fact, I think he was just living his life. (p. 2)

In the structure of Bollas' sentences, the naming of concepts, such as "an idiom," "idiom moves," and "private articulations of his personality potential," is subordinated to the narration of his process of discovery. Observations do lead to ideas and hypotheses—e.g., "he was who he is from scratch," "he seemed to be in possession of his own personality," "one of my functions for him was to be of use for his idiom moves"—girded by Bollas' sense of wonder. The analytic process looks to Bollas as if his analysand is "just living his life," and we, like Bollas, gather impressions. Bollas lays out narrative objects for our use as he shows us how we become objects for our patients' use. In this way his prose is enactive: It does what it describes.

The next two paragraphs shift from the narrative mode (still at play in the first sentence) into exposition (a form of the paradigmatic) as Bollas presents his ideas conceptually:

> I believed I could see a link between this patient's use of me in analysis and my son's use of his others to serve as human mediators of the articulation of the true self. It is a form of play in which the subject selects and uses objects in order to materialize elements latent to his personality, akin to a kind of personality speech, in which the lexical elements are not word signifiers but factors of personality.
>
> This book is an effort to think about this aspect of a patient's use of the analytic situation. In part one I entertain the idea that the theory of the true self will serve as a conceptual home for some of what goes on in the clinical hour: the patient's spontaneous use of the analyst as an object. He does so, I believe, to articulate and elaborate his idiom, an accomplishment dependent on the environment's sensitive presentation of objects for such use. In psychoanalysis, the objects of use are the setting, the process, the many elements of the analyst's personality, and those ideas he contains as psychoanalytic concepts. There is an urge to articulate the true self, and I name this the destiny drive which I link up to the force of the true self to elaborate personality potential. (pp. 2–3)

The concepts that Bollas links together in this last paragraph have been introduced in the preceding paragraphs, bottom up, through specific examples and the story of how he developed them. This way, Bollas' concept of the destiny drive is grounded in experience before it is presented conceptually.

Exercise 9.2

Personal Narratives

a. If you already have an idea for a clinical paper, use the narrative mode to tell your readers how your idea evolved. If your idea took shape over time, give your readers a sense of that history. If you had an epiphany, tell that story.

b. If your ideas are not yet developed enough to follow the suggestions above, take a clinical situation you want to write about and tell your readers the story of how that situation became interesting, problematic, puzzling, or significant for you.

Narrative Summaries

Narrative summaries are the most frequently used narrative technique in clinical prose. They are useful if not essential in setting the context for the presentation of immediate scenes (Stein, 1995) and present moments (Stern, 2004) and for establishing transitions between them. They compress time and condense history, identify patterns and telescope themes (Alberts, 2010). Thus they are indispensable in presenting the sweep and dynamics of longer segments of clinical work and are often called into service as rhetorical evidence to illustrate an idea. But like a plodding workhorse, they may be overused and lack vitality. So let's see how you can bring them to life.

As you know from reading Eigen (my pp. 32–34), narrative summaries can be charged with emotion and may be evocative and enactive. But they can also be effective when they are quieter as Rogers (1995) demonstrates when she gathers her impressions from her first session with Ben and reflects on what happened (my pp. 19–20).

Exercise 9.3

A Narrative Reflection

a. Imagine you have just written an immediate scene (my pp. 15–19, 21) that presents a psychotherapy session or a part of one. You could also write that scene if you like.
b. Summarize enough of what happened in the session you are thinking about (or just wrote about in part *a*) so your readers can track your process of linking what you remember to what you make of it as Rogers does (my pp. 19–20).
c. Like Rogers, you might be sitting at your desk taking notes. Or like McLaughlin (1993), you might be puttering in a woodshop, garden, or other "transference sanctuary" (p. 79) that supports your self-analytic work. Consider locating yourself for your readers so they can place you as you do that reflective work.

Textures

The opening paragraph of Helen Grebow's (2008) vignette "My Meeting with a Mafia Moll" is animated by her subjectivity and textured with vivid language and an evocative image:

> Gloria arrived for our initial consultation thoroughly armored in her tough and edgy façade, successfully assuming an intimidating stance. I immediately felt suffocated by the amount of space this small, 35-year-old woman filled in my office. I was overwhelmed by feelings of intimidation and

trepidation, as if I were, in fact, in the presence of a mafia moll. Gloria had a breathtakingly artful facility to use colorful language as a means of silencing rather than engaging me. Her manner of speaking was caustic, shrill, and pressured. Her imperious demeanor rendered me impotent and dumbstruck. She took charge of the session and did not hesitate to let me know that she had no more patience for "fucking therapists" who thought they knew it all! (p. 20)

In the next few paragraphs, which are also written as narrative summary, Grebow sketches Gloria's history in broad, jargon-free strokes, emphasizing her previous therapies and hospitalizations. The simplicity of her prose may reflect her quiet presence as an analyst, while the eruptions of colorful language enact the outbursts of affective intensity in the treatment process:

Gloria had begun treatment with her prior therapist, Therapist A, after a serious depressive episode that required hospitalization. Again, Gloria provided me with her own definitive analysis of the cause of her depression. Her depression was the culmination of years of emotional and physical abuse. Her abuse began in childhood and had continued through adulthood, played out in abusive relationships with numerous men. Medication had been prescribed with no appreciable results.

Finally, Gloria had moved to escape her last emotionally and physically abusive relationship. However, she had not anticipated feeling isolated and even more depressed in the absence of her support system of friends and family. It was then that she slipped into a state of deep depression and fragility. Initially she had tried to self-medicate, using combinations of medications, both prescribed and "procured," from hospitals in which she had worked. Finally, unable to function at work and sufficiently frightened by her state of mind, she voluntarily admitted herself into a hospital for treatment. Upon release from the hospital, she was referred to Therapist A and continued to see him for a couple of years until he moved out of the city. Therapist A had tried to provide referrals for her so that she could continue her therapy. She "despised" these referrals. She quickly and dismissively terminated each treatment, discarding Therapist B, Therapist C, and Therapist D in rapid succession. I, then, became the next link in this chain of eviscerated therapists—of analytic road kill. (p. 20–21)

A few choice words make this last sentence pop. Grebow's selection of details is instructive in other ways as well. She doesn't specify the details of the abuse her patient suffered as a child. Sketching in history more generally, as she does, may be fine as long as her main ideas are adequately illustrated. That, of course, is a judgment call to be made in light of her argument and her paper's rhetorical mode.

But if Grebow were to include more particularizing details (Stein, 1995, p. 254), her summary might lose its enactive force. Details that "individualize" and "differentiate" one feature from another (Stein, 1995, p. 254) could reduce the sharp contrast between the contours of her general descriptions and the bite and surprise of her more colorful phrases. Too many details could obscure her focus, distract her readers, and dissipate momentum. To write an effective narrative summary, the selection, number, and texture of the details you include need to serve your purpose and your readers' need to know without sidetracking or overwhelming them.

Knowing that very brief summaries can do important work may help you be more concise. Sometimes only a few sentences are needed as Havens (1993) demonstrates in "Some Gestures" when he tells us the patient he calls "the quiet woman" remembered that for the whole morning she hadn't wanted to die (my p. 38) and as Rogers demonstrates when she includes a brief narrative summary in her description of her first meeting with Dr. Sachs (my p. 28).

Exercise 9.4

Textures of Narrative Summaries

In this exercise I suggest that you write a narrative summary several times. Start with only a few broad strokes. With each successive revision, make your details more abundant and specific. Do this several times until you have too many details to be effective. In other words, let your production of details get out of control, so you will know what that's like. Then scale back and write a version that's a keeper.

Dynamics of Personality and Process

Writers often use narrative summaries to introduce a patient's presenting problems, character, history, and relational patterns. Notice the balance Philip Bromberg (2006) strikes between generality and detail and how he focuses his readers' attention:

> Helen was a patient in her mid-30s whose history of severe trauma had led to a reliance on dissociation so longstanding that she was unable to experience herself with a past that felt like hers, a present that she breathed life into, or a future that she could imagine. To ensure that the protective function of her dissociative solution remained reliable, she had defined the scope of her existence in a manner so limiting that she allowed herself almost no interchange with the outside world other than her work. When not in her office, she secluded herself in her small apartment, saw few friends, had virtually no social life, and was sexually inactive. (p. 74)

Two paragraphs later, Bromberg selects a few specific, telling details to mark important changes that occur in Helen's ability to relate and reflect:

> After about five years of work we reached the point where Helen was able to hold in conscious awareness the existence of moments when her thinking just stopped, when her sense of reality faded, and she was able to reflect on her own dissociative processes and the functions they served. Not surprisingly, she also began to share with me aspects of herself that were now safer to allow into our relationship, including her growing ability to make self-reflective use of some of my writings in a way that was dramatically different from her storing them away as protection against discovering their existence unexpectedly and being helpless to prevent their assault on her mind. (p. 75)

These two paragraphs are incisive narrative summaries that tell a story, trace a trajectory, and set the stage for Bromberg's more scenic, dialogue-filled presentation of a surprising session that follows them.

Although the events of a narrative summary are "told about rather than shown" (Stein, 1999, p. 239), some summaries create the illusion of our witnessing what has transpired. Look again at Grand's (2010) narrative summary of how her family told endless stories when giving directions (my pp. 49–50). Their exuberant behavior comes alive as if the scene were being played out before us on stage. In Phillips' "Clutter: A Case History" (2001a), I sense that I am hearing or "overhearing" (Northrop Frye quoted in Atwood, 2002, p. 126) what's going on:

> The person I want to write about, a painter in his early thirties, referred himself to me because he thought he was becoming 'mildly agoraphobic'. It was, he said, difficult to be sure because, obviously, he spent most of his time at home painting. He was not, he thought, a loner but had, ever since early adolescence, a passion for painting. He had a world of friends and a girlfriend; he knew something about psychoanalysis and it was clear to him, as far as he knew, that he did not especially have relationship problems. As he said, what 'people call relationship problems should just be called relationships'. I couldn't help agreeing, while also assuming that he was locating something about desire—about his link with other people—in his apparent symptom. His mild agitation about going out, and in particular the way he found himself steering clear of wider open spaces like parks and countryside, made him wonder, as he put it, 'what there was out there that he didn't want to see.'
>
> Since, perhaps unsurprisingly, he thought of his fear in visual terms I asked him if he could see any links between his fear and his work. When I asked him this in our first meeting a curious thing happened. He said, 'When you asked me that, I suddenly had a very strong image of that famous photograph of Francis Bacon's studio. And I remember thinking when I first saw the picture, "How could he find anything in all that mess?" Then he paused and said, as an afterthought, 'And his pictures are

so uncluttered.' I said, entering for some reason into a seminar on Francis Bacon, 'Yes, it's odd, isn't it? The paintings are uncluttered but rather claustrophobic.' And he replied, rather amazingly to me, 'You feel like the figures can't get out, but Bacon got them into it so presumably he could get them out.' There was a pause then, and I had so much to say that I couldn't think of anything to say. It was as though we had suddenly done a lot, and there was too much already. The word I want to use now is 'cluttered'; but as it turned out, a sense of impossible excess was to be integral to this man's predicament, and hence the predicament he would put me in. What I did say was: 'Are you worried that I might get you out of painting?' And he replied, 'I will be in a mess if I come here with agoraphobia and you cure me of painting!' As is often the case, I think, when people fear that psychoanalysis will destroy their talent—and symptoms are a talent, if only for survival—they are often having to manage a very powerful wish to be cured of it. (pp. 61–63)

Phillips' first paragraph provides important background information in the form of a narrative summary, which is focused on particular issues that have occurred over some time. Narrative summaries are great vehicles for doing that, because they can emphasize "the recurrent nature of an action rather than an event" (Alberts, 2010, p. 110). When I read Phillips' clinical material, I hear his voice as if he's speaking. Many of his sentences are interrupted by parenthetical phrases, e.g., "as far as he knew," "I couldn't help agreeing," "perhaps unsurprisingly," "as an after-thought," and "as it turned out." These function as "involvement strategies" (Elbow, 2012, p. 78): They show Phillips taking his listeners into account, guiding them, and giving them access to his and his patient's thoughts and feelings. They contribute to the illusion that Phillips is speaking, that the text has an audible voice (my pp. 88–90, 130–135) and an audience. I seem to hear his patient too. When Phillips doesn't quote him directly, his language projects his patient's voice and dry wit.

In his second paragraph, Phillips shifts from narrative summary to portray an event. The shift comes in the second sentence, with the introduction of a time stamp ("in our first meeting") and the inclusion of more dialogue. In these two paragraphs, Phillips demonstrates how to create a narrative summary in an audible voice and use it to set up a scene. Even though the information in the first paragraph is summarized, I feel that I am eavesdropping on an intimate analytic conversation in which this information has been exchanged.

Images and Themes

As you have seen, narrative summaries may be used to establish temporal contexts, identify ongoing patterns, and/or focus on a patient's psychodynamics. Summaries may also be used to create expectations, introduce themes, and zero in on aspects of the treatment process. In "Bearing the Unbearable: Ancestral Transmission through Dreams and Moving Metaphors in the Analytic Field," Judith Pickering (2012) introduces her patient with a narrative summary of the imagery that emerges in her analysis:

Introducing Rachael

> I was thrown in the deep end with Rachael, plunged into subterranean realms of experience beyond anything I had ever previously encountered. In her first session she said, 'It's been a watery year for me, full of tears. I'm really depressed, like I'm stuck in some kind of drain'. She spoke of 'treading water', unable to fully enter the 'swim of things'. Sometimes she felt submerged in a watery grave which she called her 'deathy mode'.
>
> She brought many dreams of swimming pools representing both terror and fascination with plumbing her depths. There was a sense that we were feeling our way together into such zones: sometimes tentatively dipping our toes in the water; sometimes colluding in an unspoken reluctance to dive into the unknown; sometimes drawing breath ready to take the plunge. A sense of immersion permeated our imaginal and affective space, a necessary induction into her internal world. A recurring dream of a waterless concrete swimming pool signaled a malignant 'heart of darkness', whose significance only gradually emerged.
>
> Throughout six years of analysis watery motifs, images of pools and drains welled up recurrently in Rachael's dreams, evoking recovered memories and generating the metaphoric vocabulary between us. Why did Rachael and I unconsciously use so many metaphors concerning water, pools, drowning to describe her internal landscape? (pp. 576–577)

What you choose to summarize sets up your readers' expectations and indicates what you deem relevant. Pickering's focus on the images and metaphors of Rachael's analysis is a telling choice. It goes to the heart of the process as it unfolds for this analytic couple and suggests some of the affects that are stirred up before they are understood. The language of metaphor also opens potential space for Pickering's readers to inhabit. Her first and last sentences create multiple motives in narrative terms that propel readers into her story. What were those subterranean realms? Why was this analysis so watery? As Pickering demonstrates, a narrative summary may serve more than one purpose.

An Artful Interweave

Well-written narrative summaries can gracefully shift between experience-near close-up shots, wider views, and more panoramic perspectives. Joye Weisel-Barth (2006) demonstrates how you can change the depth of field to create a vivid and varied narrative summary:

> It's a bad sign when I dread an appointment. But here it is, dread rumbling inside like a storm warning. It is Thursday, a cool early evening in fall. Anticipating winter, the sky is already growing dark as Sally arrives for her 6:30 appointment. I feel a shiver and wish to be done working and inside my warm, bright house. Instead, I rub my hands together and hug my arms in preparation for another likely icy session with Sally. It has been

rough going for a few months, a negative, angry transference in full tilt, ever since I returned from my three-week summer vacation. Sally had come for twice-weekly therapy for only six weeks before I took this vacation; but during that time she had struck a sympathetic chord in me, touched me, and challenged me to help her. She seemed to have made a beginning connection to me as well.

Sally had come to therapy for two main reasons. The first reason: she was in a failing relationship with a married man who did not love her. This liaison typified Sally's relational history. The second more general reason for therapy: she wanted to know why she feels so dead in her life. Hard working and professionally accomplished, successful by social and economic measures, she feels nothing except alien, disappointed, and empty. The mother of high achieving adult children, whom she likes well enough, she claims to feel no particular love for them. One child recently married; and while Sally orchestrated the wedding, she felt nothing particular at the occasion, except perhaps a moment of displeasure at not being adequately acknowledged in the wedding toasts.

During the first few weeks of therapy, her lover of several years terminated their relationship. Sally spent several sessions grieving, her tears expressing an array of feelings: sadness, loneliness, emptiness, but noticeably, no anger. At that time she thanked me for understanding her and for the few simple interpretations I made. Then, over a single weekend, she shut down her feelings. She told me at our Monday meeting that she no longer felt anything about the loss. She has never again mentioned her ex-lover.

Sally embodies stark contradictions. She shows capacity for both fiery feeling and frigid withdrawal. Although she claims to "feel nothing," I read in her intelligent face and deep eyes sadness and longing. Sally has one of those "rubber faces" with large eyes and a wide mouth, an elastic face that expands and contracts, crinkles and stretches to encompass a wide range of emotional experience. Her voice, too, is full of feeling. Even in a straightforward narration, it has a pleading quality. Her sentences end on raised notes, their music like a continuous stream of questions. And her strong pull on me for focused attention and cognitive understanding seems to belie her claim to "feel nothing." However, after certain empathic responses on my part, responses in which I amplified Sally's feelings with my own, she made clear that she neither likes nor wants that kind of empathy from me. It was shared emotional resonance that upset her. The experience of emotional resonance, in fact, makes her angry. (Weisel-Barth, 2006, pp. 373–374)

Let me identify the various moves Weisel-Barth makes as a writer in this well-honed narrative. First she describes the setting, her emotional state, and the current icy atmosphere. In the process, she brings us into the present moment, makes evocative use of the storm metaphor, and creates suspense. With the sentence that begins "It has been rough going for a few months," she focuses on a broader perspective. In the beginning of the second paragraph, she brings another aspect of the treatment into focus. When presenting a patient, especially in a case conference, clinicians often begin with the patient's reasons for seeking therapy. Because Weisel-Barth introduces those after she's established the emotional climate, we can import what we know of that atmosphere into what she tells us, infusing it with more affect.

With the sentence that begins "Hard working and professionally accomplished," Weisel-Barth describes the striking contrast between her patient's outward success and inward deadness and then introduces evidence to support the claim that her patient feels dead. The next two sentences provide two tiers of evidence. The first statement (she doesn't feel any love for her children) is broader than the next: She "felt nothing" at her child's wedding except a little "displeasure" at being slighted.

The third paragraph brings other contours of this treatment to the fore. "During the first few weeks," "several sessions," "no longer felt" and "never again" indicate a sweep of time and use of narrative summary. Details of specific emotions and a couple of specific interactions are interwoven and framed with time markers: "at that time," "She told me at our Monday meeting." In the last paragraph, Weisel-Barth begins with the idea that Sally is a study in "stark contradictions." Then she lays out her evidence, which is effective, because it is specific, vivid, abundant, and multidimensional. Feelings, voice, qualities of her patient's expressive face, and the "pull" her patient exerts on her analyst build that evidentiary base. The paragraph closes with the observation that Sally gets angry when Weisel-Barth is empathic, which in turn makes us wonder how these two will work together.

Telling and Knowing

As Bruner (2002) remarks, the verb *to narrate* has two intertwined roots: to tell and "to know in a particular way" (p. 27). A narrative is told from a particular point of view, sometimes even more than one. But it is always told from the point of view of a narrator as teller *and* knower, however imperfect and unreliable the narrator may be. When narrative summaries present few vivid details and mostly tell rather than show, readers are more confined to what they are told and the meanings the narrator asserts. Little or no room is left for them to draw their own inferences, entertain alternative possibilities, or evaluate the narrator's perspective. Narrative summary is dependent on the narrator's word, not just the words we read but the narrator's subjectivity and the trust we feel in the narrator as knower. Narrative summaries that are more detailed and textured give us access to the narrator's subjectivity, and those that show as well as tell will give us more opportunities to understand and evaluate the reliability of the narrator's knowledge.

Immediate scenes are even more open ended, because a scene presents more than it tells, sometimes more than the narrator may know. The more your narrative summaries approach scenic writing and are combined with scenes that show, evoke, and/or enact what you experience, the more your readers will be able to sit in your place, try on your experience, and draw their own inferences.

Exercise 9.5

Degrees of Freedom

a. Write a narrative summary of a single clinical episode that interweaves your interpretation of what's going on and offers little or no freedom for your readers to make up their own minds about your interpretation. Tell them, don't show them; be authoritarian in this part of the exercise.
b. Using the same clinical material, provide more details and greater access to your subjectivity; *show as well as tell.*
c. Using the same clinical material, create an immediate scene that *shows more than it tells* and offers your readers even more degrees of freedom than the two versions you just wrote.

---

10 Voice

> *In all the poets here, there is presence rather than absence, force rather than slackness, daring rather than timidity, idiosyncrasy rather than typicality. In almost all of these cases, one can say, "That's Bidart," or "Gary Snyder, of course," or "Graham, unmistakably," or "Heaney, yes." That is, one could not mistake Snyder for Dove, or. . . . Each has left a mark on language, has found a style. And it is that style—the compelling aesthetic signature of each—that I respond to as I read, and want to understand and describe.*
>
> Helen Vendler, *Soul Says*

It's no wonder that voice receives a lot of attention in writing classes and the revision process. It is the primary vehicle through which we feel we come to know an author and authors come to know themselves in more profound ways. But finding your voice doesn't come easily—or all at once. "For a writer, voice is a problem that never lets you go," A. Alvarez (2005) observes, "—if for no other reason than that a writer doesn't properly begin until he has a voice of his own" (p. 11). Having begun, the challenge of voice renews itself—with each creative effort, each clinical intervention. Ogden (1998) associates voice with "the *use* of language: voice is an action, not a potential—more verb than noun. The individual voice is not resting dormant, waiting for its moment to be heard. It exists only as an event in motion, being created in the moment" (p. 445). For Ogden (1998), who has written extensively about voice in literature and the consulting room,

> creating a voice with which to speak or to write might be thought of as a way, *perhaps the principal way*, in which an individual brings himself into being, comes to life, through his use of language. This conception of voice applies to all forms of language usage, whether in poetry, in fiction, in prose, in drama, in the analytic dialogue, or in everyday conversation. (pp. 426–427; emphasis added)

As important a concept as voice is for writers, its meaning is hard to pin down. Connotations proliferate; some are elusive, others, all inclusive. Paradoxes, even confusions, abound (Elbow, 1994; Yancey, 1994). The words on the page are silent, yet we seem to hear a voice in the text, sometimes more than one (Elbow,

1994; Yancey, 1994). Sometimes a textual voice emerges spontaneously in our writing while we are busy doing something else, yet developing a voice of one's own takes time and effort. Experienced writers have distinctive voices, often strikingly so; yet each writer's voice, like a singer's, extends through a range and is influenced by any number of variables. Whose voice(s) do we hear in a text anyway? The author's, narrator's, or that of our reading self (or selves)? Or maybe "a third voice that is generated in the creative conjunction of reader and writer" (Ogden, 1998, p. 444)?

In this chapter, we will explore these paradoxes and questions, focusing on what will be useful to you as a clinical writer and reader attuned to the writer's craft. I will elaborate the meaning of an "Audible Voice," "Distinctive Voice," "Voice with Authority," and "Resonant Voice" (Elbow, 1994) as they apply to our specific concerns. We will return to some of the voices we have already heard and listen to others. Exercises are included.

A Voice in the Text

The metaphor of a voice in the text is grounded in our understanding of human voices—how they develop in the company of other voices; become distinctive and also change; reflect feelings and self states or attempts to mask them; and are shaped by bodies, cultures, audiences, and occasions. Some papers more than others (whether heard at a conference or read on one's own) seem to be more audible (Elbow, 1994), creating the illusion that the writer is speaking directly to you. What makes them so?

Exercise 10.1

Listening to Audible Texts

a. Listen again to Barbara Pizer's voice in each of her two lyric narratives (chapter 7).
b. What do you notice about the way her "speaking tone of voice [is] somehow entangled in the words and fastened to the page for the ear of the imagination" (Frost, 1995, p. 713)? What specific characteristics of her prose contribute to your sense that you *hear* her speaking?
c. What other clinical writers create the impression they are speaking to you? What do you notice about the way they write that creates their audible voice?
d. How audible is your voice in your clinical prose? What contributes to its audibility or inhibits it?

A silent reading "evokes a silent voicing in the reader" (Kahane, 1995, p. xiii) that paradoxically activates the muscles and nerves of vocal production (Elbow, 1994) while simultaneously suppressing "enunciation" (Stewart, 1990, p. 1).

A sense of someone speaking is heard however silently. We animate the text—and not surprisingly. Speech "contains more semiotic channels than writing . . . more channels for carrying meaning, more room for the play of difference," like volume, pitch, speed, accent, intensity, timbre, and silence, which are all infinitely variable and part of patterned sequences (Elbow, 1994, p. 5). Giving voice to a silent text is our first act of interpretation however involuntary it may be.

To facilitate the illusion that a text has an audible voice, a writer has to convey speech-like qualities with "fewer resources" (Elbow, 1994, p. 5). Barbara Pizer creates her audible voice by drawing on the cadences and intonational patterns of informal, even colloquial, speech, on what Elbow (2012) calls "vernacular eloquence." Even though her sentence structure is varied, her sentences, like Havens' (pp. 37–42), seem to be "uttered" rather than "constructed" (Elbow, 1994, p. 9). Sentences that are "idiomatic," "easy to say" (Elbow, 1994, p. 7), and "sculpted into intonational units" (Elbow, 2012, p. 113) will seem more audible. Elbow (2012) defines an intonational unit as "a phrase that's comfortably sayable in one nonstop piece of rhythm: a phrase with a bit of musical shape or intonational rhythm to it, and a phrase that probably ends with at least a tiny natural pause" (p. 114). Sentences whose intonational units more closely resemble speech will be more readily understood. When I broke the sentences in *Scum* into intonational units (pp. 59–60), I found them easier to take in. Perhaps you did too.

Audible texts use *I* more prominently, may address readers directly, and contain fewer nominalizations and more "parentheticals" that "make the text seem an enactment-of-thinking-going-on rather than a record-of-completed-thinking" (Elbow, 1994, p. 31, fn. 2). Audible texts often incorporate the kinds of involvement strategies that characterize conversation: "all kinds of ways in which speakers use words that communicate their connection with the listeners and also their own connection to what they are saying" (Elbow, 2012, p. 78). The last two lines of my previous paragraph reflect involvement strategies as I comment on my own experience and ask you about yours.

Like Pizer (chapter 7) and Havens (pp. 37–42, 99–100), Nina Coltart employs involvement strategies in her writing. See if you can spot them along with other qualities that contribute to the audibility of her prose. The following excerpt is from "Psychoanalysis vs. Psychotherapy?" (1993):

> In the course of a large number of consultations I have done during the last twenty-five years, I am often asked, "What is the difference between psychoanalysis and psychotherapy?" The rather oddly placed question mark in the title of this chapter appeared because I have never been able to formulate a clear, concise answer to this question. I wish I could. Consultations would flow on more easily if I could produce a brief, explanatory paragraph which satisfied the intelligent questioner.
>
> What I usually say, though not at all satisfactory to me, does address some of the more practical points which are relevant, and which are in the mind of the patient, jostling with imaginative anxiety about whatever I am currently prescribing. It is something along the lines of. . . . (p. 13)

Coltart casts these paragraphs in the narrative mode, which is ubiquitous in conversation. She connects with her readers as she tells her story and lets us know what she thinks about what she does. I discern her attitudes in "the oddly placed question mark," "I wish I could," and "not at all satisfactory to me." Coltart is a seasoned consultant, but her prose reflects humility, humor, and a respect for what she doesn't know. The conversational quality of her writing is also evident in its lack of jargon and in the simple rhythms of her sentences and their natural and easily articulated intonational units.

There's another aspect of Coltart's sentences that contributes to their audibility. To show you, I have laid one out in figure 10.1.

Consultations would flow on
    more easily
        if I could produce
            a brief,
                explanatory
                    paragraph
                        which satisfied
                            the intelligent questioner.

Figure 10.1 Layout of Coltart's (1993) right-branching sentence from "Psychoanalysis vs. Psychotherapy?"

Not only are Coltart's thoughts easy to follow, but her thinking unfolds along with her sentence (figure 10.1). This is a right-branching sentence: It "start[s] with the main clause and then add[s] phrases or clauses *afterward*. If you diagram such sentences, the added bits will be to the right" (Elbow, 2012, p. 85). Conversation and audible texts tend to have a greater proportion of right-branching than left-branching sentences. Right-branching sentences reflect the writer's mind adding as it goes. "Left-branching sentences 'pre-add' phrases or clauses—they come *before* the main clause—and they are to the left when the sentence is diagrammed" (Elbow, 2012, pp. 85–86). Left-branching sentences require more forethought on the author's part and demand more of the listener, who has to hold information in working memory until the main clause completes the author's thought.

Coltart (1992) begins the following paragraph with a left-branching sentence, which has a complex narrative structure with several moving parts that amble toward its main clause:

Sometimes, now, when I look back over the early years of building up a practice, when one gratefully accepted whatever came one's way, and just got stuck in, I shudder and wonder at some of the gross psychopathology that revealed itself on our proud, young couches. Or at times, of course, *off* them, as we sat through session after session of violent acting-out, with the patient storming, crying, crouching, throwing things, in one case cutting herself—either in one's room, or God knew where. Across my mind's eye, there lurches such a procession—the woman who brought a long kitchen knife, and sat in the chair opposite me, twirling it and humming a careless little tune; this same woman, maddened with anger because I 'tricked' her into handing over the knife, leaping out of the chair and with one great sweep of her arm, hurling everything on my mantelpiece off it on to the floor and all over me—a carriage clock, two silver vases filled with water and freesias, a little box which sprung open and poured out pins, brooches and kerbigrips; an ivory carved netsuke, several postcards, and a cut-glass scent jar. She sat over me triumphantly as I sat and dripped among the ruins. 'There!' she spat out. 'You *minded*, didn't you? I can see you blushing . . .' (pp. 99–100)

Audibility exists on a spectrum, but I imagine you can hear Coltart's characteristic voice and humor in this passage despite its greater grammatical complexity. When she uses a number of elements to create a series, her sentences are still quite audible. "Storming, crying, crouching, throwing things, in one case cutting herself" is one. Then there's that vividly detailed procession of patients in the next sentence and her catalogue of collateral damage her patient exacts. As you can see, right-branching sentences (or sentences with more right-branching than left-branching parts) may contain many components, but the sentences will be audible if the parts can be easily assimilated and what's added is simply connected (e.g., by commas or coordinating conjunctions). If you are writing a paper for oral presentation, consider creating an audible text, because it will be easier for your audience to take in.

Before we close the book on how to recognize audible texts, let me note that writing that is "speakable even if it is not spoken" (Gass, 2012, p. 151) may also be audible. Such writing may not sound the way you usually do in conversation but the way you would like to sound (Kidder & Todd, 2013). Rather than " 'write the way you talk,' " Kidder and Todd (2013) advise writing "the way you talk on your best day. Write the way you would like to talk" (p. 125).

Here's an example of a speakable voice in the narrative mode. Do you recognize this writer? If so, how?

I cannot give this patient a false name, and I cannot use his real name. What he wants is to be recognized, identified, and identifiable. But he needs to persist as no one. He is an identical twin in a family of 11 children. Sent to work, called to dinner, these were two boys in tandem. Always fused, always fungible, always referred to as "the twins." Inseparable, indistinguishable to his own parents, my patient's own mother never called him by his name. Invisible, uncertain of his own specificity and existence, he would open the family Bible. There, on the front page, he was listed with the other children. He would read the names and appear. But the reassuring inscription would turn upon itself. His family was Christian fundamentalist. They preached hellfire. The Bible burned with the prospect of damnation. Named, the devil could locate him; he would be a "sinner in the hands of an angry God." He closed the family Bible, and disappeared.

While he was avoiding Hell in the afterlife, he was living Hell on this earth. The ninth of eleven children, he was born to White evangelical farm laborers. His parents were depleted by poverty but prohibited from birth control. They had no love for their offspring. Children were hired out as day laborers. At home and at work, children were beaten; they went hungry; their bones broke from harsh labor; they collapsed from dehydration. Sometimes infants died, and sometimes they didn't. Toiling in the fields, small hands bled from picking cotton. Looking up from his work, my patient saw gnarled limbs, bent backs, an infinite series of hands, reaching. If he worked, he got to eat. When the harvest was over, there was nothing to eat. They moved, and moved again and again. For years they were homeless.

If any comfort existed, it was not from his parents. Comforting had to occur in secret, in stolen moments, between the siblings. They nursed each other's wounds. They carried each other's burdens. They shared food, and took beatings for each other. These children met other children, gathering the harvest. All of them dehumanized and reduced, and still, they seemed to recognize one another. As Orange (in press) described such children, they transmitted trauma; but they also consolidated their own resourcefulness and resilience. Sometimes, they even laughed. In other families, there were parental gestures of warmth and protection. With my patient's parents, there was only grimness, brutality, and neglect. And there was no such thing as God's love. Suffering was sanctified by religious rhetoric. Satan was purged by hard labor, by hunger, and by the fist. (pp. 449–550)

This is another example of Sue Grand's (2013) evocative, narrative voice. You may have recognized her incantational style, her rhythmic cadences propelled by short, easily voiced intonational units, and the powerful punctuation of each paragraph's end line. Her descriptions are richly detailed, yet her prose is economical, even taut. She anchors her patient's psychological realities not only in the textures of family dynamics but also in the harsh realities of social class, poverty, and religious fundamentalism. Most of her sentences are right-branching. In the left-branching ones, the rhythms of her prose move us easily through introductory phrases and dependent clauses to facilitate comprehension.

Of course, we hear a written text subjectively, so no two silent readers will assess its audibility exactly the same way. To my ear, Grand's autobiographical text (my pp. 49–50) has a more audible voice than her writing about Rosa (my pp. 46–49) or than Eigen's incantational voice (my pp. 52–54). But you may not hear their voices the same way, even though we would probably agree that the excerpts from Havens (pp. 38–43, 99–100) and Pizer (chapter 7) are closer to the high end of the audibility spectrum than either Grand's or Eigen's. Being aware of the differences—however you parse them—may help you evaluate the sound of your own voice in your writing.

"Other things being equal," Elbow (1994) remarks, "most readers prefer texts that they hear—that have an audible voice. After all, when we *hear* the text, we can benefit from all those nuances and channels of communication that speech has and that writing lacks" (p. 10). If you want your papers to be more audible, you may revise them with these principles in mind. Yet you can't generate an audible voice by following a set of rules. That's not how we learn to talk, and rules, writers say, are meant to be broken (Maso, 2000; Prose, 2006).

The process of generating an audible text might be approached by stepping out of your own way and putting other expectations aside—to sound like an authority, pass muster, be polished or impress. If speaking "into the page" (Elbow, 2012) stymies you like the injunction to be spontaneous, try setting the stage for yourself. Imagine that you are sharing your ideas with a trusted colleague, working them out in the presence of a receptive listener. Such a real or imagined interpersonal context is likely to influence you subliminally if not overtly and help you incorporate more involvement strategies and conversational rhythms into your prose. It may encourage you to think out loud and reveal more of your thought process.

Feeling attended to, you may risk being more expressive, which in turn could increase the intonational quality of your prose. Elbow (1994) draws on Bakhtin for this idea: "As he puts it, intonation is the point where language intersects with life. And he points out that we often lose intonation in our speaking, if we lack 'choral support' from listeners—that is, if we have an audience that doesn't share our values" (Elbow, 1994, p. 9). However you experiment with producing your first draft, when you are ready to evaluate whether it is as audible as you want it to be, you won't have to depend on imagining the sound of your own voice. You can look for the evidence on the page.

While audible texts have many advantages, I would not want to forgo the pleasures of Henry James's fiction, Grand's (2003) literary depiction of Rosa and the postwar Brownsville neighborhood, or the dramatic and incantational voice of Eigen, among others, whose texts may be heard in different registers.

Character and Distinction

Our voices usually give us away. People who know us can identify us by how we sound. They may be able to tell how we are feeling. Even people we don't know may sense if our words are connected to our feelings and what some of those feelings are. Because human voices reflect personalities and self states, we tend to project character onto textual voices (Elbow, 1994), often equating a textual voice with the author's presence. For Aristotle, personal character, or ethos, functions as a means of persuasion (Abrams, 1985, p. 136). Ogden (2001a) identifies several character traits in Winnicott's voice: his informality, respectfulness, intelligence, humility, and playfulness. Winnicott's voice is

> casual and conversational, yet always profoundly respectful of both the reader and the subject matter under discussion. The speaking voice gives

itself permission to wander, and yet has the compactness of poetry; there is an extraordinary intelligence to the voice that is at the same time genuinely humble and well aware of its limitations; there is a disarming intimacy that at times takes cover in wit and charm; the voice is playful and imaginative, but never folksy or sentimental. (Ogden, 2001a, p. 301)

Ogden (2001a) hears this voice as "the most distinctive signature of Winnicott's writing" (p. 301). Yet Ogden's characterization of Winnicott's voice applies almost attribute by attribute to Havens' (1993) voice in "Some Gestures" (my pp. 37–42). Both writers elicit our trust, suggest rather than insist, and invite their readers to collaborate in the creation of meaning. Both writing styles are deeply rooted in psychoanalytic sensibilities. Ogden (2001a) observes that while Winnicott's "writing is personal, the voice has a certain English reserve that befits the paradoxical combination of formality and intimacy that is a hallmark of psychoanalysis" (p. 301). Havens (my pp. 35–42) is wary of trespass and gives his readers, as he gives his patients, room to think their own thoughts. Yet we would not mistake one writer's voice for another. Each is "recognizable or distinctive" (Elbow, 1994, p. 13).

Exercise 10.2

A Distinctive Voice

We can usually recognize a writer's voice even when he or she writes in a different mode. Can you identify who wrote the following paragraphs? What tips you off?

Without sensitivity what would life be like? Sensitivity nurtures us, gives life color, expressiveness, charm—provides a basis for terror. Sensitivity, feeling, and thinking feed each other, are part of each other. Thinking and feeling are ways sensitivity unfolds or grows. We speak of emotional sensitivity, reflective sensitivity not just the raw life of sensations. But without the sensory sea we take for granted, feeling and thought would dry up and die.

We have the capacity to focus on different aspects of our experiential matrix, to select a bit of experience for a time and try to see what it is made up of. . . .

One can tease out sensory elements from the perceptual flow and imagine them to be building blocks of experience, as if what we see is made of sensation bits compounded into unities. It is, indeed, possible to decompose the world into bits and pieces, focusing on intensity of hue, textures, line fragments. Stare at a surface long enough and it loses form, dissolves, changes contour, challenges categories. But the fact that we can tune into and break up our experiential field in lots of ways does not make any one way primary.

We can focus on the rise and fall of sensations or on the wholeness of objects. Or we can try to relax focus and let the perceptual flow splash through us. The fact that such an attentional capacity exists at all is amazing. That it provides us with the ability to create worlds of experiencing by subtly blending sensation, perception, feeling, and thought is even more amazing.

M. Klein and W. R. Bion apply the bits-and-pieces vs. wholeness categories, which characterize earlier writings on sensation and perception, to emotional life. Klein believes unconscious fantasy mediates affective movement from part to whole object experience, for example, seeing mother as breast or nipple vs. seeing her as an actual person, a subject in her own right. In the first, the other exists in terms of a partial function or service. If the function runs well, the other is felt as good, and good feelings result (or, vice versa, good feelings produce a sense of a good object). If things do not go well, affect is negative, allied with negative object perception. It is as if, Klein suggests, there are two worlds of feelings and objects, good and bad, depending on the emotional sensation dominant at the moment. If things go very badly, affect may not only split into positive and negative valences, but fragment and disperse (proliferation of splitting), dovetailing with a sense of self and object fragmentation. If affect dispersal goes far enough, feeling diminishes and, finally, is lost. (2004, pp. 3–4)

Turn to page 142 to learn whose voice this is.

Exercise 10.3

Another Distinctive Voice

Do you recognize the following writer's voice? How do you know whose it is?

Cognitive empathy, where the therapist silently completes the patient's sentences, is both the most precise and the least used method of testing. It is a form of mind reading. The therapist who shares a patient's world listens, at the same time, to the patient and to his own resonances with the patient. He can test immediately and exactly the extent of that resonance by the closeness of his own inner voice to the spoken words of the patient. It is most accurate when the patient uses familiar and habitual phrasing—others are elusive. Yet, in fact, reading minds with a measure of accuracy is generally possible.

What I term imitative statements are nothing more than these inner voices of the therapist speaking out loud for the patient, what is called "doubling" in psychodrama and work with children. Thus: "How can I decide?" might be said to the doubtful person; "What hope is there?" to the depressed one; or "Where does one find the courage?" to fearful ones. There are as many imitative statements as there are thoughts to be shared, but for clinical use they sort into types that have specific purposes.

The first objective is to indicate that the therapist is with the patient, specifically with those who both need someone and yet find it difficult to have anyone close. To such individuals, imitative statements must above all be *bland*. The goal is to comfort by our presence, not to startle by our prescience. Not everyone knows that minds can be read or that only a few people are so creative and unique that their thoughts could surprise anyone. Many people are deeply private; they believe their thoughts should never be known, often not so much out of shame or fear but rather out of a sense of possession. These are the people whose self-possession has been eroded from the start; they have been forced to move further and further into themselves, like a defeated populace retreating to mountain or jungle country. When we read minds, we are once again threatening self-possession. (1986, pp. 27–28)

Turn to page 143 to find out who this writer is.

Style

Style encompasses the innumerable ways in which "a piece of writing is formed—the choice of a quote, a single word, the honoring or dishonoring of a grammatical nicety" (Kidder & Todd, 2013, p. 108). Like voice with which it is often equated, "it's not as if a style is a one-time discovery. It is created and re-created sentence by sentence, choice by choice" (Kidder & Todd, 2013, p. 108). For Ogden (2012), style and content are inseparable aspects of one whole:

Neither content nor style exists without the other. Nevertheless, if, for the moment, we think of content as the anatomy of writing, then style is its physiology. Content, in the absence of style, is a lifeless corpse; style, without content, is an insubstantial wraith. Together style and content comprise the living, working body of writing waiting to be read. It is for this reason that . . . I treat writing style and ideational content as two qualities of a single entity—one cannot say the same thing in two different ways: to say something differently is to say something different. (p. 7)

Because the same principle applies to the relationship between a paper's form and content, Ogden (2005a) observes, it's essential for us to "begin to experiment with developing original forms for giving shape to one's ideas. . . . A fresh idea demands a fresh form in which to say it" (pp. 24–25).

Tone

Tone is a useful literary term that refers to the relationship between the voice in the text and its listeners and also between voice and the material that is presented. Monitoring whether your voice is apologetic, critical, moralistic, defensive, or other than you would like it to be may require enlisting another reader's opinion or putting your writing aside for a while so you can hear your voice with greater acuity. Brower (2013/1951) asks several questions that may help you locate your voice: "Where in the social hierarchy" do the fictional speaker and auditor stand in relation to each other? (p. 22). How does the speaker address his or her imagined listener? For example, with ease, respect, tact (Young-Bruehl, 2003), presumption, or . . . ? Brower differentiates between tone as a reflection of a social relation and manner as the way "the speaker adopts within this relationship" (pp. 22–23). "Lapses in tone are, simply put, lapses in respect" for your readers, your subject, or yourself (Norton, 2009, p. 164). How you address your readers, express your relationship to the material you present, incorporate self-reflection, and use yourself in your writing will all contribute to how your readers gauge the transparency, trustworthiness, and character of your voice.

A Third Voice

We experience another mix of voices when we read, because we bring the voice in the text to articulation with our own voice as silent as it may be. Whose voice(s) do we hear? The voice that is shaped through the sounds, cadences, and intonational units of the text? Our silent reading voice? Ogden (1998) identifies the voice we hear as a third, jointly created by writer and reader and unique to each pair.

If this third voice emerges from a unique synergistic process, how can you help your readers hear the voice you want them to hear? Margaret Atwood (2002) reminds us that when a reader is reading, the writer "is not in the same room" (p. 126). So you have to create tone by "musically scor[ing] your text" (Atwood, 2002, p. 158). If you don't write a text that "is a score for voice" (Atwood, 2002, p. 158), you might erroneously assume the surplus meaning you convey when you talk is available to your readers. Stein (1995) learned this lesson the hard way. Stone "read our stories to us in a monotone as if he were reading from the pages of a phone directory. What we learned with each stab of pain was that the words themselves and not the inflections supplied by the reader had to carry the emotion of the story" (Stein, 1995, p. 4).

If you can't read your drafts as Stone would, Stein (1995) recommends asking a friend "who has the least talent for acting and is capable of reading words as if they had no meaning" (p. 4). I remember asking a writer how his readers would know that he and his patient were angry with each other, and he read the passage in question aloud. I could hear the anger in the tone of his voice and the way he paced his words, but that's not what "the evidence of the text," "the givens" on the page supplied (Rodenburg, 2002, p. 4). He revised what he'd written by interspersing "acting and character clues" (Rodenburg, 2002, p. 4) in and around the lines of dialogue to make that anger stand out. He also shaped some of his sentences to enact the edge he felt. With his revisions, even a Stone-flat reading wouldn't leave anyone in doubt. You may certainly temper Stone's and Stein's advice. Elbow advises against having your paper read in a monotone, but don't assume the expressiveness of your speaking voice will be heard in the language of your text if you don't inscribe on the page the intonational units and musical effects that you want your readers to hear.

A Voice of One's Own

A woman in the late nineteenth-century English-speaking world who raised her voice to speak to power was considered "angry" or "strident"; her voice, "shrill" (Heilbrun, 1988). Articulate women face the same accusations today. Gilligan (1982) found that girls entering adolescence learned to dampen or mute their voices to preserve relationships. Some boys, it turns out, would do the same. For women, having a voice of one's own has long been associated with resistance (Gilligan, Rogers, & Tolman, 1991; Gilligan, 2011) and with women's struggle to assert their authority and have it recognized by others (Elbow, 1994). Feminism highlights this sense of voice as having a place at the table and the authority to speak from the seats of power. But the idea of creating a voice of one's own to resist confinement of any kind (Gilbert & Gubar, 1984/1979) applies to all kinds of writers who challenge hegemony and the dominance of particular literary forms. Developing such a voice may begin with listening to other voices. "Reading," writes Prose (2006), can give writers "the courage to resist all the pressures that our culture exerts on you to write in a certain way, or to follow a prescribed form" (p. 258), because other writers can "show you how these rules have been ignored in the past" with impressive results (p. 250).

A Resonant Voice

When we sense a genuine relationship between the author and the voice in the text, we speak of authenticity or resonance (Elbow, 1981, 1994). But how can we assess resonance when all we may have is a text? No wonder this is the most problematic meaning of the concept of voice that Elbow (1994) identifies. Yet it is also the most compelling. The resonant chambers of our body amplify the sounds we make. Resonance also refers to the way sound and movement are increased or prolonged by sympathetic vibration between bodies. Intriguingly, resonance may be considered both a one-body *and* a two-body metaphor (Pizer, 2012). A resonant voice has the capacity to move others, because it is a voice that is connected to feelings, depth, weight, significance, and liveliness—to the presence and body of the speaker or writer.

When Heaney (1980) describes the first poem he wrote in which his "feelings had got into words. . . . the first place where I felt I had done more than make an arrangement of words: I felt that I had let down a shaft into real life" (p. 41), he is expressing a poet's view of finding a resonant voice. The poet's voice, he continues, "may not even be a metaphor, for a poetic voice is probably very intimately connected with the poet's natural voice, the voice that he hears as the ideal speaker of the lines he is making up" (Heaney, 1980, p. 43). For Barth (1978), "the grain of the voice" is "the body in the voice as it sings, the hand as it writes, the limb as it performs" (p. 188). That grain is "the materiality of the body speaking its mother tongue" (p. 182).

When Rich writes that "every honest word" in a poem has the "sheer heft/of our living behind it" ("Poetry III" from *Your Native Land, Your Life*, quoted in Elbow, 1994, p. 32), we can hear associations to both the weight of experience and the body's weight. "Existentialists used to call 'authenticity'—a sense of the weight of the whole person behind the words" (Alvarez, 2005, p. 44). Elbow (1994) hears the human voice as "more resonant when it can get more of the body resonating behind it or underneath it" (p. 20). Resonant voices—in analysis, clinical prose, and literature—are embodied voices associated with "the true-speaking self" (Alvarez, 2005, p. 20). This is what Alvarez (2005) means by voice or "true style," and it "can come in any form provided it is alive and urgent enough to take hold of the reader and make him understand that what is being said really matters" (p. 44).

The idea of a resonant voice can be heard as a clarion call. Of all the meanings of voice, it inspires the most evocative associations, as you can see, and ones that are grounded in the body and its affects. How then do you develop your resonant voice—and keep developing it? There are many ways: by listening, imitating, experimenting, getting out of your own way, rejecting what may be too familiar, surrendering, attending to what emerges, revising (chapter 17), and listening even more.

We construct our voice in dialogue with ourselves, in anticipation of a listener, and in relation to the subjects we are writing about. If our emerging voice has the "sheer heft/of our living behind it" (Rich quoted in Elbow, 1994, p. 32), it is likely that our readers will hear its resonance and have a greater sense of our presence.

Exercise 10.4

a. Find several examples of your writing in which your voice expresses what Rich calls the "sheer heft/of our living behind it."
b. What are the qualities of your prose that contribute to creating that impression?

c. Now take a piece of your writing that doesn't have as much of a resonant voice as you would like and experiment with ways to make it more resonant, daring, and distinctive.

Coda

After reading this chapter (and the two answer keys below), you may want to reread some of your favorite writers with an ear even more finely attuned to their voice and an eye on the page to see how they scored their text (Atwood, 2002). I talk about voice throughout this book, because it's the principal way we sense an author's presence. For Ogden, the voice in the text is "the privileged portal" through which you "get to know a piece of literature" (Ogden & Ogden, 2012, p. 12). "Imaginative literature," Alvarez (2005) writes, "is about listening to a voice" (p. 17). Clinical literature is also about listening to voice, not exclusively, but importantly so.

Yet setting out to write in a particular voice may inhibit the emergence of a more resonant one. Kidder and Todd (2013) are even more explicit:

> You cannot, must not, try to design and create a voice. The creation of voice is the providential result of the writer's constant self-defining and self-refining inner dialogue. When it happens, let someone else tell you and be grateful. Yet it is undeniable that good writing must have a human sound. Maybe that is the more modest word to keep in mind: sound. You try to attune yourself to the sound of your own writing. (p. 124)

Let the sound of you emerge as you write without consciously attempting to sound a particular way. No doubt influenced by the writers you admire, you will find your voice, perhaps even break "the skin on the pool of yourself" (Heaney, 1980, p. 47), and draw up waters from deep in your well. Keep writing from your embodied self. Later you can listen, refine the sounds you make, and polish the shapes your thoughts take.

Answer Key to Exercise 10.2

Did you recognize Eigen's incantational voice in the iterative style of this excerpt's first paragraph? You may also see the influence of the paradigmatic mode in the way he structures this material and explicates Klein's thought. This passage does a lot of conceptual work, but it doesn't seem like heavy lifting. His sentences are right-branching, and their cadences move us along through speakable intonational units.

Answer Key to Exercise 10.3

Here is an example of exposition and the paradigmatic mode that is written and read with the same ease as a narrative. If you listen carefully, you will recognize many narrative elements, of a story being told about how a therapist uses language empathically. The writer's balanced cadences, graceful intonational units, and use of everyday language contribute to a sense of ease. The prose is economical but not hurried. This writer is respectful of his readers and those he describes. His respect for his readers and for the privacy and vulnerability of the self may remind you of Leston Havens. This is his voice, his unmistakable signature (Heaney, 1980; Vendler, 1995).

11 Introductions

Every writer knows that the choice of a beginning for what he will write is crucial not only because it determines much of what follows but also because a work's beginning is, practically speaking, the main entrance to what it offers. Moreover, in retrospect, we can regard a beginning as the point at which, in a given work, the writer departs from all other works. . . .

Edward W. Said, *Beginnings: Intention and Method*

Your paper's introduction establishes crucial points of contact with your readers. Effectively written, it engages their attention, entices them to continue, and lays out an implicit contract about what you will deliver. With your readers' expectations established, writing your paper becomes a process of fulfilling and perhaps exceeding them. An introduction in the paradigmatic mode often includes

- a good lead—the opening sentence(s)—that pulls your readers in
- a motive that creates the need to know what you have to say
- ideas worth noticing and elaborating
- reasons why these ideas are important—the so-what? factor
- a context, which may include references to relevant literature
- a sense of your paper's direction and possibly its organization

Introductions in the narrative, evocative, and enactive modes may look very different, often resembling the beginning of a short story. A relational conflict, clinical dilemma, or evocative image may serve as the impetus for their unfolding. Introductions in these modes may set the scene, introduce the patient/therapist relationship, stimulate readers' curiosity, or build suspense.

Writing any introduction may feel overwhelming for some of you, precipitating chocolate binges, procrastination, and panic. At one time or another, all kinds of writers, including published authors, may be prone to stalling rituals and self-defeating doubt. Having too many ideas may make it difficult to organize your thoughts. Developing your thinking over a long time may cause you to undervalue your ideas because they are no longer fresh. Or taking the "back-end view of writing," as Hart (2006) calls it, and comparing your nascent ideas and early drafts to "the finished work of accomplished writers" (p. 4) can leave you vulnerable to narcissistic injury and paralyzing defeat.

One way to avoid such pain is to believe in writing as a process of discovery and ideas as emergent properties, thoughts that find their own form in the process of writing. So don't sweat getting things right in the beginning or getting the beginning right the first few times. Just get going to see what emerges, knowing you can shape and develop your ideas as you go. You probably have much more experience trusting your implicit self and the unfolding of process in your consulting room than you do when you sit down to write. I encourage you to bring the same trust to your writing process.

If you typically get blocked writing your introduction, consider using a question, the description of a problem, a quotation, or a tentative hypothesis to serve as a placeholder. You could also start with a clinical vignette, tell the story of how you came to write about your subject (as Bollas does in *Forces of Destiny*, my pp. 117–119), or skip your introduction for now and jump into writing the rest of your paper. If you tend to get stalled because you can't stop revising your introduction, go with what you have rather than perfect it. However you get started, when you get to the end of a draft, you are likely to find more of what you need and be able to write your introduction more easily.

This chapter will teach you how to identify the elements of effective introductions, analyze opening moves in different modes of clinical prose, and experiment with specific ways to jumpstart an introduction. If you are ready to write an introduction, this chapter will increase your options.

Opening Moves in the Narrative Mode

Good storytellers know how important beginnings are. Newspaper writers have a special word for the opening move on which a reader's quick decision to continue is made. Leads may be as short as a sentence or as long as several paragraphs. Good ones engage and excite readers' interest and pull them in. They are page turners. Once hooked, you want to read on. They don't have to be elaborate. Here are two short leads in the narrative mode:

> The patient sat down promptly, decisively, as if my office were the right place to be. I was not all that sure. (Havens, 1996, p. 3)

> I had just returned from my summer vacation. My office was cool and still and expectant, the way an analytic room is when it has long been empty of stories. (Grand, 2000, p. 115)

Both writers stimulate our curiosity. Why is Havens' narrator unsure? What is about to fill Grand's office? Let's take a closer look at Grand's first paragraph to see how she crafts her introduction to "The Depravities of the Nonhuman Self: Greed, Murder, Persecution" (2000). You might want to read her text (on the left) all the way through before reading my commentary, so you can feel how her prose affects you without interrupting its flow.

I just returned from my summer vacation. My office was cool and still and expectant, the way an analytic room is when it has long been empty of stories.

Grand's first sentence is matter-of-fact, marking the setting's essentials. In the second sentence, the description of the atmosphere is richly textured and suggestive. That sentence unfolds luxuriously, playing on the trope of personification. By endowing the inanimate environment with human qualities, Grand suggests a world turned upside down.

Claire and I took our seats. She studied each object in its place. Then she began to speak.

The pace of the narrative quickens as these short, simply constructed sentences follow without reflective detail. I am struck by what is not happening and not said. The patient's attention is focused on inanimate objects, another clue that something is out of kilter. Another foreboding.

Over the next few sessions, I listened for the man who was missing from her stories.

The analyst listens for the man noticed in absentia, expected but not in his place in her patient's narrative. Our attention is drawn back to the patient's scrutiny of objects, each in its place in contrast to the man who is missing, like a concrete object that has been removed.

Prior to my vacation, he had consumed her. Where he was present, now he was absent.

The presence of the man who had "consumed" Grand's patient is now replaced by his absence. Emptiness, space, and absence become even more richly textured.

As I listened, the room's tranquility filled with dim perception. I sensed, rather than knew, that he was gone.

A different kind of stillness—tranquility—is filled with a dim perception of a different kind of absence—"that he was gone."

First, gone; then, dead; then, finally: murdered.

In rapid fire, three short phrases echo the three brief sentences that cut short the flowing reflectiveness of the paragraph's second sentence. Here each word is followed by a punctuation mark. There is no connecting tissue. No subject. No agent. Everything is stripped away and negated. The plot in one powerful sentence.

Murdered by my patient, during my vacation.

Two more turns of the screw.

And she had told me nothing. (p. 15)

A powerful end line that ups the ante. Now there is a murder mystery. A crime, a suspect; no motive, no proof. Something terribly, terribly wrong. And nothing was said.

Grand's prose is highly charged. Its minimalist style creates a Hitchcock-chilling suspense. Her narrative generates more questions than it answers. Having applied narrative skills to make the clinical experience come viscerally alive, Grand suggests more than she states. Hers is an eerie "conjuring of the nominated" (Bollas, 1999, p. 195) of an ominous, accusing absence made hauntingly present. How does Grand manage to pull this off?

Everything in this paragraph contributes to creating "a unity of effect" that Poe would admire. "Of the innumerable effects or impressions, of which the heart, the intellect, or (more generally) the soul is susceptible" (Poe, 1846, p. 1), Grand concentrates on a constellation of images of stillness, emptiness, absence, and violent negation. The structure of her sentences also enacts negation, a world turned upside down, reflections cut short, the plot condensed in a single taut sequence: "First, gone; then, dead; then, finally: murdered." My guess is that Grand did not sit down and carve out a strategy to solve the problem of how to depict such a palpable absence. I imagine instead that she wrote from inside her experience of being with this patient and that the writing found its own form, presumably polished in the process of revising her text.

A couple of paragraphs later Grand explains how she knew her patient had murdered "the connection," a drug dealer who camped out in her apartment, refusing to leave. After her patient tells her "in the language of things: 'I had to kill him for the apartment' " (Grand, 2000, p. 118), Grand reports:

> Now I recalled that my first clue to the murderer was in the context of things and their human violation. I did not find my first clue in her silence about the "connection." I found it in my office, just prior to our arrival. Then, my office was as her apartment: its empty tranquility was derived from human absence. Later, its violation was derived from the renewal of human presence. I knew this as she made her confession. (p. 118)

When an introduction contains "in germinal form the entirety of the story that would follow" (Ogden, 2005a, p. 18), as Grand's does, it not only contains important information but also has "the feel of the inevitable" about it:

> Deciding how and where to begin a case description is no small matter. The opening of a clinical account, when it works, has all the feel of the inevitable. It leads the reader to feel: how else would one begin to tell this story? The place where one starts, in addition to providing an important structural element to the story and to the paper as a whole, makes a significant implicit statement about the writer's way of thinking, the sorts of things he notices and values, and, in particular, which of the infinite number of junctures in this human experience deserves pride of place in the telling of the story. (Ogden, 2005a, p. 17)

Davies' (2012/2004) introduction to "Whose Bad Objects Are We Anyway? Repetition and Our Elusive Love Affair with Evil" (quoted below) is written in a different style than Grand's, befitting the drama that is unfolding. Let's see what Davies' style anticipates and suggests. Once again, you may want to read her text before reading my comments.

It was a Thursday afternoon, the kind of day on which the coldness simply could not be stopped. Sweaters, space heaters, and the assorted accoutrements of winter were insufficient to the task.

The first sentence announces the narrative mode and begins to establish the setting with a time tag (Alberts, 2010). The unstoppable cold and the insufficiency of the analyst's space to provide warmth foretell trouble and are stand-ins for the participants in the drama that will unfold. Descriptive words accumulate, hinting that something else might become as unstoppable as winter's cold.

I had a sore throat and a terrible head cold. Achy and irritable, I was unsure how I was going to make it through my four remaining sessions that afternoon. I wanted only a pillow for my head, a warm comforter for the aches and pains, and a thermos full of hot tea and honey. To make it worse, Karen was coming next. At that moment I needed someone "easy"; someone who would be willing to cut me a little slack in my present condition. But that was not to be. One could simply never hide from Karen's keen and unrelenting eye. She was never easy!

We are invited to listen from the perspective of an analyst whose body aches, who longs for comfort and feels trapped. The contrast between a vulnerable analyst and a difficult patient builds suspense. Details continue to overflow, enacting a dynamic of the treatment.

We had been working together for almost 3 years, and though much of our analytic work had been productive, our relationship itself had remained tense and unpredictable, fraught with unexpected twists and turns, seemingly impossible demands, sudden disappointments, frustrations, and angry outbursts. There was little that was fluid and comfortable.

A narrative summary sets the context for a scene that is about to be played out. The tumultuous relationship between participants takes center stage. Notice how many words Davies uses to describe their relationship and how highly charged they are, adding to the dramatic effect, increasing tension, implying excess.

As I came into the waiting room, Karen was hunched over inside an enormous down jacket. Her face was particularly stormy and brooding, even for her. My heart sank, and my spirits took a nosedive.

Davies tells us what she sees so we can imagine this scene and understand why she is feeling the way she does.

"You're still sick?" she asked, half complaint, half admonishment. "I can't believe you haven't shaken that thing yet."

Dialogue creates the effect of an immediate scene. Karen strikes out with words, calling Davies' cold "that thing." Small matters become overblown as the excess of Davies' prose has enacted and foretold.

I felt suddenly slow and stupid, my cold a matter of immunological ineptitude.

We are invited to follow the shifts in Davies' self states and learn how she perceives her patient's experience of her. We are privy to the feelings of both participants. I love the ironic exaggeration of "immunological ineptitude" that adds humor without diminishing suspense.

She sat in the chair facing me, ensconced within her ballooning jacket. We were silent.

The strong verb "ensconced" and the image of "her ballooning jacket" help readers sense what Davies is up against.

From deep within her stare I detected a gleam—a noticeable quantum leap in energy and excitement. In response, my stomach churned and my muscles stiffened. Even before words could explain, it seemed as if my body knew that *something* was coming, and my body told me it wasn't good.

Despite the exaggeration of Davies' description and her analytic savvy, her body tenses in real time in anticipation of what is about to happen.

It must mean that we had occupied this place before—that my muscles were remembering, before my mind could catch up, that something dangerous loomed ahead of us. (Davies, 2012, pp. 163–164)

Davies makes three moves in this sentence. She provides a narrative summary—"we had occupied this place before"; notes that memory is more quickly triggered along sensorimotor pathways than through cortical networks; and foretells danger, providing a narrative hook into the next paragraph.

Davies' abundantly descriptive language enacts a note of exaggeration even before she describes her cold as "a matter of immunological ineptitude." She might have mustered such humor to break the tension she feels as she anticipates her patient's stomach-churning attack. Her language tells us how visceral her encounters with Karen are. Yet something is overblown, out of proportion.

To capture readers' attention, first paragraphs of narratives, Stein (1995) suggests, should "excite the reader's curiosity, preferably about a character or a relationship," "introduce a setting," and "lend resonance to the story" (p. 16). The opening paragraphs of Grand's and Davies' papers do that in different ways. Each introduction is superbly crafted to evoke and enact the specific nature and emotional climate of each clinical encounter. Although the excerpt I quoted from Davies' paper is not long enough to demonstrate, she deftly alternates experience-near presentations of clinical material with theoretical discussions of it; that is, she alternates between the narrative and paradigmatic modes throughout her paper.

Opening Moves in the Evocative Mode

The evocative mode (chapter 5) works by invitation and suggestion. Evocative writing stimulates an emotional response. We are moved to imagine, feel, and experience what an artful use of language suggests. Metaphor and imagery are usually brought into play, and the rhythm of the prose may also contribute to its effect. Evocative writing beckons, calling on the reader's active participation as the contemporary incantational styles of Grand, Loewald, and Eigen demonstrate (chapter 5).

In the first chapter of *Theaters of the Mind*, "Stepping onto the Psychoanalytic Stage," McDougall (1991/1985) describes the analytic process by drawing on the evocative power of language to conjure things:

The scenarios are written in an unknown language; the dialogue is inaudible, sometimes reduced to mime; the characters are as yet unnamed.

Each of these elements defies language. Nothing yet is known. Here the evocative works by conjuring what is unspoken. How apt for the stage on which shame and dissociation are often played out.

The psychic dramas of the theatres of the mind thus await production on the analytic stage. In the hope of finding meaning and easing pain, two people step out on that stage to bring the drama to life as psychic reality. (p. 3)

We learn what kind of painful dramas "await production," where they are produced, and why. Theater metaphors guide our imagining, bridging from the known to the not-yet known, and lending substance to such an elusive term as psychic reality.

As many reader-response critics have taught us, literary narratives and evocative prose like McDougall's demonstrate how much readers participate in the creation of a text's meaning. Meaning does not lie inert upon the page (Ogden, 1997, pp. 6–7). Like the deft strokes of a Chinese brush painting, so much more is implied than is actually drawn. We bring our own feeling-toned experience to McDougall's prose to round out her picture under the guidance of the text, transforming black ink into imagined dramas and lived experience.

Exercise 11.1

An Opening Move in the Evocative Mode

To practice writing about an idea in the evocative mode, pick one that lends itself to metaphoric elaboration. Let McDougall, the writers featured in "Moving Matters" (pp. 99–101), and the incantational styles of Grand, Loewald, and Eigen (chapter 5) serve as models.

Exercise 11.2

Another Opening Move

To practice writing about a patient in the evocative mode, let Grand's depiction of Rosa inspire you (my pp. 46–49). Plan what you write as an introduction. Draw your readers in.

Opening Moves in the Enactive Mode

The first sentence of Ogden's (1985) "On Potential Space" appears to be a straightforward:

> Perhaps the most important and at the same time most elusive of ideas introduced by Donald Winnicott is the concept of potential space. (p. 129)

This sentence has a graceful shape and artful cadence, and it also contains an implied paradox: The concept of potential space is important and at the same time elusive. Since paradox is at the heart of Winnicott's concept, this lead not only states but also enacts its meaning. Even the first word announces the enactment, letting the paradox amble into view and inviting readers to consider what follows. A potential space is opened from the get go. Any of the techniques of enactive writing may be employed in your introduction to create an experience to be lived as well as thought (chapter 6).

Opening Moves in the Lyric Narrative Mode

Because a lyric narrative (chapter 7) may begin in any number of ways, its introduction may not give its mode away. But you may find hints in its core ideas or the way the story highlights the uncertainties of the present moment and the limitations of present knowledge that set its introduction apart from the paradigmatic or narrative modes. Papers are usually written in more than one mode even though one usually structures the whole and governs its aesthetic. To get started on a lyric narrative of your own, go to exercise 7.1 (p. 93).

Leads in the Paradigmatic Mode

Leads in the paradigmatic mode serve the same purpose as leads in any other mode: to actively engage your readers' attention and pull them in. Notice how these writers do it:

> This is a strange time to be insisting on the importance of siblings. (Mitchell, 2003, p. 1)

> There is bad blood between psychoanalysis and attachment theory. As with many family feuds, it is hard to identify where the problem begins. (Fonagy, 2001, p. 1)

> Joseph Campbell once said that the gods are not in Greece, or in books about myth, but instead are right on the corner of Broadway and 42nd Street, waiting for the light to change. (Hillman, 2004, p. 70)

These idea-driven leads stimulate questions, propelling readers into the text in search of answers. Juliet Mitchell's readers may want to know why it is a strange time to assert the importance of siblings. Fonagy's readers may want to know what the feud is all about and whether a rapprochement is possible. Hillman's readers may want to know how to recognize the gods on 42nd Street and what they will do when the lights change. As these writers demonstrate, effective leads in the paradigmatic mode may spark readers' curiosity and create tension that is similar to suspense.

Straight Up

Let's say you want to start your paper in the paradigmatic mode by making a point boldly, perhaps underscoring its importance, as the following writers do:

> It would be hard to find an issue that has generated more controversy during the history of psychoanalytic ideas than aggression. (S. Mitchell, 1993b, p. 351)

> No concept is more central to psychoanalytic practice than transference. (Gabbard, 2000, p. 2)

Or let's say you want to make a point that contains more information and write a lead like this one:

> The nature of sibling relationships, in all their complex forms of love and hate, still remains more of a mystery than the passions and developmental vicissitudes of parent-child relationships. (Sharpe & Rosenblatt, 1994, p. 491)

Notice how much is packed into this well-balanced sentence. A comparison adds richness: Sibling relations are more mysterious than parent-child relations. An implied question draws readers in: What is at the heart of the mystery of sibling relations? Notice too that the terms "sibling relations" and "parent-child relations" are each qualified by compound descriptive phrases.

In contrast to these leads in the paradigmatic mode, a lead such as "We begin with two propositions" does little work, does not contain an idea to explicate or debate, and merely points in a general direction. "There are many ways to lose a parent" is also just a pointer. One might expect a list to follow, but there are no surprises, paradoxes, or puzzles to solve, and little that is memorable about the writer's voice.

Notice how much more definitive the following leads are. You know exactly where each writer stands:

> Few issues in psychoanalysis are quite so muddled, or tend to generate quite so much confusion in the mind of the clinician, as the relationship between theory and technique. (Greenberg, 1986, p. 89)

> Gender is one of the most contested concepts in contemporary social thought and social life. (Harris, 1991, p. 197)

> One of the most contested topics in contemporary discourse is the constitution of subjectivity. (Flax, 1996, p. 577)

These leads do more work than the sentences I labeled pointers, and they do so with confidence. Because they identify the writer's position so directly, I characterize these leads as straight up.

Exercise 11.3

Straight Up

"You would learn very little in this world," writes Oliver (1994), "if you were not allowed to imitate. And to repeat your imitation until some solid grounding in the skill was achieved and the slight but wonderful difference—that made you *you* and no one else—could assert itself" (p. 13).

a. Try writing a handful of straight-up leads. Pick any subject for which you can quickly form an argument or make an assertion, beginning perhaps with some of the concepts that are central to your discipline or theoretical orientation. You will not have to write a paper to back up your lead, so practice getting off the starting line with a strong, deliberate lead and see what it feels like to do so.

b. Once you get comfortable writing a lead straight up, try writing several specifically for your writing projects.

Motive

Ideas are compelling when set in motion. The motive does that work. It generates a need to know what you have to say, for example, by identifying a gap that needs to be filled, a problem that needs to be solved, or a paradox that needs to be understood. Your motive creates momentum, motivating the ideas that follow. It implicitly sets up your readers' expectations that you will address if not resolve the problem(s) you raise. Gordon Harvey (1996), former Assistant Director of Harvard's Expository Writing Program, defines the motive as "a problem, difficulty, dilemma, over-simplification, misapprehension, or violated expectation that the writer defines at the start of the essay, and to which the essay's thesis acts as an answer, solution, correction, or clarification" (p. 51; see also Booth, Colomb, & Williams, 1995).

The motive is not limited to an opening move. It may be used elsewhere and more than once in a paper to provide the impetus and structure for what follows. Motives are used in all of the modes of clinical prose. Most of the examples that follow are drawn from introductions that are written in the paradigmatic mode. As we have seen, a crisis, conflict, anomaly, or the introduction of suspense may function as a motive in one of the other modes.

Motive as Gap

Identifying a gap in our knowledge prompts the need for new understanding, perhaps a new concept, a review of diagnostic categories, or new theory. Ogden (2003) demonstrates his strategic focus in his two-sentence introduction to "On Not Being Able to Dream." The first sentence, which is shaped like a funnel, identifies the subject of his paper and the gap that needs to be filled. The second sentence alerts us to the direction and organization of his paper:

> Much has been written on what dreams mean; relatively little on what it means to dream; and still less on what it means not to be able to dream. What follows are an idea, a story, and an analytic experience, each used as points of entry into the question of what it means—on both a theoretical and an experiential plane—not to be able to dream. (p. 17)

Notice how Craige (2002) identifies two gaps in our understanding of the treatment process in "Mourning Analysis: The Post-Termination Phase" (see also my pp. 222–225, 228–232):

Post-termination is the least understood phase of the psychoanalytic treatment process.	Craige identifies a significant gap in our understanding of the treatment process, creating a strong lead and motive.
While over a hundred psychoanalytic articles and books have been written about termination (notably Freud 1937; Firestein 1978, 1982; Loewald 1988; Peddler 1988; Novick 1982, 1988, 1990; Viorst 1982; Blum 1989; Orgel 2000), only a few writings discuss the fate of the analysand and the completion of the analytic process after termination.	She establishes a context for her subject by noting the abundance of literature on termination and the scarcity of literature on the post-termination phase. (my pp. 222–225 for an analysis of her literature review.)
In the psychoanalytic literature, post-termination is considered to be a phase of the analytic process during which the analysand mourns the loss of the analyst and creates internalizations of the analytic relationship that supports the analysand's capacity for continued self-analysis.	Craige quickly and efficiently defines what is meant by the post-termination phrase.
Little is known, however, about how analytic patients actually experience post-termination mourning.	She immediately identifies another gap—that little is known about how analysands experience the mourning process that is characteristic of the post-termination phase.
The present study attempts to fill this gap by investigating how analysands who are psychoanalytic candidates negotiate the loss of the unique analytic relationship after termination. (pp. 507–508)	In the fifth sentence of this concise introduction, Craige tells her readers how her paper will address these gaps.

It's easy to see the strategic purpose of each sentence in Craige's well-honed and effectively focused introduction. Nothing is extraneous.

Motive as a Problem

While identifying a problem is one of the most obvious and effective kinds of motives to employ, the form such a motive takes may be more subtle or complex than the obvious. Notice how Havens (1996) finesses his motive-as-problem lead:

> The work of healing begins in a safe place, which then exposes what is false and what is real. It is no easy task to exchange one for the other. (p. 1)

If your patient feels safe enough, the work of healing may begin to expose the difference between what's false and what's real. The problem comes in exchanging one for the other. The motive in this lead is an implied one: What makes that exchange possible? The essays in Havens' book respond to this question.

Here is another example of the motive cast as a problem to be solved:

> Among the concepts commonly associated with C.G. Jung, few are more widely recognized, nor more poorly understood, than the theory of archetypes. This state of affairs leads many, both within the Jungian community and among Jung's critics, to speak with confidence about this central concept while talking past each other. (Hogenson, 2004, p. 32)

Hogenson's first move is similar to Ogden's (1985) in the opening lines of "On Potential Space" (my p. 152). Paradoxically, a widely recognized concept is poorly understood, prompting a need for clarification. Hogenson addresses the so-what? factor in the next sentence when he explains why this is an important issue.

A Short List of Motives

Here is a short list of possible motives for your clinical papers. Please add more of your own:

- a clinical example that calls out for new understanding
- a gap in knowledge that needs to be filled
- a problem that needs to be solved or at least addressed
- a paradox that needs to be understood
- a complication that has been missed
- implications that have not been thought out
- complexity that has been overlooked
- a need for the reevaluation of terms, concepts, theory
- a need for alternate interpretations of clinical material
- a need for a new concept, theory, or paradigm

The motive is one of the most effective organizing principles you can bring to your writing. Just as creating a good lead draws your readers in, articulating a motive, even more than one, creates momentum, pulls your readers into and through your paper, and builds structure and coherence. If I had to choose one principle as the most important take-home message from a writing workshop, I would choose the motive. Too many papers I am asked to read suffer for lack of one. If only they had that impetus and sense of direction a motive creates. Instead they offer information or descriptions without a sense of purpose. An introduction that lacks a motive is "humdrum" as one writer said of hers.

Exercise 11.4

Reading for Motive

a. As you read clinical papers, identify each writer's motive.
b. If a paper is particularly well written, you might find more than one. Be sure to identify all of them.
c. If a motive is not apparent or only implied, write one for that paper's introduction.
d. If the motive is not clearly articulated, write a more effective one.
e. If the paper has a motive in the introduction but doesn't incorporate any later on, add one or more as if you are the author.

Exercise 11.5

What's Your Motive?

What's the motive for your writing project? Does a gap in knowledge need to be filled, a problem solved, a paradox understood? What prompts the need for your clinical paper to be written and read?

a. Jot down as many possible motives for one of your writing projects as you can and write leads that introduce each one.
b. Use one of the motives you just identified to write an introductory paragraph that eases into your motive over the course of the paragraph instead of starting out with it as a lead.

Ideas Fit to Print

Paraphrasing *The New York Times* banner line—"all the news that's fit to print"—let's think about what makes an idea fit for publication. We'd probably start by ruling out what's obvious, uncontested, old hat. In the humanities, your main idea or thesis needs to be "arguable . . . an assertion someone could reasonably argue against" (Walk, 2008, p. 49). If it is, then it may provide "unexpected insight [that] goes beyond superficial interpretations, or challenges, corrects, or extends other arguments" (Walk, 2008, p. 49).

The So-What? Factor

When you refer to why the subject you are writing about could matter to your read-ers, why it is important to solve the problem(s) you are trying to solve, or what the consequences would be if it couldn't resolve them, you are addressing the so-what? factor. If Jungians and their critics talk past each other when they talk about arche-types because they don't have a shared understanding of them, as Hogenson (2004) argues (my p. 157), they will find it more difficult to learn from each other and will perpetuate the unfortunate split that Freud and Jung set in motion.

When you draw out the implications or significance of the ideas your paper will address, you demonstrate why your paper needs to be written for others. You answer the implied reader's question—so what? Note how Ogden (1985) does that in his introduction to "On Potential Space":

Perhaps the most important and at the same time most elusive of the ideas introduced by Donald Winnicott is the concept of potential space.	Ogden invites us to consider a paradox: that Winnicott's most important concept is also his most elusive.
Potential space is the general term Winnicott used to refer to an intermediate area of experiencing that lies between fantasy and reality.	Ogden defines potential space.
Specific forms of potential space include the play space, the area of transitional object and phenomena, the analytic space, the area of cultural experience, and the area of creativity.	Examples follow and, by implication, further underscore the concept's importance, addressing the so-what? factor.
The concept of potential space remains enigmatic in part because it has been so difficult to extricate the meaning of the concept from the elegant system of images and metaphors in which it is couched.	Here's another problem that serves as an additional motive.
The present paper is an attempt to clarify the concept of potential space and	Ogden's paper is presented as a solution to the problem of understanding such an important, elusive, enigmatic concept.
to explore the implications that this aspect of Winnicott's work holds for a	Ogden tells us there are several implications of this study, further addressing the so-what? factor.

psychoanalytic theory of the normal and pathological development of the capacity for symbolization and subjectivity.

They involve

• the theory of normal and pathological development of symbolization and subjectivity and

Although potential space originates in a (potential) physical and mental space *between* mother and infant, it later becomes possible, in the course of normal development for the individual infant, child or adult to develop his own capacity to generate potential space.

• individual's capacity to generate potential space. Ogden also describes the developmental origins of potential space.

This capacity constitutes an organized and organizing set of psychological activities operating in a particular mode.

This capacity to generate potential space also has implications.

The concept of the dialectical process will be explored as a possible paradigm for the understanding of the form or mode of the psychological activity generating potential space. (p. 129)

What's more, Ogden will explore a possible paradigm for understanding the psychological activity generating potential space.

Every sentence of Ogden's introduction serves a strategic purpose. What he does as a writer and why he is writing about potential space are exceptionally clear.

Exercise 11.6

The So-What? Factor

a. Why does your paper need to be written? What is gained if it is? What is lost if the issues you raise are not addressed? What's at stake?
b. Once you have answered these questions, go back to exercise 11.5b and develop the introductory paragraph you wrote by addressing the so-what? factor if you haven't already done so. Draw out the implications of what you are proposing so your readers can begin to understand the importance of what you set out to do.

Creating a Context

Let's play with the idea of context for a moment. Imagine you have a camera in your hand and zoom in for a tight focus, zoom out for a more panoramic shot, and shoot from a number of angles. Let's see how Gabbard (2000a) does this as he frames his subject and creates several motives in "What Can Neuroscience Teach Us about Transference?"

No concept is more central to psychoanalytic practice than transference.

Gabbard's lead couldn't be more direct.

Cooper (1987) once noted, "Despite the diversity of analytic views that abound today, analysts seem to agree on the centrality of the transference and its interpretation in analytic process and cure, differing only in whether transference is everything or almost everything" (78).

He cites a source to corroborate his statement, one that adds a touch of humor.

The essence of transference, however, has undergone a variety of transformations as psychoanalytic theorists of diverse persuasions have attempted to understand it.

Here's a problem that propels the project of Gabbard's paper: Things aren't as simple as they appear to be. This is one form of motive.

Many of the debates on the concept of transference remind one of religious zealots who are arguing that their view of God is the correct one.

Here's another problem—creating even more momentum.

We have had very little success in approaching the problem scientifically and finding a rigorous method to adjudicate which perspectives on transference are more clinically useful or scientifically accurate than others.

Another catch and another motive, with the same effect. The problem is getting more difficult with each new input—all the more reason this important concept needs new attention.

As a result of the burgeoning field of cognitive neuroscience, we now stand on the threshold of being able to fulfill Freud's dream of the integration of mind and brain.

Given a new angle provided by cognitive neuroscience, we may begin to do what Freud couldn't do.

In this communication I will review the development of the concept of transference, provide a brief overview of our understanding of neural network models, and then suggest ways that transference can be translated into modern tenets of cognitive neuroscience.	Gabbard points in the directions he will go: providing a historical context to understand the concept of transference; introducing the perspective of neural networks; and indicating that we can now understand transference in terms of cognitive neuroscience.
My hope is to ground the notion of transference in our contemporary understanding of how the brain works. (p. 2)	Gabbard addresses the so-what? factor, demonstrating how transference works in terms of how the brain works, thus beginning to fulfill Freud's dream of integrating mind and brain.

A Sense of Direction

An effective introduction will give your readers a sense of your paper's purpose and direction as Gabbard's (2000a) does. However, you do not have to spell everything out or give everything away in your introduction, but you do want your introduction to be isomorphic with your paper. That is, you want the ideas in your introduction to be presented in the same order as you present them in the body of your paper. Some introductions are quite short, as examples in this chapter demonstrate, and the sense of direction in papers written predominately in the paradigmatic mode may be suggested rather than thoroughly rehearsed.

Abstracts

Many journals require an abstract. I recommend that you write your introduction as if your article will not be published with an abstract, because you are likely to write a more complete introduction if you do. Abstracts literally abstract the argument from your paper. They tend to be dense more by default than prescription. For an experiment, try reading a number of abstracts to see how readable they are and how many reflect the same voice and tone that are used in the article. Can you detect any hints of the author's personality in the abstract?

Occasionally, I am delighted to find an abstract that sounds like the author rather than some unidentifiable voice. Below is Westen's (1999) abstract, one of my favorites, from "The Scientific Status of Unconscious Processes: Is Freud Really Dead?"

At regular intervals for over half a century, critiques of Freud and psychoanalysis have emerged in the popular media and in intellectual circles, usually declaring that Freud has died some new and agonizing death, and that the enterprise he created should be buried along with him like the artifacts in the tomb of an Egyptian king. Although the critiques take many forms, a central claim has long been that unconscious processes, like other psychoanalytic constructs, lack any basis in scientific research. In recent years, however, a large body of experimental research has emerged in a number of independent literatures. This work documents the most fundamental tenet of psychoanalysis—that much of mental life is unconscious, including cognitive, affective, and motivational processes. This body of research suggests some important revisions in the psychoanalytic understanding of unconscious processes, but it also points to the conclusion that, based on controlled scientific investigations alone (that is, without even considering clinical data), the repeated broadside attacks on psychoanalysis are no longer tenable. (p. 1061)

How can you make your abstract less dense than the ones you are used to reading and more like Westen's? I suggest you let some of your personality and commitment show. In writing your abstract, be guided by what you know about introductions. Incorporate a good lead and motive. Feature your paper's core ideas and the reasons why they are important—the so-what? factor. Give your readers a sense of you paper's direction and organization. You don't have to lay everything out, because you want your readers to get hooked and read on. Feel free to use the first person singular (*I*) in your abstract, write in a distinctive rather than generic voice, and use active rather than passive constructions. Belcher (2009) advises that you "include as many relevant keywords as possible, since many search engines search by abstract and title only" (p. 55).

Like an introduction, your abstract offers an opportunity for you to make contact with your readers and begin to shape their expectations. Writing in a detached, anonymous voice will distance you from your readers and create the impression that you are holding them and your subject at arm's length. Don't be afraid to show up on the page, beginning with your abstract, and to be heard speaking in your own voice.

12 The Narrative Axis

Even more than with plot, no doubt, I shall be concerned with plotting: with the activity of shaping, with the dynamic aspect of narrative—that which makes a plot "move forward," makes us read forward, seeking in the unfolding of the narrative a line of intention and a portend of design that hold the promise of progress toward meaning.

The closure demanded by narrative understanding—the closure without which it can have no coherent plot—is always provisional, as-if, a necessary fiction.
Peter Brooks, *Reading for Plot: Design and Intention in Narrative*

I think of clinical papers as having two axes. The horizontal or narrative axis is organized temporally and is composed of clinical phenomena, description, and narrative details at the first level of abstraction (pp. 106–109). Arranging these for presentation is an exercise in plotting in Brooks' (1992) sense of the word. The vertical axis of your paper is organized conceptually and is composed of the links you create between what's on your paper's narrative axis (at the first level of abstraction) and your ideas about that material in the form of interpretations, concepts, and theory, etc., that are represented at higher levels of abstraction (chapter 13). Most clinical papers can be distinguished by the *relative* emphasis on the work they do along one of these axes. Clinical narratives emphasize the lived experience of psychotherapy as a story that moves *through time* (chapter 3). Lyric narratives explore clinical experience as it unfolds *in the lyric present* (chapter 7). Conceptually organized papers put narrative details in service of ideas at higher levels of abstraction.

Where you locate evocative and enactive passages will depend on how they are used. I would place the evocative details of the Brownsville neighborhood in which Grand (2003) and her patient grew up (my pp. 46–47) on her paper's narrative axis. The prose that enacts Rosa's disjunctive self (my pp. 48–49) could be placed there too. But Grand's use of the images of that immigrant world to demonstrate how Rosa "lived the changing seasons of Brownsville" (Grand, 2003, p. 315; my pp. 48–49) is interpretive, so I would place that material on the second level of abstraction. Evocative and enactive prose may function at even higher levels of abstraction, as we have seen in their use at the conceptual level in Ogden's prose (my pp. 67–68) and as Ogden (2001a) has noted in Winnicott's (my pp. 68–70).

Relative is the operative word in comparing different modes of clinical prose, different papers in the same mode, and the balance a paper strikes between its narrative and conceptual axes. Conceptually organized papers usually present some clinical material chronologically, and writing that is organized temporally can accommodate self-reflection, interpretations, ideas, and theory without losing its narrative orientation. When you look closely at the clinical material writers present along the narrative axis, you are likely to find inferences and interpretations interwoven. Given such relativity, you may wonder why it's helpful to make such distinctions at all.

Conceptualizing the structure of a paper's two axes and analyzing how writers connect and negotiate the levels of abstraction may help you understand the strategic moves a writer makes (my pp. 184–188); develop moves of your own; and assess your paper (or another) in terms of its structure, evidence, integrity, conceptual clarity, and persuasiveness (chapters 13 and 14). In this chapter, we'll look at what might be mapped along your paper's narrative axis. We will also return to Bruner's (1990) idea of a narrative's dual landscape (my p. 5), identify other narrative lines you could trace, and consider the use of vignettes and "thick description" (Geertz, 2000/1973; Ryle, 1990/1971) in clinical prose. Exercises will be incorporated.

Rhetorical Evidence

I think of the narrative details and clinical phenomena that form the narrative axis of your paper as data points or rhetorical evidence in which you ground your ideas (thinking from a top-down perspective) or on which you build your ideas (bottom up). They are the particulars that are so valued in the narrative mode. When teaching writing, I do not demand that evidence be hard edged. Instead, I ask if it is adequate to the task at hand. Is it ample, detailed, and specific enough to allow your readers to understand your perspective?

Let's take a look at several examples, beginning with Jody Davies' (1999) introduction of her patient Daniel, and notice how each writer uses literary techniques to lay down rhetorical evidence along the narrative axis of their paper:

> Daniel was twenty-seven years old when he first came seeking psychotherapy with the vague sense that he needed some help "putting things together." Indeed, my first impression of him was of a young man for whom nothing quite went together: clothes somewhat wrinkled and mismatched, long arms and legs that didn't quite work together in coordinated motion, thoughts that seemed scattered and undirected. He came for the first time on a bitterly cold day, and some of the first things that struck me were the thin socks and sandals he wore on his feet. Though I asked him about this, he simply replied offhandedly, "Oh, I never, ever get cold." Daniel was exceedingly bright, remarkably well read, and potentially attractive under his somewhat rumpled, ragged, and disorganized exterior: an interesting combination of creative genius and neglected little boy. I entertained both fantasies. (pp. 188–189)

Davies lets us know how she sees Daniel and what she initially makes of what she sees: Nothing comes together for him, and he gets away wearing sandals and thin socks in winter without feeling cold. Davies' evidence is subjective as one would expect in our field and as she implies with the words "impressions" and "fantasies" and more indirectly in the qualifiers "somewhat," "quite," and "seemed." Yet she gives us enough evidence for us to understand how she comes to entertain her fantasies.

See if you can spot the relationship between Davies' ideas and her evidence in her next paragraph:

> Daniel took to analysis as if he had been waiting for this moment all his life. Within the first month he was coming three and then four times a week, a schedule he has maintained to this day. However, despite the manifest eagerness, there was an odd, disconnected quality to the story of his life as it emerged in the first months of working together. In telling his story, Daniel seemed to be relaying a series of separate, unrelated events—well remembered, even emotionally full, but oddly disjointed from other occurrences or from any overriding attributions of meaning that would enable him to draw conclusions or construct any patterns of motivation and significance. There was a kind of intermediate dissociative process between the awareness of certain events and the attribution of meaning to those events. For example, Daniel told of coming home from school one day, around the age of fifteen, to find his mother lying on the kitchen floor with the gas on, all the windows closed, and a towel stuffed into the doorjamb. "You mean she had attempted suicide?" I naïvely asked. The patient looked shocked and then tearful. "Do you really think that's what she was doing?" He was incredulous. (pp. 188–189)

The structure of this paragraph is tight and clear, and Davies' evidence is easy to spot. The assertion of the first sentence is grounded in the details of the second. Davies' sense that Daniel's story had a "disconnected quality to it" is explicated in the next two sentences and illustrated with her vignette.

In the next example, Steven Knoblauch (2000) describes the music of his patient's voice and what it conveys to him. Let's look at the links he makes between the narrative details (on the first level of abstraction) and his inferences and ideas (on the second):

> "I don't want my body to become big." "I," "don't," "body," and "big" marked high tones spoken with earnest fear. They were sharp and demanding. "Want," "my," and "to become" floated along a lower sound channel. They were softer, more tentative, a background drone, holding and placing the notes of intention in time and place. The sentence as a discrete utterance flew out the way Charlie Parker would extend the harmony of a blues phrase, an afterthought inflection, which retextured the entire feeling, mixing paradoxical anguish and hope into the unexpected mastery of surprise.

I heard a little girl's voice. This voice surprised me, different from that of the strident African-American adult who would usually address me as one who could not know, could not understand, the journeys and sensibilities of a human marked female and black. Lacy was afraid to become pregnant. (p. 17)

Knoblauch interweaves a detailed description of the sounds of Lacy's words with his thoughts about their meaning—e.g., "spoken with earnest fear"; "demanding"; "I heard a little girl's voice." Knoblauch's intuition that Lacy is afraid of becoming pregnant comes in a flash. He shows us how he gets there—or almost there—through his associations to jazz; listening to the music of her sentences; and factoring in their relational patterns. The gap between these details and Knoblauch's insight points to an intuitive leap that Bion (1984/1965) would call "a selected fact," because it brings together "by a sudden precipitating intuition" seemingly "unrelated incoherent phenomena" to form a new understanding (p. 127).

Exercise 12.1

Rhetorical Evidence, Fantasies, and Intuition

Think of a fantasy or intuition you have about a patient and write a short paragraph about it so your readers will understand what you put together to get there. If an intuitive leap is involved, show that. Let Davies and Knoblauch be your guides.

The Narrative Axis as Plot

Sequences of clinical material presented chronologically form a plot. Their meaning may be implied in your narrative's unfolding or interpreted more explicitly. If you are writing in the evocative, enactive, narrative, or lyric narrative mode, your interpretations and ideas about what's happening may appear primarily in self-reflections or as a function of selecting and sequencing your clinical material rather than formulating hypotheses. Narrative order is telling. A plot, Brooks (1992) explains, "shapes a story and gives it a certain direction or intent of meaning. We might think of plot as the logic or perhaps the syntax of a certain kind of discourse, one that develops its propositions only through temporal sequence and progression" (p. xi).

We select the elements that form our story's plot based on the perspective time bestows. How else would we know what to select as salient? We infer causes by their effects however subject to revision both may be. The lyric narrative mode highlights the tentativeness and uncertainties of the present moment and does not rely on retrospective knowledge to create meaning. The narrative mode puts hindsight to work not only in the plot's construction but as a guide to interpretation and meaning. The way you select and plot a series of clinical episodes (what Brooks, 1992, calls plotting) will depend on the mode of clinical prose you employ, how you want retrospective knowledge to inform what you present, and what your clinical and conceptual points of focus are.

Where your story begins and ends contributes to its meaning. Do you want to begin in the beginning (wherever that may be), *in medias res*, or later? At the end of your narrative, do you want to leave things up in the air or tie them down and with what certainty, passion, caution, or wonder? Ogden (2005a) advises clinical writers to start writing before they know where their story will end and

> allow it to take form in the process of writing it. Not knowing the end of the story while at the beginning preserves for the writer as well as for the reader a sense of the utter unpredictability of every life experience: we never know what is going to happen before it happens. The equivalent in writing is to allow the piece 'to tell how it can. . . It finds its own name as it goes' (Frost, 1939, p. 777). (pp. 18–19)

Exercise 12.2

Plot

a. Imagine that you will write a new paper about your work with one of your patients.

b. Think of 3–5 sets of narrative details, clinical phenomena, or segments of your clinical work that are relevant to the story you want to tell. For each set of synchronous materials, make notes on a separate page.

c. On the top of each page, write the time in the course of treatment in which each set of materials belongs to remind you to orient your readers.

d. Lay these pages out in chronological order, with the earliest on your far left and the most recent on your far right. Look at what defines your story's beginning, middle, and end.

e. What are the implications of what you have selected and plotted?

f. Now try this thought experiment: Imagine that you are not the clinician who has made these notes but someone who does not know the story the writer is about to tell. From this perspective, what does this plot imply? What questions and thoughts do you have about what you see plotted out?

g. Returning to your own perspective as the storyteller, review your choice of clinical material and make any changes you want.

h. Looking at your plot now, does your story incorporate the traditional elements of dramatic action: exposition, rising action, crisis, falling action, and resolution? Do you want to include any of these elements that you haven't addressed?

i. Given your plot, is yours a story of triumph, doubt, impasse, stumbling along or. . . ?

Multiple Plots

Stories often have more than one plot, because the intricacies and conflicts of characters' lives cannot be contained within a single narrative line. The dramas we play out in our minds, relationships, and lives would people many plots and are often recursive. In retrospect, Winer (1994) identified five "story lines" running through his analytic work with Elizabeth:

> The first of the four narratives that can be constructed from my work with Elizabeth is the story she would easily tell of her life if you asked her, the autobiography she might write. . . .
>
> The second story is actually, from her point of view, a number of bits and pieces that don't fit well with the autobiography. They are memories of experiences, or stories she has been told, which to the listener cast the first report in a different light. They don't jeopardize the first telling for her because she keeps them split off from the main current of her self-understanding. For the listener, however, they come together to form another narrative of her life, a darker, more problematic one. . . .
>
> The third narrative can be constructed from reading the analytic tea leaves—listening to dreams, tracking associations, following the events of her life. This narrative must also be assembled by the listener, and it is composed of elements that, unlike those in the first two narratives, are not within Elizabeth's awareness. We might call this, imprecisely, the narrative of the unconscious. . . .
>
> The fourth narrative is the one that emerges in the process between patient and analyst, specifically in the transference-countertransference unfoldings, and I have chosen to trace this from the vantage point of the countertransference. So this is the enacted story, a lived telling. (pp. 96–97)

After detailing each of these storylines, Winer (1994) identifies a fifth:

> The degree to which these alternate versions of the story can be teased apart was unusual, and actually suggested a fifth, integrative narrative in which I was to be the container for Elizabeth's dissociated versions of herself and her life. Her unconscious intention was for me to wrestle with her fractured experience; I was to drown or find a handhold in the swamp. The separating of the strands, in this telling, was part of my effort to adapt to this disorganizing situation. I then wondered whether this had been Elizabeth's fate as a child: being made container of her parents' split experiences. There was much to suggest this. (pp. 107–108)

As a writer, you may separate the different storylines of an analysis, as Winer does, or weave distinctive threads together as Wright (2009) explains that she does in "Going Home: Migration as Enactment and Symbol":

> The analogy of weaving best explains the structure of this paper, in which the 'warp', or fixed parallel threads are of home, migration and the analytic

journey of a woman whom I will call Ana. The 'weft' thread is a discussion of the symbolization process. Just as in weaving the weft runs over and under the fixed threads, so I hope to track a process of symbolization as it weaves between the external and internal worlds where home and migration resonate with meaning. Symbolization is a creative process of mind that enables the free emergence of expressions of being: like weaving it can bring new patterns into existence, a fabric individually crafted. (p. 475)

Setting Your Plot in Motion

Beginnings, like endings, may be discovered in the act of writing or revising as Ogden (2005a) explains:

> The [first] sentence 'came to me' in the act of writing as a dream comes unbidden in sleep. . . . Moving that sentence from the third paragraph of the original version to the position of opening sentence allowed it to take on more dramatic force—thus creating in the writing something of the emotional impact that Mr. A had had on me at the very beginning of his analysis. Only after making this sentence the opening sentence of the story did I recognize that it contained in germinal form the entirety of the story that would follow. (p. 18)

Let's look at the narrative details and gaps three writers present to set their plots in motion, beginning with the opening of Hazel Ipp's (2010) "Nell—A Bridge to the Amputated Self: The Impact of Immigration on Continuities and Discontinuities of Self":

> The thick Afrikaans accent crackled through my answering machine. Immediately, I tensed, froze, hearing little more than the startling guttural tones. The bare bones of the message filtered through. An Afrikaner wanting to enter therapy with me; *me*, the South African, English-speaking, protesting other, who, by definition, would be pitted as the natural enemy of the Afrikaner. Suddenly, the 30 years since I had left my homeland collapsed, and I felt catapulted back into that world of divisiveness, hatred, pain, suffering, horror—a world of angst and terror. The feeling was powerful, visceral. In those next moments I became painfully aware of the alarm and reflexive feelings of hatred and rage this accent triggered for me. Of course, I would not respond to this message, let alone even *contemplate* being this woman's therapist. (p. 373)

Just as Ipp is thrown into the unexpected, she catapults us into a particular moment in time, infused with emotions that draw on deep roots suddenly exposed. The action takes place primarily within the analyst narrator. Although there is an initiating event, the narrator's experience of it is paramount. Together these two perspectives create what Bruner (1990) identifies as the dual landscape of literary narratives: "That is to say, events and actions in a putative 'real world' occur concurrently with mental states in the consciousness of the protagonists. A discordant linkage between the two. . . provides a motive force to narrative. . . . For stories have to do with how protagonists interpret things, what things mean to them" (p. 51). Ipp recreates both landscapes so we can understand her discordant experience.

The beginning of Melanie Suchet's (2011) "Crossing Over" grabs our attention and propels us forward. Suchet focuses more on her patient than on her analyst self, and yet she too presents a dual landscape:

> I look across the room to cold eyes and a body steeled. There is no glimmer of a smile. My few attempts at engagement with Rebecca, a young lesbian lawyer, are rebuffed. I push back in my chair and brace myself for a difficult first session. She has been in one form of therapy or another since the age of 6 after intimidating other children on the playground. She informs me that she is quite adept at playing mind games, one of the benefits she has gained from therapy. Near the end of the session she manages to tell me that this is the longest time she has felt depressed. Although conflicted about starting therapy again, she has only come out in the last few years and wants to try working with a lesbian therapist. When the session ends I am convinced I will never see her again.
>
> I am surprised, and intrigued, when a few days later she calls, "I was really an asshole," she says to the answering machine. "Will you give me another chance?" Wolverine, her favorite superhero, is named after wolves for his heightened animal senses, and his mutual healing powers which enable his body to regenerate and his mind to heal by driving trauma from his memory. I will, over time, come to appreciate this very complex identification. She tells me very early on that she doesn't like her body, especially her breasts. She feels particularly vulnerable when people stare at them; it makes her feel as if she could be raped. Simultaneously she finds herself riding subway cars alone late at night. (p. 172)

Suchet effectively combines experience-near details with narrative summary and intimations of what's to come. By providing evidence that is intriguing but fragmentary, she creates several motives. We want to read on to see what happens next. When we learn that the Wolverine is her patient's favorite superhero, we may wonder why. When we learn that her patient feels vulnerable yet rides the subway late at night, we may want to know what drives such risky behavior. Suchet shows us how evidence that is incomplete can be used as a hook.

Helen Grebow's (2010) introduction of her patient Electra demonstrates the power and pull of the analyst's subjectivity:

> Opening my waiting room door, I am prepared to greet a new patient—a 20-something-year-old woman. I am startled, instead, by a vivid fantasy accompanied by visual and visceral associations. I have the sense of greeting a child—a shamed child, head hanging, tentatively rising from her chair. I feel disoriented by the presence of this child—this bewildered woman-child—a woman-child frozen in time, I think. As she slowly turns toward me, I am stunned. I struggle to contain my impulse to step back and, instead, present

what I hope is some semblance of steadiness. Her face and body appear asymmetrical. Her head is framed by a tangled mass of wiry, electric hair—a complex system of antennae, I think—a kind of motion detector, or an emotion detector! Nothing will escape her notice, her senses, or her keen vigilance. Her head, with its complex circuitry, appears disproportionately larger than her shriveled body. As she jolts upright, turning toward me, it requires great effort to maintain my composure. I feel that I have come face to face with some grotesque feminine incarnation of the elephant man. I look into her eyes as I introduce myself. My gaze is silently met by the eyes of a 'blind' person—glazed, teary, and unfocused. The deafening silence pounding in my ears produces a vertiginous sensation—a disequilibrium that again forces me to steady myself. The blind person staggers into my office with a listing gait, one arm partially uplifted as if fending off blows. She navigates the short distance from my waiting room to my consulting room couch, head thrust forward, antennae bobbing, scanning, searching—keeping a safe space between us.

My fantasy and associations are jarringly discrepant from my perceptions. I recognize that my visual impressions do not match the objective appearance of the woman I face. Reeling from this discrepancy, I am flooded with questions and speculations. Am I experiencing the sensate impact of a body tightly shrouded in trauma? What are her developmental issues, unarticulated and unexplored, worn like a misshapen shield? How did her head overcome her body? Has she been compelled to overuse her enormously disproportionate mind to defend against some nameless horrors? What was the cause of her 'blindness?' Is there something she cannot allow herself to see? What past horrors have so deformed her mind and body? (pp. 312–213)

Even though Grebow (2010) explains in her paper's first sentence that "this article emerged from an encounter with my own subjectivity upon first meeting my patient, Electra" (p. 307), her writing conveys the force of that encounter so effectively that many of us may be unaware of the "jarring" discrepancy between her "visual impressions" and her patient's "objective appearance" until she tells us about it a second time. Her writing highlights the highly subjective and contingent nature of perception. Thoughtfully but not indulgently giving your readers access to your subjectivity and acknowledging its influence will contribute to your credibility.

Exercise 12.3

Discordant Links and Gaps

a. Think of a moment in your clinical work in which you sensed a discordant gap between what happened and your experience of it. Give your readers enough to go on so they can appreciate the contrast you felt. Let Ipp, Suchet, and Grebow be your guides.

b. Read what you have written to see if you laid out enough rhetorical evidence for readers to appreciate the contrast you felt. If you haven't, provide whatever your readers will need to appreciate your subjectivity. Whether you are writing about something that fits together or hasn't yet come together, you need to create a good-enough fit between your rhetorical evidence and what you are trying to convey.

Vignettes

A vignette is often used to link focused clinical material along the narrative axis with an interpretation or explanation to illustrate an idea or concept at a higher level of abstraction. The advantage of using a vignette is that it is short and to the point. You craft it to illustrate just what you need. But that is also its liability. Clinical material is rarely uncomplicated. With a short vignette, readers will need to draw on their own experience for nuance and confirmation.

Nevertheless, vignettes may be effective. They are also often necessary, since you may not have the space to develop an extended clinical example for each point you make or may want to focus on a concept rather than the particulars of specific examples. Even if a vignette is economical, it may bring a concept to life if it is well written and may be more valuable than its size suggests. Because "psychoanalytic material commonly has strikingly self-similar aspects," a relatively small portion of analytic material may reflect the larger whole as a fractal (Galatzer-Levy, 1995, p. 1107) or a dream does. "Arguably, vignettes may be viewed as fractals of an analysis, in the same way that a single dream can condense internal object relations, the transference, the history of the treatment, and issues of current concern in everyday life" (Scharff, 2000, p. 424). Reiterating Daniel Stern's (2004) ideas, Weisel-Barth (2006) writes "that examining small momentary units of intersubjective experience, examining especially the emotional charge in these momentary units may yield more powerful information about relational/therapeutic change than broad narratives of therapeutic process" (p. 373).

Although Scharff (2000) argues that "there is no substitute for the detailed description of fold upon fold of analytic process, the rhythm of chaos and order, over a lengthy treatment" (p. 424), a vignette can do its work in a compelling fashion as Joan and Neville Symington (1996) demonstrate when they illustrate Bion's concept of the container/contained:

> An analyst once had this experience when treating a mentally handicapped man. The patient was aged 33 and went each day to a sheltered workshop where he performed the most menial tasks. The analyst and some of the staff believed that he had a mental capacity that was capable of higher-grade work. In the sessions these words would sometimes dribble out from the corner of his mouth:

I am 33 years old and is that nothing?

And a moment later:

Can't you give me a picture of who I am?

The analyst said:

> The fact that you feel they have been thirty-three years of emptiness, waste and nothingness is so painful that it is better to have people's pictures of you than to face this ghastly nothingness.

He replied:

> Well, if you won't give me a picture what do I come here for?

The analyst stood up, placed himself alongside him and said:

> It is like this. There in front of us is thirty-three years of waste, nothing and emptiness. It is like sitting in a train and opposite sits a man with a wounded and diseased face and it is so horrific that you have to hold pictures up in front of you because it is more than you can bear. But the reason you come to see me is that perhaps there is just a possibility that if you have me beside you then you can look at it.

The matter that could not be contained was pain: thirty-three years of waste, nothing and emptiness. The incident is also an image of a mother interacting with the distressed infant in such a way that there is the possibility of the pain being held in the infant's mind. (pp. 51–52)

I find this sequence compelling. The dialogue is framed with the barest essentials, highlighting the starkness of this patient's life. A particularizing detail (Stein, 1999, p. 56) surprises: the patient's words sometimes "dribble out from the corner of his mouth." Dialogue predominates, giving this minimalist vignette the feel of an immediate scene (Stein, 1995) despite its lack of visual details. Affect is emphasized, although paradoxically we don't know if the patient expresses emotion as he talks. The sparseness of the scene not only reflects the patient's empty life but also draws us in by stimulating our imagination to wonder about or fill in what isn't described.

Because the vignette's purpose is to illustrate Bion's concept of the container/contained, the patient's uncontained suffering (dribbling out) and the analyst's response are the most important elements that need to be presented. The analyst's empathy and containing responses are expressed in action (taking his place beside his patient); in words that repeat, extend, and interpret his patient's language; and in images that extend his patient's imagery. The vignette's last two sentences pinpoint the interpretive and conceptual ideas the whole sequence illustrates. I don't think the vignette's economy jeopardizes its effectiveness, because it is experience near and helps us see what the analyst sees. Its starkness poignantly illustrates and enacts the patient's experience. Nor do I think the vignette's power as an illustration is diminished by its standing without benefit of more contextualization. We don't need any more information to understand the outlines of Bion's idea. The vignette completes the work it sets out to do.

In Eigen's (2009) hands, an image-infused narrative summary is used to create an evocative vignette:

In my book, *Psychic Deadness* (1996, Chapter Twelve), I write about a man who recalls a moment when he died, i.e., when his feelings numbed, froze. It was after an unexpected paternal rage, a capricious rage at dinner over something trivial, something that had no value except in the patient's imagination. The patient recalls shock, momentary trembling, then a spreading psychic anaesthesia which never fully went away. He lived on the other side of this frozen state ever since.

Someone might say, "Get over it, get on with it. Why dwell on things like that?" My patient became a successful man, and lived a full enough life on the other side of the freeze. But he came for help to reclaim himself, to thaw out. In a secret, important way he felt he was a corpse who wanted to live. We all die, to some extent, in order to live, to survive. Psychic deadness is part of life. But perhaps some of us die more than we have to, in worse ways than necessary. Some of us hope that, with help, we might find more life. (Eigen, 2009, pp. 37–38)

Exercise 12.4

Vignettes: Bottom Up and Top Down

In *The Zen of Seeing* (1973), Franck writes, "It is in order to really see, to see even deeper, ever more intensely, hence to be fully aware and alive, that I draw what the Chinese call 'The Ten Thousand Things' around me. Drawing is the discipline by which I constantly rediscover the world" (p. 6).

a. Pick an ordinary moment that you would like to see more fully and describe it in words.
b. Consider what clinical concept or wisdom your writing illustrates and incorporate it into your vignette if you haven't already done so. If you start with the description of what you see and then articulate an idea, you'll be presenting your material bottom up. If you start with an idea and illustrate it with a vignette or other kind of description, you'll be presenting your ideas top down.

Setting a Context

If the clinical session or moment you want to present needs a larger context, how large does it need to be? Theodore Shapiro (1994) found that the presenting analyst and his colleagues were able to reach more of a consensus on what transpired in a specific session when the context of the three previous ones was presented. For them, three sessions constituted "the ecology of the hour." Rather than present all three sessions, you may use a narrative summary (my pp. 15, 120–128) to establish the ecological context.

Spence (1982) distinguishes between the analyst's "privileged competence" that comes from being in the analytic process with a patient and the "normative competence" of others in the field who are not privileged to that private experience. Over time the analyst's privileged competence shades into normative competence, because it is hard to hold on to the nuances, affective gradations, and fleeting nonverbal qualities of a session. Spence's distinction can serve as a reminder that the specifics you will need for experience-near writing could easily slip away even if you have a tape recording. The subjective meaning of what is said (or not said) in a clinical moment is essential to capture, as Spence (1994) explains, "because meanings, not words, compose the gist of our data, and unless we capture the meanings *as they were sensed in the clinical moment* by analyst and patient, we are looking for the key under the wrong lamppost" (p. 294).

As the lyric narrative mode reminds us, privileged competence may be characterized by uncertainty, ambiguity, and the limits of present knowledge. Privileged competence in this sense doesn't mean having it all together. Spence (1982) actually warns against "narrative smoothing," the urge, however unconscious, to write defensively or make things fit together, especially with our theories. Sue Shapiro (2004) encountered such narrative smoothing when a resident wrote up an interview Shapiro had done:

> The intake interview was one of the more distressing—though not *that* uncommon—experiences of barely contained chaos, intense emotional tension, barely comprehensible psychotic ramblings. I was glad I didn't have to present the various versions of reality and history described by two distraught parents and their acutely psychotic child. The [resident's] presentation the next morning was beautiful, a seamless coherent narrative. She included some of the facts of the case, but left out the most salient quality—the tension and confusion that any person new to this system would experience in the face of shorthand and conflicting reports described by three people locked in a desperate emotional struggle. The truth in this instance wasn't neat, and an accurate report would not get high grades for narrative coherence. But a coherent report failed totally to convey what went on in that consulting room. (pp. 669–670)

Shapiro continues: "It is that very messiness—the kind that defies simple storytelling—that keeps the work fresh" (p. 670).

Tuckett (1993) notes another problem with a clinical narrative that fits too neatly together:

> In particular, there is the possibility that a good, well-told and coherent story creates the risk of seduction, which in the context of communication to others can be summed up thus: the more a narrative is intellectually, emotionally and aesthetically satisfying, the better it incorporates clinical events into rich and sophisticated patterns, the less space is left to the audience to notice alternative patterns and to elaborate alternate narratives. (p. 1183)

In Coen's (2000) vocabulary, clinical writing that fits too neatly together is closed, because it doesn't allow readers to collaborate with authors. For that to happen, clinical writing needs to be open enough to allow readers "into our minds and experiences sufficiently for them to see what we see, to see what we do not fully know we see, and to see what we do not and cannot see for ourselves" (p. 464). Writing that is open shows as much if not more than it tells.

"The Local Level"

As you know, the view of the therapeutic process "from being in the thick of it, in the middle of the session" looks very different from "a cleaned-up after-the-fact version" (Boston Change Process Study Group, 2010, p. xvii), from a perspective afforded by subsequent events and the wisdom time may bestow. The view from the local level is "indeterminate, untidy, or approximate" (BCPSG, 2010, p. 95), because the local level itself is "sloppy, nonlinear, noncasual, and unpredictable" (p. xvii) as complexity theory suggests. If you want to depict what's going on at the local level, you may want to leave some "loose ends" (Plaut, 1999, p. 390) and ragged bits that may never cohere and in their raggedness reflect the nonlinearity of clinical process and "the mystery of things" (Bollas, 1999).

Exercise 12.5

"The Local Level"

a. For starters, make a list of a handful of the smallest details at the local level of a single session: e.g., tiny narrative bits; the quality of a gesture; a tonal shift; a somatic clue; an association; or micromovement in your relationship dance. You might want to make this list while a session is still fresh. Include some details that may not yet fit together or whose meaning is still unclear.
b. Using some details that fit together and some that don't, write about this session in a way that highlights the messiness of your experience and the provisional nature of your understanding in the present moment.

"Thick Description"

For Goldstein (1998), clinical writing is associated with the creation of "a virtual reality" (p. 452). As vivid ethnographies demonstrate, creating such a virtual reality necessitates "something more than the force of their arguments" (Geertz, 1994/1988, p. 4). For Geertz (1994/1988), that something more is an ability to convince readers of the writer's deep involvement in others' lives and the literary skill necessary to create a sense of "truly" having "'been there'" (p. 5). Geertz (1994/1988) explains what's involved:

The ability of anthropologists to get us to take what they say seriously has less to do with either a factual look or an air of conceptual elegance than it has with their capacity to convince us that what they say is a result of their having actually penetrated (or, if you prefer, been penetrated by) another form of life, of having, one way or the other, truly "been there." And that, persuading us that this offstage miracle has occurred, is where the writing comes in. (pp. 4–5)

Geertz sees human beings "suspended in webs of significance" they have spun, and his work as an anthropologist, like ours as psychotherapists, is "not an experimental science in search of law but an interpretive one in search of meaning. It is explication I am after, construing social expressions on their surface enigmatical" (p. 5). Geertz's language makes me think of Havens' (1993) patient's small gesture and the meaning he discerns in that grain of sand (my pp. 40–41).

How do you convey your understanding of what on the surface appears enigmatic? How do you depict the "webs of significance" in which you, your patient, and your clinical work are suspended? One way is to create "thick description." Ryle (1990/1971) coined the term, which Geertz (2000/1973) brought into prominence. It refers to the quality of a description that "entails an account of the intentions, expectations, circumstances, settings, and purposes that give actions their meanings" (Greenblatt, 1997, p. 17) and allows one to distinguish between two behaviors that look alike but mean quite different things, such as a wink and twitch of an eye to cite Ryle's famous example.

While Ryle applies thick description to the characteristics of a text, Geertz also uses the term to apply to the object described (Greenblatt, 1997). Some things are thicker than others, more "compressed and hence expandable," more amenable to interpretations that "widen out into larger social worlds" (Greenblatt, 1997, p. 19) and more complex meanings. For writing about other people's lives to be persuasive, "the dense networks of meaning charted in an effective thick description had to be traceable back to the anecdote initially held up for scrutiny" (Greenblatt, 1997, p. 19). Thick description in clinical writing brings compressed and expandable objects of analytic scrutiny into focus. The objects we select, their thickness, and the thickness of our descriptions and explications will vary. But we too must select out of the "confused continuum of social [and therapeutic] experience" small-enough units of subjectivity, intersubjectivity, social action, and culture— "enacted statements of. . . particular ways of being in the world" (Geertz, 2000, p. 17)—to hold within the boundaries of attention.

Exercise 12.6

A Writer's Sketchbook

Many vignettes are interweaves of clinical material and an interpretation, explication, idea, or concept. Like a sketch, they suggest the shape and character of what you see and feel that stimulate the senses of the beholder to complete.

a. As you read other clinical papers, notice what kinds of vignettes they use, what objects of attention they bring into focus, how compressed and expandable those objects are, how thick the writer's description is, and what makes the description effective if it is. See what you can learn from other writers' techniques.

b. I invite you to begin a writer's sketchbook. Experiment by writing different kinds of vignettes and detailed descriptions of clinical moments. To begin, keep the scale small. Try writing a sketch that is as nimble and sparse as the Symingtons' vignette (pp. 174–175) and another that is an evocative narrative summary like Eigen's (pp. 175–176). In others, try creating slivers of vivid clinical process thickly described. Even though you may be working on a small canvas, you can still give your readers a sense of your "having been there" in that moment.

c. If you'd like to practice setting a narrative or conceptual context for any of these sketches, by all means do.

Your ideas don't have to be fully baked for them to be worthy of capture. Cooking them takes time. Bollas (1987) explains how he makes notes of emergent ideas whose meaning he has not yet realized:

> In the evening after work, while driving in my car, listening to music or simply engaging in the pleasant humdrum of ordinary life, an idea derived from work with a patient will cross my mind. I enter the idea in my notebook without straining to push myself beyond what I know exactly at that moment. I prefer it this way because it allows me to imagine an idea without, as it were, knowing exactly what I mean. I often find that although I am working on an idea without knowing exactly what it is that I think, I am engaged in thinking an idea struggling to have me think it. (p. 10)

Keep your sketchbook handy. Writing practice can heighten your attention, sharpen your senses, and help you hold on to experience-near details and emotional textures that reflect your "privileged competence" (Spence, 1982). "Capturing" the specificity of what you experience before it evaporates or the surprise of an idea that suddenly arrives is one way to develop your "creative competencies" (Epstein, 1999).

13 The Conceptual Axis

What we call concepts *are neural structures that allow us to mentally characterize our categories and reason about them. . . . What makes concepts concepts is their inferential capacity, their ability to be bound together in ways that yield inferences.*
George Lakoff and Mark Johnson, *Philosophy in the Flesh*

All life is a dance between levels of abstraction.
Alfred Korzybski, *Science and Sanity*

I visualize the conceptual axis of a paper as a network of ideas arising out of the narrative axis (thinking bottom up) and extending vertically through the levels of abstraction that are relevant to the work of that paper (p. 244). The relative importance of each axis depends on the work you do along each one. Whether you move your readers through the levels of abstraction bottom up or top down, your paper's integrity depends on how you link these two axes and how cogently you connect your ideas all along the conceptual axis. I can't emphasize this point enough. *Your paper's integrity rests on establishing sturdy and compelling connections.*

Concepts and categories play an important role in the organization of ideas and the way we "make sense of experience" (Lakoff, 1990). They "are the structures that differentiate aspects of our experience into discernible kinds" and allow us to make inferences, reason, and build systems of understanding (Lakoff & Johnson, 1999, p. 19). Theories may be seen as a system of categories and concepts organized at different levels of abstraction.

While concepts help us identify commonalities among particulars and develop inferences, they may also obscure the particulars that make each person and situation unique. Nietzsche wrote that " 'Concepts are formed by forgetting what distinguishes one object from the next' " (quoted in Pontalis, 2003, p. 3). Pontalis (2003) elaborates:

The necessary condition for the formation of a concept thus is forgetting: a forgetting of property, of singularity, of difference. I say "table" and I forget this table. I say, "He's obsessional," and I forget the one who is speaking to me. I say, "identification with the father," and I haven't said anything at all. I say, "transference," and I think I have been saved from the uncontrollable love or this merciless hate. I say "maternal transference," and I don't know to which mother he or she is referring. (pp. 3–4)

Pontalis (2003) points out that the word "concept in German is *Begriff*. The concept has claws (*Griffe*). It is a predator, a tyrant" (p. 4). Concepts are prone to reification, impose closure, and may be recruited for the exercise of power (Quinney, 2003, p. ix). When concepts are gathered into belief systems we call theories, the danger increases: "More dreadful still is the ambition to construct a large edifice of concepts, very coherent, sturdy, and resistant. There's a strong risk that the edifice will offer only the 'strict regularity of a Roman columbarium' (Nietzsche again)" (Pontalis, 2003, p. 4), a structure of vaults and recesses to hold the urns and ashes of the dead.

An antidote to conceptual tyranny lies in the vitality of language:

> Language saves us from the grip, the influence, and the tyranny of the concept . . . . Words are travelers in every way (whereas the concept tends to claim just one meaning, it defines, it circumscribes its field of application). Language breathes; it is mobile; and rich or impoverished, it can say everything; it is a meeting with the unexpected. It disconcerts the concept, mocks it. (Pontalis, 2003, p. 4)

We can't do without concepts, but we can hold them "lightly" as Orange (1995) suggests we hold our theories; preserve their connection to the clinical details and particulars that give rise to them; keep them alive in our continued interrogation of their meaning; and resist being "subjugated to them, so we can stay open to the inconceivable" (Pontalis, 2003, p. 4). "Words, when they are living and breathing, are like musical chords," Ogden (1997) writes. "The full resonance of the chord or phrase must be allowed to be heard in all of its suggestive imprecision. We must attempt in our use of language, both in our theory-making and in our analytic practice, to be makers of music, rather than players of notes" (Ogden, 1997, pp. 4–5).

Sandler (1983) sees concepts as highly elastic. They can be "stretched to encompass new insights and new ideas" (p. 35) and extend the life of a theory by "tak[ing] up the strain of theoretical change, absorbing it while more organized newer theories or part-theories can develop" (p. 36). But using old terms like transference, projective identification, and representation in new contexts, Orange (2003) argues, means carrying a lot of baggage from the metapsychology, philosophy, and epistemology of bygone days, creating dissonance rather than the chords Ogden describes.

What is a writer to do when working at the conceptual level? This chapter will help you think about ways to develop and negotiate the conceptual axis of your paper. The conceptual axis should be explicit in papers written in the paradigmatic mode but may be implicit in papers written in other modes. Even if your paper's conceptual structure is implied, it needs to be well thought out and coherently organized.

"Dimensions of Meaning"

An analytic concept, Sandler (1983) proposes, "has a set of *dimensions of meaning*" that exist "in a meaning-space, in which it moves as its context and sense changes" (p. 36). Concepts, key terms, or words, to quote Gass (2009) on words, "really don't have an independent life. They occupy no single location. They are foci for relations. Imagine an asterisk made by innumerable but inexactly crisscrossing lines: that's one image of the word. Tokens take on meanings as well as contribute their own by the way they enter, then operate in and exit from, contexts" (p. 337).

Many of the contexts of the concepts you employ may be visualized using the levels of abstraction. Doing so may help you develop the meaning space of a concept or evaluate how another writer has created one. Let's see how this works.

Evocative terms like Bollas' (1987) "unthought known" are potential spaces in which meaning arises out of the interactions between writer and reader, observations and ideas, clinical examples and personal associations. One journal editor I interviewed (2000) admired clinical writers who are " 'elusive and elliptical enough in their writing that they get their idea across without nailing it down' " (p. 84). He cited Winnicott, Phillips, Sanville, and Grotstein as examples. A reader's " 'willingness to be confused' " by more elusive prose opens space for the writer's " 'making contact with the reader in ways that go beyond cognitive recognition' " (quoted in Naiburg, 2000, p. 84). Writing that draws readers into a meaning space, as the evocative, enactive, and lyric narrative modes can do especially well, invites readers to expand that space for themselves. For Ogden (2001a), Winnicott's "indefinite, enigmatic language does not fill a space with knowledge; it opens up a space for thinking, imagining, and freshly experiencing" (p. 317). Winnicott's prose also demonstrates how evocative and enactive writing may be incorporated into the paradigmatic mode.

I think of a meaning space as an area and a concept as a meaning space rather than a point. When high school students are taught to write a five-paragraph essay, they are told to make a point in the first paragraph, illustrate it in each of the next three, and hammer it into the ground in the fifth. When teaching college students, I presented a different approach. Instead of planting an idea as a stake in the ground and returning to the same point at the end of their paper, I invited them to build their ideas progressively so they became richer, more nuanced, and complex. As they developed as writers, they learned to elaborate dimensions of meaning throughout their papers, extending them beyond their first words.

We have already seen how a number of clinical writers do that. When writing about the word conversation, Ogden (2001b) shows us how to use its " 'fossil poetry,' " "itself a chorus of accumulated meanings" (p. 4), to explore and extend the word's meaning (my pp. 218–219). Loewald's (1980) evocation of instincts (my pp. 51–52) and Eigen's of emotional storms (my pp. 52–53) are examples of using the evocative mode to open up the meaning space of a concept. Bollas (1991) uses a personal narrative to introduce the meaning of the destiny drive (my pp. 117–119). Grand (2003) employs the evocative and enactive modes to portray the noisy, colorful world of Brooklyn's post-war streets and the dim interiors of Rosa's family home. Then she uses these vividly rendered scenes to describe the textures of Rosa's self experience (my pp. 48–49). Whether working at the level of a single word, personality, concept, or the intersections of culture, history, family, and self, each of these writers opens up the space of meaning far beyond the one dimensionality of a single point.

Exercise 13.1

"A Meaning Space"

a. Pick or name a concept to practice developing a meaning space.
b. Following the directions for the clustering exercise (pp. 6–7), use the concept you just selected as your central term and brainstorm ideas and associations that enrich its meaning. If I want to explore the meaning of a recent enactment, I might include notes about what happened, my feelings and associations, the repetitions I sensed were being played out, relevant bits of theory, neighboring concepts, and lookalikes.
c. After you've completed your clustering process, notice what has emerged and write a few paragraphs to develop your concept's meaning.

Lateral and Vertical Moves

Making distinctions and drawing boundaries are essential to establishing conceptual meaning. Gass (2009) explains how one word rubs up against another to "shave" meaning and be "shorn" in the process: "If the word is an accretion formed from its history of use, then when it scrapes against another word, it begins to shave the consequences of past times and frequent occasions from its companion, as well as being shorn itself" (p. 337). When Racker (1957) distinguishes concordant and complementary countertransference or another writer differentiates procedural, declarative, narrative, and autobiographical memory, they are making what I call a lateral move to distinguish one term from another at the same level of abstraction. When you move from the general to the particular (top down) or from the particular to the general (bottom up), you make what I call a vertical move.

Visualizing a concept on the levels of abstraction may help you analyze the moves someone else makes and consider those you would make. When Barbara Pizer (2003) distinguishes Russell's crunch from her relational (k)not, she explicitly makes a lateral move (my pp. 189–193), but she also implicitly makes a vertical one, because her idea and Russell's now form two subtypes of the Crunch with a capital *C*. Both kinds of moves are implied in Ghent's (1990) title "Masochism, Submission, Surrender: Masochism as a Perversion of Surrender."

Concepts like resistance and the Oedipus complex have different meanings in the context of different theories and may even have different shades of meaning when used by clinicians of the same theoretical stripe. So you may need to do some work at the level of theory, metapsychology, philosophy, or epistemology to clarify what a specific concept means to you. Bromberg (1998; my pp. 216–217) makes both vertical and lateral moves when developing a contemporary under-standing of resistance as the layout of his ideas in figure 13.1 suggests.

Analytic Tradition

Classical Analytic Thought   Postclassical Analytic Thought

Metapsychology

Model of Mind

Based on Repression   Based on Dissociation

Concept

Resistance

Freud 1925   Bromberg 1998

Unitary account of transference   Dyadic experience of transference/
                                           countertransference matrix

Archeological barrier   Enacted dialectical process of meaning
                                           making

Avoidance of insight   Dialectic between preservation and change
Fear of change   Negotiation of incompatible domains of self
                                           experience

Figure 13.1 Layout of Bromberg's (1998) ideas from *Standing in the Spaces*

Figure 13.1 does not represent all the ideas Bromberg discusses in the excerpt I quote in chapter 15 (pp. 216–217), but it does map the primary structure of its intellectual field and mark both the lateral distinctions and vertical moves he makes. It also visually represents a meaning space.

Let's consider an example from Gerson's (2009) "When the Third is Dead: Memory, Mourning, and Witnessing in the Aftermath of the Holocaust" (see also my p. 101):

The "third", "thirdness", & the "dead third"

The theoretical concepts of the 'third' and 'thirdness' have been, in recent years, the subject of numerous formulations from a variety of theoretical perspectives, and have been applied to a host of clinical, developmental, pathological, and social realms of concern (Aron, 2006; Benjamin, 2004; Green, 2004; Ogden, 2004). In the process, we have gained a plethora of meanings that enrich the conceptual base of psy-choanalysis even as they, at times, threaten to move us from clarity to confusion. In an issue of the *Psychoanalytic Quarterly* devoted entirely to 'The Third in Psychoanalysis' (2004), the eight articles offered a total of 22 different types of the 'third'. In an attempt to find order amid this proliferation of usages, I suggested that all of the types of the 'third' belonged to one of three major domains of concern—the developmen-tal, the relational, and the cultural—and that all usages of the concept could be accounted for within these categorizations, albeit with some overlaps between these three broad domains (Gerson, 2004). Briefly, the three major applications of the concept of the third are delineated in the following way. First, the 'developmental third' includes those processes and structures through which the child moves from dyadic to triadic relating, the prime exemplar of which is the oedipal configuration. Second, the concept of the 'relational third' refers to the unique configuration in which self and other combine in every relationship and can be considered to be the inter-subjective process and product of each relationship. The concept of the 'analytic third' (Ogden, 2004) can be thought of as a specific form of the broader category of the relational third and illustrates that in all relationships unconscious structures are created that transcend the individuality of the two participants and that these are partially determined by the context within which the relationship exists. Third, the concept of the 'cultural third' designates the existence and impact of all of the non-personal contexts and process within which each individual lives and that shapes the nature of their development; included here are linguistic forms that exert powerful influence on the structures of thought and affect. It should, of course, be borne in mind that these usages of the concept of the third exist both in external and psychic realities, are configured both objectively and subjectively, and are registered and maintained in both conscious and unconscious configurations.

In this article, I apply the notion of the third to that entity—be it personal, social, or cultural—that exists in relation to an individual and his or her experience of massive trauma. The concept of the 'witness' is used as an exemplar of a 'live third'—simply put, this is the other whose engaged recognition and concerned responsiveness to the individual's experience creates livable meaning. The 'dead third' is conceptualized as the loss of a 'live third' upon whom the individual had previously relied, had entrusted with faith, and in relation to whom or which, had developed a sense of personal continuity and meaning. In this regard, the third—again, whether person, relationship, or institution—serves the elemental function of solidifying an individual's sense of person, place, and purpose. We each develop within this crucial set of orienting functions provided by the 'thirds' in which we exist, and while their presence is internalized throughout the lifespan, we all remain vulnerable to their abrupt loss. External traumas call forth our need for the containing and meaning-making functions of all the 'thirds' in which we live; when such needs are ignored, we then face the internal traumas of living with the absence of that which made life comprehensible. Under such circumstances, the living thirds in which the person was nested, now become a nest of dead thirds from which he or she cannot escape. (Gerson, 2009, pp. 1341–1342)

My map of Gerson's (2009) first paragraph appears in figure 13.2.

The Third/Thirdness

Developmental	Relational	Cultural
processes and structures through which child moves from dyadic to triadic relating	configurations of self/other in relationships	nonpersonal contexts and processes
	an intersubjective process	
e.g. Oedipal Configuration	e.g. Ogden's Analytic Third	e.g. language

All categories involve external *and* psychic realities, are configured objectively *and* subjectively, and are registered and maintained in both conscious *and* unconscious configurations.

Figure 13.2 Layout of Gersons's (2009) ideas from "When the Third Is Dead"

Tracking Gerson's ideas in figure 13.2 from the top down, you will see that he makes a vertical move, dividing the third into three subtypes, which I represent at a slightly lower level of abstraction than the core concept. Then he makes lateral moves to define and differentiate each subtype. He makes another vertical move when he provides an example of each subtype and rounds out his paragraph by identifying three shared characteristics of thirdness. If you read his paragraph with this map in view, you can see how he moves through his intellectual field. You could trace a line through the map to represents how his ideas travel through this meaning space, defining it as he goes.

I've mapped the ideas in Gerson's next paragraph in figure 13.3.

Third in Relation to Person's Experience of Massive Trauma

Live Third	Dead Third
trusted, relied upon recognition and responsiveness creates livable meaning, personal continuity	
solidifies individual's sense of person, place, purpose	loss of live third
functions internalized in normal development	

Witness

Intrusion of External Trauma

Presence of Live Third	Absence of Live Third: Dead Third
nesting protection	creates internal traumas
containment, meaning	a nest of inescapable dead thirds

Figure 13.3 Layout of next paragraph of Gerson's (2009) ideas from "When the Third Is Dead"

Moving from figure 13.2 to figure 13.3, you can see that Gerson shifts his attention from the differences between the personal, social, and cultural thirds to the difference between a live and a dead third. He also explains how the presence of a live third leads to different consequences than its absence. Approaching the notion of a third from different angles in each paragraph, Gerson demonstrates how we may spiral around an idea, opening up its meaning space on different planes.

Exercise 13.2

Necessary Contexts

a. Imagine either of the maps of Gerson's ideas with a chunk of the material missing and notice the consequences of that erasure. Now put that chunk back, erase a different one, and notice the effects.
b. What does this exercise show you about the importance of establishing a concept's contexts at different levels of abstraction (vertical moves) and making distinctions at the same level of abstraction (lateral moves)?

If you erase one of the three subtypes that Gerson identifies in the first paragraph I quote, his categories won't be inclusive enough to account for the twenty-two kinds of thirds he found in the *Psychoanalytic Quarterly* articles. If you dropped out the examples of each subtype, his ideas would be that much more abstract. Connecting ideas at higher levels of abstraction with those at lower ones is grounding, especially so when you present vivid clinical material; when the two axes of your paper meet in the presentation and interpretation of clinical material (my pp. 190–193); and when the links you make between levels of abstraction don't span large gaps.

Stepwise

When a writer's ideas fit snugly together, as Mitchell's (my pp. 108–112), Bromberg's (my pp. 184–185), and Gerson's (my pp. 185–188) do, I think of the verti-cal moves they make as a stepwise progression. Here's an example in which that progression is built sentence by sentence and sometimes even clause by clause:

One may nevertheless wonder why mentalisation is seen by us as so important, and we offer some thoughts on this here. Firstly, it enables the child to see people's actions as meaningful through the attribution of thoughts and feelings. This means that their actions become predictable, which in turn reduces dependency on others. This is an important component of the process of individuation. The child of around 4 or 5 is frequently able to understand what the mother is doing and why, without her needing to bear his limited perspective constantly in mind ('I can't do that now because I am worried about granny's illness', etc.). This allows both child and caregiver to attain increasing mental and physical independence, needing to refer far less to each other in order to allow the child to borrow the mother's understanding. (Target & Fonagy, 1996, p. 462)

Sentences like these remind me of building with Lego blocks. Can you see how the third sentence in Target and Fonagy's paragraph carries the meaning of the second a little further? It does so in two steps, the first in its main clause, the next in its dependent (which) clause. The fourth sentence caps these two with the concept of individuation, which is then exemplified in the description of the child's capacity to understand the mother's actions and intentions. The last sentence plays out the consequences of the child's new mental capacity, taking one conceptual step in each clause. Take any of these sentences out of this paragraph or drop out a smaller unit of meaning that I visualize as a Lego brick, and you leave a gap. Gaps that are too wide for readers to cross sure-footedly may cause them to slip and question your guidance and authority.

Exercise 13.3

Minding the Gap

a. Lay out a set of ideas as the basis for a paper, using the template of the levels of abstraction.
b. Notice if you jumped any levels or left any gaps that would make it difficult for your readers to follow you along the conceptual axis of your paper. If so, fill in what's needed.

Crucial Intersections

We might think of the intersection(s) where the two axes of your paper meet as zones in which attention shifts or alternates between clinical material and what you make of it. Writers present clinical material in innumerable ways as the modes of clinical prose and the examples I quote suggest. For Jacobs (2008), "The task of the analytic writer. . . is to render the analytic experience so fully, in such vivid colors, that the reader enters into, and, for a time, lives, that experience; knows it, and, understands it—through his imaginative immersion in the interplay of patient and analyst; interactions that are at the heart of the analytic process" (pp. 510–511).

Vividly rendering analytic experience is often a priority of the narrative, lyric narrative, evocative, and enactive modes. How writers share with their readers the tasks of making sense of that experience depends on their choice of clinical mode and how they execute it. Some writers, like Rogers in *A Shining Affliction* (chapter 3), may hug the narrative axis and extend their reach along the conceptual axis into the level of interpretation but leave most of the conceptualizing to their readers. Other writers may pay more equal attention to both axes, while some may tilt the balance more toward the conceptual. Although Henry James wished that an artist would select the "richest" of subjects, he advocated honoring each artist's choice and based his criticism on the artist's execution: "We must grant the artist his subject, his idea, his donnée: our criticism is applied only to what he makes of it" (quoted in Miller, 1972, p. 115).

Let's return to Barbara Pizer's (2003) "When the Crunch is a (K)not, A Crimp in Relational Dialogue" (my pp. 54–55) to see how she connects the narrative and conceptual axes of her paper. Her article begins on the conceptual axis as she makes a lateral move to distinguish between Russell's crunch and her concept of a relational (k)not. The crunch is an intense yet necessary repetition and mutual enactment that threatens the viability of the treatment. The therapist's job is to survive it, still the confusion, and interrupt the repetitions—hers and her patient's. But she can't do that from the sidelines. "For the person sitting in the analyst's place, the capacity to contain and negotiate the treatment process requires, as Russell emphasizes, *involvement*" (Pizer, 2003, p. 173). "The most dangerous part of the treatment process is when both parties wish for, invite, non-involvement. That is the most dangerous repetition" (Russell quoted in Pizer, 2003, p. 173). It is exactly at this point in Russell's theorizing that Pizer turns in a new direction:

> We might surmise that the noninvolvement Russell describes has to do with the potential consequences of too much affect in the consulting room. I mean here, however, to identify a particular situation, a microprocess related to the crunch, that silently dictates disengagement, a kind of petrified distortion from the past that enters present dialogue and contributes to what I have come to call a relational (k)not. (Pizer, 2003, pp. 173–174)

Pizer presents her theory of how relational (k)nots develop before concluding the first three-page section of her paper with this extended definition:

> In the title of this paper, "not" is a play on the word knot (see Laing, 1970), which refers to that form of relational dialogue that subverts authentic, open communication. As a consequence, the apparent dialogue presents merely an image of two people in conversation; what one person is really saying remains unspoken, and the other person's response—if not already scripted—becomes distorted. Recognition, acknowledgement, and genuine affect necessarily drop out. Without a true dialogical space in this relationship, internal reflection, the

capacity for mentalization, is compromised; the possibilities for negotiation between participants are diminished, knotted up, or nullified (see Pizer, 1992, 1998). Informed by the double bind construct originally coined to describe the etiology of schizophrenia in family discourse (Weakland, 1960), I use the term relational not(s) to describe a crimping form of communication that occurs between and within persons along the entire spectrum, from pathology to health, from notably disturbed to relatively well-functioning people. (Pizer, 2003, p. 174)

By defining a relational (k)not as a particular kind of crunch "that silently dictates disengagement" (p. 173), Pizer does several things at once. She builds on the conceptual power of Russell's term to develop and differentiate her own and borrows its dynamic energy for hers, transferring its charge to the negating power of a (k)not. As Pizer presents four brief examples of relational (k)nots and one extended clinical example, the force of her term accrues the kinesthetic energy of a crunch.

Let's take a look at one of the intersections Pizer creates between the two axes of her paper:

Inevitably, relational nots appear as repetitions in the treatment situation. But the repetition I refer to here is not the content of a particular interaction, but the process; a process of uninvolvement; a process that consists of the "notting" or negating of the original anguish or affect and is, therefore, not "rendered" for negotiation between patient and analyst. A relational not, a crimp in thinking, feeling, or interacting, coerces noninvolvement. Persistent relational notting produces a crisis of detachment involving both participants. We might see it as the negative, or underside of a crunch, wherein genuine affect is subtly, imperceptibly dropped out. The relational not deletes relational space. Whereas a crunch consists of a confusion of time, a foreclosure of space in the relationship between two people, the not conflates time and space and erases relationship. Here is a hypothetical example of a series of interconnecting (k)nots from the consulting room:

"I don't want an antidepressant because if all it takes is a little pill, then I should be able to do it myself."

Something is missing in that thought process, but it's hard to figure out exactly what. And then—

"If it turns out that I feel better on your pills, then I'll really be upset that I didn't take them sooner!"

How did that happen? The therapist reorients, attempts to grab at the lost stitch. "*My* pills?"

"You know what I mean, the antidepressants."

"*Forget it!*" thinks the therapist to herself, and then the intensity of that instruction is almost imperceptibly replaced by, "It's best to let that go for now; it will come up again."

We might infer from this example that there may be something in the patient-person's past that coerces him to assume a correlation between the size or sign of an antidepressant pill and the size or sign of his ability for manly accomplishment. And, furthermore, there is something in the past or present situation that causes a particular vulnerability to a perception of coercion; but he is unable to think so or say so directly. And what about the therapist-person's state of awareness? Might her past contain a fear of assertion? Does the presence of latent anger or detachment frighten, or anger, her? What do we have to go on? The repetitions here consist of interlocking instances of dialogical crimps that make up a series of relational (k)nots. There is a jamming of relational space. Sometimes these nots will silently, subversively evade or negate involvement until patient and therapist terminate—both wondering what they somehow left out or missed, and why a pretty good experience did not seem good enough. The relational not is a drag on the necessary crunch; both in its outrageous and its subtle forms, it pulls for disengagement, noninvolvement. (pp. 176–177)

Pizer begins this excerpt with a conceptually rich paragraph that continues to expand the meaning space of relational (k)nots, crimps, and notting. Notice how she continues to contrast a (k)not with a crunch to elaborate the meaning of both. Then she makes a vertical move and drops down from the conceptual level into clinical material at the first level of abstraction—that is, along her paper's narrative axis. She doesn't leave any gaps between these two *non*contiguous levels (of a concept and a clinical example). Instead, she links them, first by interpreting the unspoken correlations between "the size or sign of an antidepressant pill [that her patient doesn't want to take] and the size or sign of his ability for manly accomplishment." Then she adds an understanding of the relational dynamics at play in the conjunction of the patient's unspoken or unthought past and present "vulnerability to a perception of coercion" and the therapist's possible past and present contributions to "this jamming of relational space." She ends by noting how this dynamic "pulls for disengagement, noninvolvement." Rather than assume the connections between concepts and clinical material are self-evident, Pizer carefully links the conceptual and narrative axes of her paper step by step.

Two brief examples later and just before she introduces her longer clinical example, Pizer makes another vertical move. She asks, "How do we allow ourselves, or gain the ability, to recognize and remain open to the actual lived pain or perturbation experienced in the therapy relationship when we come up against the sly repetitious negations that inevitably rub us the wrong way?" (p. 179). Then she moves up the levels of abstraction to draw on theories of mentalization for an answer, which in turn leads to an understanding of the mutative effects of the patient-therapist relationship to foster the patient's capacity to mentalize. Mentalizing can guide the therapist in righting herself and developing her patient's ability to stay engaged, creating a way out of their relational (k)not.

Theories as Modes of Perception

Theories (and the concepts that are part of them) are modes of perception (Bollas, 2007). They are not absolute truths, "but the best guesses we can make for the moment" (Tuckett, 1994, p. 1176). Russell (1994) sees theories as the clinician's "transitional objects," which "serve, more than anything else, the function of letting the therapist in whatever way he can, be *in* the relationship" with his patient (p. 3). For Bollas (2007), "each theory sees something that the other theories do not see" (p. 5). So "if we develop new theories we enhance our perceptual capacity" (Bollas, 2007, p. 5). Knowing more than one theory is similarly enriching, because the analyst will have "more perceptual capacity in his preconscious than an analyst who remains within only one vision" (Bollas, 2007, p. 5). Foehl (2010) takes this idea one step further when he advocates that we "ground our theoretical pluralism in an *epistemological* pluralism, which entails embracing layers of perspectives by weaving together a rich fabric of understanding that includes what is irreducibly ambiguous about psychoanalytic experience" (pp. 77–78).

Sandler (1983) believes that psychoanalysis "will never be a complete theory" (p. 37). Instead, we have "a body of ideas, rather than a consistent whole" (p. 37). In practice, we combine "theoretical and clinical propositions" from a myriad of sources representing different points of view. Sandler (1983) contends that clinical practice is governed more by partial, private theories that operate outside of awareness than by consciously held and publically espoused theories. "Such partial structures may in fact represent better (i.e. more useful and appropriate) theories than the official ones" (p. 38). Hence, Sandler urges, "the more access we gain to the preconscious theories of experienced analysts, the better we can help the advancement of psychoanalytic theory" (p. 38).

Conceptualizing

Following William James, Johnson (2007) suggests "we should speak of conceptualizing (as an act), rather than of concepts (as quasi-things). Conceptualizing is one of the things we *do* in and with our experience. . . [that] makes it possible for us to make sense of and to manage our experience. Conceptualizing involves recognizing distinctions within the flow of experience" (p. 88). It's hard to imagine how we could get a handle on experience without making distinctions. Conceptualizing also contributes to our ability to make inferences and create larger, more complex perceptual systems we call theories. Johnson (2007) elaborates: "It is our ability to abstract a quality or structure from the continuous flow of our experience and then to discern its relations to other concepts and its implications for action that makes possible the highest forms of inquiry, of which humans are uniquely capable" (p. 92).

Exercise 13.4

Your Conceptual Axis

Return to the clinical material you generated for exercise 12.2 (p. 169) and identify the horizontal and vertical moves you will need to make to develop the conceptual axis of your paper. Use the template of the levels of abstraction to make your notes.

Publication Standards

Let's take a different tack and consider some of the standards your clinical writing will be expected to meet if you want to publish it. The most frequently cited measures of a paper's worthiness for publication are originality, quality, and relevance.

Originality

Being original may feel like a tall order given all the ideas in circulation, but journal editors and peer reviewers think of originality in approachable terms, e.g., generating new meaning, drawing ideas and inferences out of unique clinical experiences that may be applicable to others, and making a modest contribution to our field. Ogden (2005a) brings the standard of originality down to earth when he says "there is nothing new under the sun but. . . it is always possible to view something old in a fresh and original way" (p. 26). Editors I interviewed (Naiburg, 2003) said a manuscript makes a contribution if it articulates " 'an interesting turn, something that isn't just stating the obvious,' " makes " 'a new connection,' " or demonstrates that the writer is thinking about something " 'in a different way' " (p. 301). One identified work with more recent formulations and specific populations that are underserved or underrepresented in the literature as innovative. Ogden (2005a) assures us that we have the capacity to be original in an achievable way: "No writer, to my mind, need worry that what he has to say has already been said. Of course, it has previously been said innumerable times, but it never has been said from the perspective that each of us might bring to it if we dare to try" (p. 26).

Feiner (1987) focuses on the reader's experience as a measure of a paper's originality: "In fact we might say that what we call originality is merely the rearrangement of something we already know, and it is actually the capacity and ability of the author (or composer) to evoke in us the experience of feeling what it is like to have the idea" (p. 680). Feiner would like to see papers stimulate readers so they, "like our patients, should have the experience of an expansion of imagination and perception, i.e., of possibilities, and perhaps, of choices" (p. 681fn).

Quality

Editors identify the usual suspects when discussing qualities that characterize well-written clinical papers: clarity; focus; thoughtful organization; coherence; solid conceptualization; adequate clinical material; persuasive links between clinical material and interpretations and theories; intelligent use of sources; readability; effective style; appropriate use of language (e.g., respectful, nonsexist, relatively jargon free); and clean copyediting. Because sloppy mechanics suggest a careless mind, be sure you don't underestimate the deleterious effects of submitting a manuscript that hasn't been well edited.

Tuckett (1998) emphasizes the importance of the rigor of a paper's argument—its premises; the logic used to support them; the selection, appropriateness, and adequacy of evidence and the meanings attributed to it; the clarity and illustration of key terms; and the argument's utility. When you make your interpretations and inferences explicit and offer readers enough evidence to support them, you create what Tuckett (1998) calls "transparency." Papers miss the mark for Tuckett (1998) if their evidence is insufficient; they contain straw man arguments; rely too much on argument by authority; contain errors of fact, methodology, or scholarship; are too narrowly conceived; or omit relevant references to the work of others.

Although Tuckett (1998) notes that the kind of argument being proposed will determine the kind of evidence needed to support it, his thinking highlights an already existing bias toward a certain kind of paradigmatic prose. Plaut (1999) expressed concern that Tuckett's emphasis on the strength of an author's argumentation contributes to overvaluing the analyst's conscious knowledge and neglecting "intuitive feeling and thinking," the preconscious, and "various loose ends, such as the analyst's fantasies and unplaceable bits of dream-thoughts" (p. 390).

A more ecumenical way to think about the quality of a paper than privileging argumentation would be to say that even abundant clinical material doesn't speak for itself. It has to be interpreted, and a context for interpretation needs to be provided. Yet reader-response criticism teaches us that the writer is not the only source of meaning making and that interpretations may arise from the interactions between reader and text. How much is explicated within a text and how much emphasis is put on the conceptual axis are not just matters of execution but also of intent, the choice of a paper's aesthetic form and mode, and the writer's strategies for enlisting the reader's participation in the creation of meaning. What constitutes a well-written paper varies across modes of clinical prose. More broadly based standards would recognize the validity of each mode of clinical prose, each of their ways of worldmaking (Goodman, 1978), and judge each according to its kind.

Relevance

The criterion of relevance generally pertains to a manuscript's being germane to a discipline, field, or specialty as well as to a journal's mission and audience, including its level of expertise. If a manuscript makes a contribution to the field but is not deemed relevant to a particular journal's aims or audience, it will need to look for acceptance elsewhere. The standard of relevance also applies to conference proposals. Your presentation needs to be relevant to the conference's purpose, theme, and audience. Import and relevance also apply to the utility of your ideas, their timeliness, and significance. When you present your ideas in the context of a compelling motive and address the so-what? factor, you make a case for your ideas to be seen as relevant and significant.

Other Guidelines

A former editor of the NASW journal *Social Work* sees a publishable manuscript as characterized by its

> *generativity*, challenging the commonplace, assumed, or taken-for-granted; *heuristic capacity*, stimulating new questions, ideas, or perspectives; *transformative potential*, proposing basic changes in beliefs and practices; and *value expression*, articulating, clarifying, or expanding the central professional values of human dignity and social justice. (Witkin, 2000, p. 6)

Plaut (1999) advises writers to address four questions when they write for journal publication:

1. What is it precisely that I want to say? Later: What are my personal reasons for wanting to write about the subject or case?
2. How much of that has already been said (i.e. published)? This will put the personal contribution into perspective.
3. How much more remains to be explained? Here, knowledge of the literature as well as vision is asked for.
4. How can I best (most cogently rather than persuasively) communicate these points to the reader? (p. 378–379)

Theodore Shapiro (1994) suggests that we think of writing for journals as answering the question "what do we wish to tell each other when we write? Writing for journals is just that. It is telling others what we see and have learned from our cases and the creation of generalizations across cases used to demonstrate that our work is an initial phase of fact-gathering" (p. 1229). The words of one of the editors I interviewed (Naiburg, 2003) come to mind in response to Shapiro's question:

> I see this is the story that the clinician is constructing based on his experience collaboratively, hopefully, with a client, or clients, or a group, and I see the way this has progressed. I can see where the practitioner has come from. I can see the story of this event, and I can follow it. If I can follow it, and it has some internal consistency and coherence for me, and the person

has attempted to put this in a body of literature in some way, put it in time and space and the context of what's known in the field, to me that meets the criteria. (p. 312)

Writing for publication can be seen as a search for knowledge rather than an announcement that you have finally arrived. Sanville (1999) writes to honor what she learns from her patients while acknowledging what she doesn't know:

> I sometimes write to find out what I think and to make peace with the fact that I am in a career where I can never know enough. . . . As I review these cases [from her book *The Playground of Psychoanalytic Psychotherapy*], I realize afresh how often I write as a way of learning from the patient, hanging on to that, and noticing how much more I would like to know. (p. 16)

Writing for publication may feel more achievable when approached from guidelines like these and when you remember that no one else can write from your perspective.

14 Shapes of Arguments

I will be seeking to demonstrate that arguments that are thought through and elaborated in some depth, that follow logical rules of inference and deduction, and that make explicit the grounds for believing in them that the author considers valid; arguments that explicate what knowledge is being claimed and how it is claimed to be known—are of a 'higher' standard than those that do not display these features.
David Tuckett, "Evaluating Psychoanalytic Papers:
Towards the Development of Common Editorial Standards"

For me—for all sorts of reasons—there has always been only one category, litera-ture, *of which psychoanalysis became a part. I think of Freud as a late romantic writer, and I read psychoanalysis as poetry, so I don't have to worry about whether it is true or even useful, but only whether it is haunting or moving or intriguing or amusing—whether it is something I can't help but be interested in.*
Adam Phillips, *Promises, Promises*

As you connect ideas along the conceptual axis of your paper, you generate an argument or a network of ideas—often more than one. Writers make these connections in radically different ways as the following two examples illustrate. As you read them, I invite you to notice your reactions to each before I identify the authors and comment on their writing.

Here's the first example:

Theory and practice always stand in dialectical relation to one another. At times, clinical observation and practice lead theory, as when, at the turn of the 20th century, Freud started to notice that his patients seemed to attribute to him qualities that did not belong to him. This observation led to the theory of transference (Freud, 1912), which then guided practice and further observation. This neck-and-neck relation between theory and practice—where one is a step ahead, and then the other—is essential for the development of both.

In psychoanalysis, we are currently in an era in which not only is practice leading theory in most domains, but also the theories that guided clinical practice and observation for decades no longer seem adequate to the task. There is no longer a consensus on the nature of motivation—a cornerstone of psychoanalytic theory, at least in the United States, through the 1980s—or even of unconscious processes—perhaps the cornerstone of psychoanalytic theory since its inception (see, e.g., Stern, 1983, 1997). We no longer have shared theories of development: Is development characterized by a movement across psychosexual stages? Ego-psychological stages? Object-relational stages (and, if so, posited by whom: Klein? Fairbairn? Kernberg? Kohut?)? Nor do we have shared theories of psychopathology: Is psychopathology a result of infantile fixations and regressions, a failure to transcend the schizoid position, the mirror stage, or the stage in which the child should be developing grandiose representations of self and idealized representations of parental figures? Or is psychopathology the result of a failure in the original inter-subjective relationship between parent and infant, which does not leave the developing child with a capacity for playful, mutual engagement?

In a collective sense, we find ourselves in an epoch of Eriksonian crisis, a period of both opportunity and danger. The opportunities can be seen in the development of new ways of conceptualizing the relationship between patient and analyst, integrations of psychoanalysis and neuroscience, and, perhaps most important of all, new ways of relating to our patients that would have been unthinkable (or unacknowledged) two decades ago. The dangers lie, on the one hand, in rigid adherence to models that may no longer work well but have the imprimatur of oedipal authority; and, on the other, in reactive and equally defensive denial of elements of theory and technique that need to be preserved and incorporated into any new synthesis, such as the importance of conflict, aggression, sexuality, and unconscious processes. A third danger lies in a defensive retreat from theory, often rationalized as a respect for the ineffability of the mind, which leaves practice unmoored in explicit theory and driven instead by unconscious, unformulated ideas and unanalyzed counter transferential pulls. (pp. 857–858)

Here's the second:

People come for psychoanalysis—or choose someone to have a conversation with—when they find that they can no longer keep a secret. What was once private has become, in spite of oneself, unbearable; has become a means of recruitment, a message. A symptom is always the breaking of a confidence. Suffering, like desire, is the secret we may not be able to keep. Because it has the potential to rupture our fantasies of self-sufficiency, suffering can be longed for, and feared, as a medium for legitimate contact and exchange between people. Pain makes us believe that other people have something we need. When we suffer first, as children, we seek people out; and our wish to communicate, and our will to believe in comfort is urgent. But as every parent—and every child—knows, what is being asked for is not always clear. The risk of having a need met—which confirms one's utter dependence (and potential envy of the person who can satisfy us)—is as great as the risk of misrecognition. If there is such a thing as help—a word which has always covered a multitude of sins, a word that is often the nice term for sado-masochism—it makes us wonder in what sense a need is something that can be known; what is it to want something (anything) from someone else? Because we can't help doing it, we can't help not noticing what we are doing.

Suffering, like desire, turns privacy into secrecy. From a psychoanalytic point of view a symptom is a (secret) way of asking for something (forbidden). This is what Freud meant when he wrote that the patient's symptoms *were* his sexual life. A symptom is the sign of a wish to make something known, but by disguising it—at once a demand and an invitation. Or rather two demands: a demand to be accurately translated, or recognized—the wish that the object of one's desire gets the joke, realizes, say that you keep blinking because you want to look at her; and a demand for satisfaction. Because desire is always, in part, constituted by the forbidden, every wish is ambivalent, its own best enemy. In this psychoanalytic picture we can't help but communicate, and we can't help but be baffled by each other. We always know too much and too little; we're always in the words of the song, the first to know and the last to find out.

So Freud presented his patients—and his readers—with two useful paradoxes. Firstly, you can only tell yourself a secret by telling someone else. And second, people are only ever as mad (unintelligible) as other people are deaf (unable, or unwilling, to listen). It's not only beauty that is the beginning of terror, it's also listening. The psychoanalyst is paid not to talk too much, because talking is a good way of not listening. Being listened to—making one's presence felt through one's words, and through one's body which is making the words—at its best, restores one's appetite to talk. Symptoms—when the body takes over from words—are a change of currency. (pp. 33–34)

These two excerpts reveal different minds at work, two distinct ways of working with ideas and engaging readers. The first, the beginning of Drew Westen's (2002) "The Language of Psychoanalytic Discourse," has the feel of a strategic march—clearly delineated, tightly organized, and forceful. Westen writes decisively and persuasively, but the rigor of his thinking does not preclude his being lively (see also my pp. 162–163). If I were back on my high school debate team, I'd want Westen as my debate partner.

I could also describe Westen's writing without using the language of a military march, but I chose that vocabulary to highlight how often our conceptualization of an argument is informed by the metaphor of war (Lakoff & Johnson, 2003/1980). Just listen for it in the language of holding a position, defending an idea, crushing your opponent, or saying "You disagree? Okay, shoot!" (Lakoff & Johnson, 2003/1980, p. 4). Because Westen's writing exemplifies the clarity with which a writer in our field can establish a thesis and marshal evidence and reasoning to support it, I will use it later in the chapter to present Stephen Toulmin's (2003/1958) model of the components of an argument.

The Shapes of Adam Phillips' Ideas

The shapes of Adam Phillips' ideas are informed by the spirit of entertaining, enjoying, and flirting with ideas rather than the metaphors of competition, debate, or strife. "Flirting," Phillips (1994) explains, "keeps things in play, and by doing so lets us get to know them in different ways. It allows us the fascination of what is unconvincing. By making a game of uncertainty, of the need to be convinced, it always plays with, or rather flirts with, the idea of surprise" (p. xii).

Westen's and Phillips' styles exemplify two different meanings of the verb to prove:

> The practice of experimenting, or trying something out, is expressed in the now uncommon sense of the verb *to prove*—the sense of "testing" rather than of "demonstrating validity." Montaigne "proved" his ideas in that he tried them out in his essays. He spun out their implications, sampled their suggestions. He did not argue or try to persuade. He had no investment in winning over his audience to his opinion; accordingly, he had no fear of being refuted. On the contrary, he expected that some of the ideas he expressed would change, as they did in later essays. Refutation represented not a personal defeat but an advance toward truth as valuable as confirmation. To "prove" an idea, for Montaigne, was to examine it in order to *find out* how true it was. (Zeiger quoted in Lopate, 1995, p. xlv)

The informal essay is an ideal medium for writers to play out their ideas and a perfect vehicle for Phillips, who began writing in this tradition without a conscious intention to do so (Phillips, 2014, p. 43) and now writes regularly for *The London Review of Books, The New York Times, The Observer, Slate*, and *Threepenny Review*. In his hands, the informal essay lives up to its reputation as "a notoriously flexible and adaptable form" (Lopate, 1995, p. xxxvii), "a kind of walkabout," and what Hazlitt described as a "rhetorical amble" (Lopate, 1995, p. xli). Phillips also turns the informal essay into "a suitable form for penetrating psychoanalytic enquiry" (Frank Kermode quoted in Phillips, 1998). For Phillips (2014), psychoanalytic sessions are "like essays, nineteenth-century essays. There is the same opportunity to digress, to change the subject, to be incoherent, to come to conclusions that are then overcome and surpassed, and so on" (p. 42).

Comparing Westen and Phillips reminds me of the contrast Elbow (1994) draws between texts that are "a record-of-completed-thinking" and those that are "an enactment-of-thinking-going on" (p. 31, fn.2). D'Agata (2003) makes a similar distinction: "Maybe every essay automatically is in some way experimental—less an outline traveling toward a foregone conclusion than an unmapped quest that has sprung from the word *question*" (p. 95). For Phillips, "things come out in the making—I don't sit there with all these ideas and then write them down. They appear as I write them" (quoted in Güner, 2010, p. 1).

Phillips' writing inspires both controversy and spirited commentary. Kermode coined the adjective "Phillipsian" to characterize essays that are "so agile and exuberant in their performance of thought that jumping in is irresistible. 'Phillipsian' would evoke a vivid, paradoxical style that led you to think that you had picked up an idea by the head, only to find that you were holding it by the tail" (Appignanesi, 2005).

Let's look more closely at what Phillips (1995) does with language in the opening paragraphs of "Symptoms," my second example. I read his first four sentences as a mini essay with a discernible progression of ideas, but what Phillips does with words is much more complex than sequence implies. How many of you read his first sentence to mean psychoanalysis is choosing to have a conversation with someone about a secret that can no longer be kept? Or did you latch on to *or* as a sign of contrast rather than equivalence, thinking some people may choose to have a conversation with someone other than an analyst when they need to reveal their secrets? How much richer the meaning is if you have it both ways and begin to wonder how psychoanalysis is both like and unlike a conversation. That's an interesting question for Phillips, who sees good conversation as a model for psychoanalysis (Phillips quoted in Molino, 1997; see also Phillips, 2014).

Phillips often links ideas laterally, at the same level of abstraction: "has become . . . unbearable; has become a means of recruitment, a message." Ideas beget other ideas in succession, in opening up space for the play of his readers' thoughts, and as interjections, interrupting and extending his thoughts ("—or chose someone to have a conversation with—"; "in spite of oneself"). His sentences and sequences often take me by surprise. They are less frequently organized in the hierarchical and subordinating structures that characterize Westen's prose. Instead, Phillips turns things on their head (e.g., *Going Sane*), approaches ideas from an unexpected angle, and transforms the ordinary into something new (e.g., flirting, hinting, clutter).

Phillips' essays are studded with aphorisms, which concentrate meaning, yet I resist identifying any as a thesis. To do so feels strange. The language of claims and evidence doesn't seem to fit. In the excerpt from "Symptoms," Phillips elaborates a network of ideas. Rather than following a strategic march, his thoughts take off on unplanned excursions punctuated by pithy aphorisms. Molino (1997) identifies a tension in Phillips' prose between "the concessions to the pleasures of writing, to its aesthetics and erotics" and "a quality of definitive 'pronouncement,' a *knowledgeable* quality, if you will, that inheres in a more subtle way" (p. 149), which his aphorisms represent.

Phillips agrees: "there is a sort of internal conversation . . . between something free-wheeling and something more formulaic" (Phillips quoted in Molino, 1997, p. 149). Like a thesis statement, an aphorism "precludes real essaying. It denies a text the possibility for reflection, digression, discovery or change" (D'Agata, 2009, p. 185). Aphorisms are "overcontained. . . . They're like a stun, they pull you up short" (Phillips quoted in Molino, 1997, p. 150). For Phillips, aphorisms function to contain his feeling that his thought is "unbounded . . . something with no end to it . . . something that goes in all sorts of directions" (Phillips quoted in Molino, 1997, p. 150).

Phillips is a very Winnicottian writer: e.g., in eschewing jargon, being playful, writing for a wide audience, creating potential spaces for readers to explore, and presenting ideas as objects for their use. These are all attributes Phillips (1988) identifies in Winnicott's prose. We may add a few more based on Goldman's (1993) assessment: "Winnicott's ideas were rarely expressed as exact logical concepts: rather, they were, in Guntrip's (1975) words, 'imaginative hypotheses that challenged one to explore further' (p. 155)" (Goldman, 1993, p. xiii). Winnicott also "reframed words to arrive at innovative concepts, often turning old ones upside down" and "standing classical ideas on their head" (Goldman, 1993, p. xxiii). We can also trace the influence of "Winnicott's controversial and apparently whimsical pronouncements" (Phillips, 1988, p. 13) in Phillips' arresting aphorisms: "Psychoanalysis is about what two people can say to each other if they agree not to have sex" (Phillips, 2002, p. xx).

Phillips' (1988) description of Winnicott's writing also pertains to his:

> When he [Winnicott] wrote, for example, that 'we are poor indeed if we are only sane'; or that 'true neurosis is not necessarily an illness . . . we should think of it as a tribute to the fact that life is difficult'; or that 'even when our patients do not get cured they are grateful to us for seeing them as they are'; he was, in his own blithe and unbeglamoured way, radically revising conventional psychoanalytic pieties. A certain arch honesty, an often willfully benign astuteness is part of Winnicott's distinctive style. (p. 13)

Phillips sees Winnicott as I see Phillips writing "against the grain of . . . [the psychoanalytic tradition's] prevailing forms of seriousness and its fantasies of methodical rigour" (Phillips, 1988, p. 15).

Phillips (1988) also notes of Winnicott:

> The need of the self to be both intelligible and hidden that he found in his patients is reflected in his style. . . . And though Winnicott sounds like no one else writing in the psychoanalytic tradition, he can often sound curiously like Lewis Carroll. It is, in fact, part of his irreverence as a psychoanalyst to be entertaining. Only Winnicott could have written as a footnote to one of his most important papers: 'When the analyst knows that the patient carries a revolver, then, it seems to me, this work cannot be done.' (pp. 14–15)

"Despite the work of Winnicott, Lacan and Bion," Phillips (1994) explains, "amusement is always secondary to instruction in psychoanalytic writing, but there is no good reason for this. Freud showed us—if we needed showing—that it is not more truthful to be serious. Psychoanalysis with a light touch, so to speak, need not be a contradiction in terms" (p. xi). When asked if he thought he "has succeeded in getting his ideas across, given the complexity of his ideas and his unwillingness to make them appear less so," Phillips responds:

> That's an interesting question . . . I mean, I don't really think like that. I don't have theories, I have sentences. I don't want people to come away thinking, this is what Phillips thinks about X and Y. My wish is not to inform people, but to evoke things in them by the way the writing works. That, I value. Ideally, I want the books to return you to your own thoughts. (Phillips quoted in O'Hagan, 2005).

As one commentator said of an experimental essay by Mallarmé, Phillips' essays demonstrate "that no act of knowing can avoid what's unknowable, that no thesis statement is without contingency, that every essay is a journey of a thought into risk" (quoted in D'Agata, 2009, p. 36). Winnicott, Phillips believes, "has made it impossible for us to copy him: he is exemplary as a psychoanalyst by being inimitable" (Phillips, 1988, p. 17). Phillips is exemplary in a similar way, inimitable as a writer and analyst who inspires us to be our most playful, idiosyncratic selves.

Exercise 14.1

Writing Good Sentences

Phillips doesn't think of himself as developing theories but as a writer of interesting sentences (Güner, 2010). With Phillips as your guide, experiment with writing a short informal essay that presents psychoanalytic ideas for educated lay readers.

Stephen Toulmin

As Westen, Phillips, and the modes of clinical prose demonstrate, arguments in the sense of a writer's core ideas come in strikingly different shapes. In the next sections of this chapter, I will present Toulmin's (2003/1958) model of the components of an argument, so if you want to evaluate the integrity of your argument (or another's) with Tuckett's advice or the values of practical reasoning in mind, you will have the vocabulary and conceptual understanding to do so. In contrast to the levels of abstraction, Toulmin's analysis of arguments provides an alternative and complementary way of looking at how ideas are put together in the paradigmatic mode. Even though your ideas may not be pitched as claims, the rhetorical structure of an argument organizes most paradigmatic writing and works behind the scenes in other modes. Your ideas need to be supported, and the nature of that support cannot be taken for granted. In the paradigmatic mode, what is called evidence needs to be explained. What qualifies it for its evidentiary role often needs to be spelled out, which warrants do, and warrants themselves may need to be backed up. Toulmin (2003) gives you ways to understand, establish, and evaluate these relationships.

Components of an Argument

In studies of argumentation, the ideas you propose and want others to accept are called claims, and the reasoning and support you muster for your claim are called grounds. The more your ideas challenge received knowledge or business as usual, the sturdier your arguments will need to be and the firmer the grounds on which they rest will have to be for your ideas to compete with other ideas and vie for your readers' attention.

Claims and Evidence

To consider ideas as claims, we will look at how Westen (2002) establishes the grounds for his idea that *the* concept of object relations is problematic in psycho-analytic discourse, because it misrepresents multiple phenomena as singular. In using this example, my objective is not to advocate for an object relations perspective but to use Westen's argument to demonstrate how claims, evidence, warrants, and backing may be effectively deployed in clinical prose. Here's an example of how Westen does that:

> One of the major problems with many psychoanalytic concepts is what might be called "the-ism" or "unitarianism"—the tendency to use a single term to describe a multiplicity of phenomena, such as object relations, the transference, the unconscious, the theory of therapeutic action, and the psychoanalytic theory of neurosis.
>
> Consider the concept of object relations. The patient is a 35-year-old actor who has difficulty forming any long-term relationships. He has superficial friendships but can describe only two friends with whom he has had a long-standing relationship, and he sees each one only once or twice a year. Dynamically, he has a number of narcissistic features and seems to thrive on the acclaim and admiration provided daily by an interchangeable audience.
>
> Here is a patient with quintessentially "primitive" object relations. His capacity to invest emotionally in others is severely impaired. He has difficulty developing mutuality in relationships and instead seems to use people in need-gratifying ways—as audiences, as temporary lovers, as superficial friends to "play" with. And dyadically, he has difficulty empathizing with other people and instead focuses ego-centrically on his own experience in a way that drives others away, constantly interjects details of his own life as they are describing their experiences, and so forth.
>
> On closer analysis, however, things are more complicated. When he talks about himself in therapy, at times he demonstrates genuine insight and shows complexity in his representations of people. Theoretically, patients with primitive object relations would not be expected to have complex representations, certainly not of themselves, particularly if their object relations are "preoedipal." Preoedipal children do not have complex representations. Nor are the patient's representations of people and relationships malevolent, a hallmark of the kind of "primitive" object relations seen in borderline and paranoid patients. The patient's views of others are, in fact, affectively fairly benign; he rather likes and expects the kind of admiration he receives, and tried to elicit it in dyadic relationships as long as he could. And, perhaps most important, this is a patient who can bring an audience to tears with phenomenal pathos, or bring them to the edge of their seats in spine-chilling fear, or lead them to laugh uproariously. At an implicit level, he knows precisely how to empathize with his audience, so that he can move them to feel whatever he wants them to feel in ways few of us can imagine. (pp. 861–862)

Westen clearly states his claim in the first paragraph, focuses on the example of object relations, and then provides clinical material as evidence for his claim. He identifies his patient's difficulties in forming meaningful relationships with others and notes features of his patient's so-called "primitive" object relations. This picture is made more complex by information he introduces in the third paragraph. Together, the descriptive and diagnostic details serve to address a hypothetical challenge: What are your grounds for making your claim that this patient's object relations is not a unitary phenomenon? In a rhetorical sense, the details Westen musters are his data or evidence, which need to be relevant, sufficient, and persuasive (Booth, Colomb, & Williams, 1995).

Westen's argument rests on two observations: that his patient presents with some features of "primitive" object relations *and* that his patient also demonstrates a capacity for more complex object relations. Typically, most arguments are made up of more than one claim (or subclaim), because ideas usually come in clusters. Each claim needs to be grounded in its own evidence as Westen's are. Just for practice, you might want to note the evidence he presents for each of his claims before I do.

Westen's second paragraph is organized around the claim that his patient has "difficulty forming any long-term relationships." In support Westen notes that his patient's friendships are "superficial," long-term friends are scarce, and he rarely sees those he has. His acting career reflects the narcissistic features of his personality and his need for an audience, which is kept at a distance and is "interchangeable" on a daily basis.

The first sentence of Westen's third paragraph presents its organizing idea, which serves as another claim. This paragraph deepens our understanding of this patient's limited capacity for relationship by focusing on more psychological dynamics, such as his lack of mutuality, the use of others for gratification, and his difficulty empathizing with others in dyadic relations. Westen adds even more detail to make his last point and describes how his patient drives others away by interrupting their comments with his own egocentric ones. All examples do not need to be treated equally. You may develop some more fully than others. Would you say that Westen's rhetorical evidence is sufficient and convincing enough to support his claim that his patient presents with *some* features of "primitive" object relations? I think so.

Warrants

Writers often make the mistake of failing to provide a warrant when one is needed, creating a weak link in the connection between their ideas. In order to decide whether you need a warrant, you have to know what a warrant is, how it functions, and estimate whether your audience needs one spelled out. Let's see what Westen does with warrants.

To complete his argument that object relations is misrepresented as a unitary phenomenon, Westen needs to add complexity to the picture he has just drawn. He does that in the fourth paragraph, beginning with its first sentence and some new evidence. To wit, his patient can demonstrate genuine insight about himself and complexity in his representations of self and others. Now we come to two sentences that do not function as evidence. They are bridging statements or warrants that support the connection between his evidence and his claim, which allow him to make the inferences that he does (Booth, Colomb, & Williams, 1995; Toulmin, 2003/1958). If patients with primitive object relations aren't expected to hold complex representations of others or themselves and this patient does, then this patient can't be said to have *only* primitive object relations. The references to the representations of preoedipal children, borderline, and paranoid patients also function as warrants.

Warrants may provide information, but they don't function as evidence. Instead they demonstrate that the link between the data and conclusion is "appropriate and legitimate" (Toulmin, 2003/1958, p. 91). Warrants may be understood as authorizing the logic " 'If D, then C.' " (Toulmin, 2003/1958, p. 91) or "When(ever) we have evidence *like* X, we can make a claim *like* Y" (Booth, Colomb, & Williams, 1995, p. 114). The evidence that Westen provides in his second and third paragraphs doesn't need a warrant to justify his claim. But in the fourth paragraph, Westen chooses to provide warrants.

Let me run through the parts of Westen's argument in his fourth paragraph so you can distinguish at a glance between claims, evidence, and warrants. I will also indicate two places where Westen assumes his audience knows enough to see how his evidence supports his claim and decides that an implied warrant suffices.

> *Claim*:   "Things are more complicated" [implying that the patient's object relations are not all primitive].
>
> *Evidence*:   "In therapy, at times he demonstrates genuine insight [about himself] and shows complexity in his representations of people."
>
> *Implied Warrant*:   Insight about the self in this context implies a complex representation of the self, and a complex representation of self and others is evidence of complex object relationships.
>
> *Warrant*:   "Theoretically, patients with primitive object relations would not be expected to have complex representations, certainly not of themselves, particularly if their object relations are 'preoedipal.' "
>
> *Warrant*:   "Preoedipal children do not have complex representations."
>
> *Evidence*:   "Nor are the patient's representations of people and relationships malevolent."
>
> *Warrant*:   [Malevolent representations are] "a hallmark of the kind of 'primitive' [split] object relations seen in borderline and paranoid patients."
>
> *Evidence*:   "The patient's views of others are, in fact affectively fairly benign."
>
> *Evidence*:   "He rather likes and expects the kind of admiration he receives, and tried to elicit it in dyadic relationships as long as he could."
>
> *Evidence*:   "And, perhaps, most important, this is a patient who can bring an audience to tears with phenomenal pathos, or bring them to the edge of their seats in spine-chilling fear, or lead them to laugh uproariously."

Evidence: "At the implicit level, he knows precisely how to empathize with his audience, so that he can move them to feel whatever he wants them to feel in ways few of us can imagine."

Implied Warrant: If the patient can empathize with his audience effectively enough to move them profoundly, his object relations cannot be that primitive in the context of his work as an actor. (Westen, 2002, p. 862; Toulmin's terms added)

Deciding whether or not to state your warrant explicitly will depend on your assessment of your readers' willingness to accept your evidence as grounds for your claim without your warranting that connection. Do you and your readers share the same theoretical orientation and a common understanding of key terms, concepts, and psychological dynamics? What can you assume your readers know? What needs to be spelled out? How much space can you allocate for making your claims, articulating your warrants, and backing them up?

Backing

Just as some evidence may need to be backed up by other evidence or warrants, warrants may also need to be backed up "by other assurances, without which the warrants themselves would possess neither authority nor currency" (Toulmin, Rieke, & Janik, 1979, p. 96). How much and what kind of backing is needed is field dependent (Toulmin, 2003/1958). Whether you use backing depends on your audience, your claims, and your warrants.

Westen sets his next paragraph up with a question and responds with his major claim about the complex nature of object relations. He provides an overview of his empirical research, a specific aspect of which serves as backing for an earlier warrant that complex representations are indicative of more complex object relationships. Here's this paragraph:

So what do we say about this patient's "level" of object relations? Empirical research suggests that object relations is, in fact, a multifaceted construct and that the same person can be high level on one object relational developmental line and low level on another—or high on one dimension in one set of circumstance and low in another (see Westen, 1989, 1990). In our own research, my colleagues and I have distinguished eight distinct dimensions of object relations, which overlap but can vary independently: complexity and differentiation of representations, affective quality of representations (which itself often varies considerably within a single individual for different types of relationships, such as relationships with peers versus father figures), emotional investment in relationships (whether they are truly mutual or primarily need gratifying), emotional investment in moral values, understanding of causality in the social realm (ability to make sense of what people do), self-esteem, coherence of sense of self, modulation of aggression in relationships, and dominant interpersonal concerns (the themes that repeatedly emerge across relationships, similar to Luborsky's [Luborsky and Crits-Christoph, 1998] core conflictual relationship themes and the transference paradigms we observe in our patients every day) (Westen, 1990; Conklin and Westen, 2001). And even this multifaceted view of developmental lines does not take into account many of the complex forms of internalization we see clinically, which are part and parcel of what we mean by object relations. (Westen, 2002, p. 862–863)

In another paragraph Westen (2002) addresses the implications of misrepresenting object relations as a unitary phenomenon and attends to the so-what? factor (my pp. 159–161):

To speak of a patient's object relations as primitive or low level may be a convenient shorthand, but it may also obscure much of the subtlety of clinical observation. The reader might object at this point that the problem is "just" with our theory, not with the way we really think clinically. Indeed, as clinicians, we are all aware of the fluctuations in level of maturity, health, and pathology our patients show along multiple developmental lines over the course of many sessions or even a single session. But theories guide, above all else, where we focus our clinical attention; and to the extent that our theories lack the sensitivity and range of our third ears, they may restrict rather than enhance the dynamic frequencies to which we are attuned. (p. 863)

Qualifications

Although Westen doesn't qualify his major claim, you may need to temper a claim you make based on various kinds of counterarguments or qualifications that "limit the certainty of your conclusions, stipulate the conditions in which your claim holds, address your readers' potential objections, and—when not overdone—make you appear a judicious, cautious, thoughtful writer" (Booth, Colomb, & Williams, 1995, p. 92). When they pertain, qualifications (e.g., often, sometimes, probably, possibly, with the exception of) may strengthen your argument rather than weaken it by keeping you from going too far out on that proverbial limb.

Exercise 14.2

Components of an Argument

a. Identify your major claims, subclaims, and evidence for each in one of your papers or rough drafts.
b. Identify the warrants you use to authorize the links between your claims and evidence. Are your warrants explicit or implicit? If implicit, do any need to be explicit?

c. Check to see if you need to back your warrants up if you have not already done so.

d. Identify any counterarguments or qualifications you introduce or may need to introduce.

How We Write

Westen (2002) is outspoken about the need for psychoanalytic writers to use more data as evidence; to test their hypotheses against more detailed case material, including full transcripts and input from large numbers of clinicians; and to draw on relevant empirical research from other fields as backing for their claims. Westen values case material while also recognizing its limitations, "especially when its evidentiary value is not maximized by the way it is typically presented" (p. 882). Westen distinguishes between generating hypotheses ("the context of scientific discovery") and testing them ("the context of justification"), which requires meeting more stringent "evidentiary demands" (p. 883).

Most of the clinical writing you and I will do will probably involve generating hypotheses rather than testing them, drawing on one case or a few clinical examples. "Cases," Westen notes, "are every bit as empirical as experiments—that is, they involve observation of events in the world, which is what empirical means—and they can yield a great deal of insight. They can be particularly useful in alerting us to the existence of phenomena we would not likely have discovered in any other way" (p. 882).

When it comes to generating hypotheses, Toulmin, Rieke, and Janik's (1979) thinking about well-made arguments comes into play:

> The claims involved in real-life arguments are, accordingly, *well founded* only if sufficient *grounds* of an appropriate and relevant kind can be offered in their support. These grounds must be connected to the claims by reliable, applicable *warrants*, which are capable in turn of being justified by appeal to sufficient *backing* of the relevant kind. And the entire structure of argument put together out of these elements must be capable of being recognized as having this or that kind and degree of certainty or probability and as being dependent for its reliability on the absence of certain particular extraordinary, exceptional, or otherwise *rebutting* circumstances. (p. 27)

Possibilities

Even if you don't want to take on the establishment or sound like a debater when presenting your ideas, holding Toulmin's model of practical reasoning in mind may help you develop logically sound connections between ideas at different levels of abstraction. Toulmin's model can also remind you to supply warrants when needed and qualify your conclusion when necessary. But as Phillips' essays demonstrate, a debater's logic is only one form of persuasion. As Rowland (2005) demonstrates, writers may also choose to disrupt the kinds of logical relationships Toulmin's model lays out to enact the limits of rationality as Jung does in "On the Nature of the Psyche." Rowland (2005) demonstrates how Jung "omits the connecting features of grounds and warrants. . . . and frequently advances claims at some textual remove from the grounds that would support them" (p. 71). In addition, Jung mixes rhetorical strategies "to invite validation from the affective and experiential" (p. 72).

Given the striking differences between Phillips' and Westen's rhetorical strategies and Jung's example of mixing things up, imagine the possibilities that are open to you, possibilities, Rowland (2005) suggests, that reflect different attitudes toward knowledge and power:

> Politically, argumentation oriented toward the logical end of the spectrum is inherently monological, closing down opposing positions or the voice of the 'other'. A rhetorical argument with an emphasis on the dialogic makes less of a claim to power through knowledge. Rather it provides a network to connect different social and epistemological standpoints. (p. 72)

Adapting Toulmin's model of argumentation in your clinical prose does not have to box you into a monological corner, although using too authoritarian a voice or dogmatically arguing your claims could put you there. However foreign Toulmin's model may be to the intuitive ways you practice and the more informal ways you may think about what you do, his model is an exercise in practical reasoning rather than formal logic. In contrast, argumentation that is monological is the heir of "Modern Science . . . whose first giant was Isaac Newton—and Modern Philosophy—the method of reflection initiated by Descartes . . . twin pillars of modern thought, and prime illustrations of the strict 'rationality' on which the modern era has prided itself" (Toulmin, 1992, p. ix). Toulmin sides, instead, with the pluralism of American pragmatists, the Renaissance humanists from Erasmus to Montaigne, and "a style of philosophy [prior to about 1640] that keeps equally in view issues of local, timebound practice, and universal, timeless theory" (Toulmin, 1992, p. 24). Throughout his career, Toulmin "argues for the need to confront the challenge of an uncertain and unpredictable world, not with inflexible ideologies and abstract theories, but by returning to a more humane and compassionate form of reason, one that accepts the variability and complexity that is human nature as an essential beginning for all intellectual inquiry" (quoted in Toulmin, 2000, back cover).

15 Using Sources

> *Knowledge never stands alone. It builds upon and plays against the knowledge of previous knowers and reporters, whom scholars call* sources. *These are not, in a paper, the source of your particular argument (you are), but rather of information and ideas that help you discover, support, and articulate that argument.*
>
> Gordon Harvey, *Writing with Sources, A Guide for Harvard Students*

Using sources reflects our appreciation that ideas exist in context, that minds exist in relation to other minds, and that thinking is a dialogic process. Like the creative use of an object, using sources can serve essential, not simply auxiliary, functions for your readers and yourself. Sources usually serve one of two complementary purposes: to set your ideas in context or to set your ideas off from another's (e.g., to stake your claims and qualify or refute counterarguments). Writers are usually more familiar with using sources to acknowledge their debts or establish contexts than they are with setting boundaries to distinguish their ideas from those of others. Yet such boundary setting is essential to establishing your ideas as your own and demonstrating your authority. In this chapter you will learn how to use sources effectively and artfully, when to consult them, and how to structure a literature review when one is required.

Setting a Context

Setting a context for your ideas may involve articulating historical or conceptual antecedents or describing the contemporary landscape in which your ideas are found. Panksepp (2009) does both in a few deft strokes when he comments on Freud's contributions to understanding the biological basis of mental life, identifies areas of new research, including his own (1998), and notes the significance of this new work:

> We are finally in an era where most thoughtful investigators agree with Freud's deep belief in the biological foundations of the psyche, but not necessarily Freud's psychoanalytic metapsychologies, with all their conceptual baggage, creatively constructed from limited, culture-bound clinical observations. At present, the most interesting discussions in psychiatry and

psychotherapy are emerging from new interdisciplinary frontiers: (1) developmental social neuroscience (Schore, 2003a; Siegel, 1999; Stern, 2004), (2) an emerging neuropsychoanalysis (Solms & Turnbull, 2003), (3) a human and animal affective neuroscience (Panksepp, 1998a), and (4) new visionary perspectives on autonomic nervous system regulations that need to be coherently integrated with higher brain processes (see Porges, [2009] . . .). These scholars are finally grappling not only with the affective nature of the human mind, but also with the deep emotional nature of the mammalian brain. It is now clear that affective values are built into the nervous system as birthrights, but not ethical and moral values, which are epigenetic emergents of developmental landscapes. (pp. 2–3)

Panksepp is in charge of his sources as he enumerates new frontiers of knowledge, cites his sources parenthetically, and uses his argument rather than his sources to structure his paragraph.

Exercise 15.1

Setting a Context

Write a paragraph or two using sources to situate a concept within one or two relevant contexts. Let your ideas rather than your sources structure your paragraph as Panksepp does.

Acknowledging Your Debts

Sometimes you may want to place your references to the work of others in a footnote so your readers aren't distracted, especially if the list is long. If the contribution of another is particularly relevant, then giving that source its due is appropriate. Donnel Stern (2010) demonstrates both strategies:

As a result of the work of a number of writers,[1] it is today a familiar idea in interpersonal and relational psychoanalysis that the self is not simple and unitary but a more or less cohesive collection of self-states. These different self-states may be simultaneously knowable; there is no implication that a person need be uncomfortable about knowing one self-state while he is "in" another. The multiple self as the expectable, everyday condition of identity is, among other things, a very helpful addition to our conceptualization of the role of context in understanding because our frequent shifts from one

[1]   Most recently, Bromberg (1998, 2006); Chefetz (2003); Chefetz and Bromberg (2004); Davies (1996, 1997, 1998, 1999, 2003, 2004); Davies and Frawley (1991, 1994); Howell (2005); Pizer (1998); Slavin (1996); and Slavin and Kriegman (1992, 1998). See also Flax (1996); Harris (1996); Mitchell (1991, 1993).

self-state to another emphasize the continuous change in the context of all understanding.

The idea of the multiple self in psychoanalysis owes much to Sullivan (1950), who suggested that the interpersonal field determines the contents of consciousness. The kind of relationship we establish with another person has everything to do with what we can be aware of in that person's presence and what the other can be aware of in ours. (I use "presence" now both in its physical sense and in the more metaphorical, intrapsychic sense as the symbolic presences of the inner world.) It was Sullivan (1950), after all, who said over half a century ago, "For all I know we have as many personalities as we have interpersonal relations" (p. 221).

Admittedly, Sullivan was not proposing a multiple-self theory at the time. He was criticizing the reification in the traditional idea that each of us has something that we are justified in referring to as a unique, unitary self. But add to this critique Sullivan's emphases on trauma and on dissociation as a defensive process, and you have the seeds of what has become the multiple self in the hands of interpersonal and relational writers. Sullivan's great insight that what we can experience is defined by the field becomes, in multiple self theory, the idea that each self-state is defined by the experience that we are capable of creating, feeling, and formulating from within it. When, for defensive reasons, we cordon off certain self-states from contact with the others, and then restrict ourselves only to some of these and not others, we also restrict our access to the fullness and depth of the experience it is possible for us to have. We thus reduce the imagination, precision, and affective nuance of the formulations of the experience we are capable of articulating. (pp. 48–49)

Stern acknowledges the debt contemporary psychoanalysis owes Sullivan, distinguishes the Sullivanian seeds from the harvest, and underscores the significance of what we have reaped (the so-what? factor). Following the paragraphs I quoted, Stern (2010) lays out a number of other ideas: about the self's multiplicity as normal, its origins in both interpersonal and intrapsychic phenomena, concordant and complementary identifications, his own (1997) distinction between weak and strong dissociation, and some implications of the idea of a multiple self for clinical practice. Given this rich line of thought, it's no wonder that he turns over the Sullivanian soil in which contemporary Interpersonal and Relational ideas germinated.

Exercise 15.2

Acknowledging Your Debts

To whom are you indebted for your core ideas? Following Stern's example, write a paragraph or two to acknowledge one of your intellectual debts in some detail and note the significance of what you've inherited.

Defining Your Terms and Staking Your Claim

In the opening paragraphs of "Resistance, Object Usage, and Human Related-ness" (1998), Phillip Bromberg distinguishes his conception of resistance from Freud's and explains that his concept "is anchored more fundamentally in disso-ciation than repression" (p. 206). He also notes a similarity with Schafer's view of "the *structure* of resistance as an account of transference itself" and distinguishes his meaning of resistance as "a dyadic experience rather than an individual one" (p. 206). By differentiating his meaning of resistance from both Freud's and Scha-fer's, Bromberg clearly stakes his claim and establishes the conceptual territory of his original work:

> "Resistance" is not a word I ordinarily use, either conceptually or clinically, and when I might hear it inadvertently pop out of my mouth it is usually when I am feeling grouchy with a patient and unaware that I wish to conceal it. Not-withstanding its illusory advantage in a countertransferential emergency, it is a term that I feel has become largely incompatible with the natural evolution in postclassical analytic thought. In effect, it traps us into preserving intact Freud's (1925) formulation of the function of negation, in which the negativ-ity of resistance is viewed as a barrier between depth and surface designed to prevent repressed images or ideas from entering consciousness. In this sense, it is a remnant of our past that I think can be usefully reframed as part of an enacted dialectical process of meaning construction, rather than an archeo-logical barrier preventing the surfacing of disavowed reality.
>   Freud (1925) observed that

> the content of a repressed image or idea can make its way into conscious-ness, on condition that it is *negated*. Negation is a way of taking cogni-zance of what is repressed; indeed it is already a lifting of the repression, though not, of course, an acceptance of what is repressed. . . . With the help of the symbol of negation, thinking frees itself from the restrictions of repression and enriches itself with material that is indispensable for its proper functioning. (pp. 235–236)

> This, of course, bears centrally on the concept of "resistance," which in my view, as I shall discuss, is anchored more fundamentally to dissociation than to repression. My conceptualization of resistance, like that of Schafer (1983, pp. 230–231), addresses the *structure* of resistance as an account of transfer-ence itself, but as a dyadic experience rather than a unitary one—an account of the transference and countertransference matrix, rather than of transfer-ence alone. It also addresses the *motivation* of resistance as not simply an avoidance of insight or a fear of change, but as a dialectic between preserva-tion and change—a basic need to preserve the continuity of self-experience in the process of growth by minimizing the threat of potential traumatization. It is a "marker" that structures the patient's effort to arrive at new meaning without disruption of self-continuity during the transition, and gives voice to

opposing realities within the patient's inner world that are being enacted in the intersubjective and interpersonal field between analyst and patient. The negativity of resistance thus represents a dialectic tension between realities that are not yet amenable to a self-reflective experience of intrapsychic conflict and are, at that moment, in a discontinuous, adversarial relationship to each other. Optimally, and most simply, it is a dimension of the ongoing process of negotiation between incompatible domains of self-experience. (pp. 205–206)

Bromberg's commentary is skillfully focused to concisely articulate his idea of resistance, yet it is ample enough for his readers to appreciate how he infuses it with new meaning. The honesty and playfulness of his first few sentences elicit my trust. The last paragraph shows how gracefully he elaborates his idea, contextualizing resistance as an example of "a dialectic between preservation and change" needed to preserve the "continuity of self-experience" and as "an ongoing process of negotiation between incompatible domains of self-experience." In just a few paragraphs, Bromberg not only distinguishes his intellectual work from two others, thoughtfully defines his term, and stakes his claim but also clearly establishes the direction of his paper. I feel I am in good hands.

Exercise 15.3

Defining Your Terms and Staking Your Claim

In one or two short paragraphs, use sources to situate a term within its theoretical or historical context and/or distinguish it from contemporary lookalikes. Let Bromberg, Pizer (my pp. 190–193), and Gerson (my pp. 185–188) be your guides.

Maintaining Your Poise in the Company of Others

Ideas don't exist in a vacuum. They keep company with other ideas. It's not easy to bring ideas from multiple or distinguished sources into your writing while maintaining your poise, your perspective, and the sequence of your thoughts. Structure is the key, and limiting and integrating what you reference or quote are crucial strategies, as the Boston Change Process Study Group (2010) demonstrates when writing about implicit relational knowing:

Implicit relational knowing has been an essential concept in the developmental psychology of preverbal infants. Observations and experiments strongly suggest that infants react with caregivers on the basis of a great deal of relational knowledge. They show anticipations and expectations and manifest surprise or upset at violations of the expected (Sander, 1988; Trevarthen, 1979; Tronick, Als, Adamson, Wise, & Brazelton, 1978). Furthermore, this implicit knowing is registered in representations of interpersonal events in a nonsymbolic form, beginning in the first year of life. This is evident not only in their expectations but also in the generalization of certain interactive patterns (Beebe & Lachmann, 1988; Lyons-Ruth, 1991; Stern, 1985). Studies of development by several authors (Lyons-Ruth & Jacobvitz, 1999; Sander, 1962, 1988; Stern, 1985, 1995; Tronick & Cohn, 1989) have emphasized an ongoing process of negotiation over the early years of life involving a sequence of adaptive tasks between infant and caregiving environment. The unique configuration of adaptive strategies that emerges from this sequence in each individual constitutes the initial organization of his or her domain of implicit relational knowing. Several different terms and conceptual variations have been proposed, each accounting for somewhat different relational phenomena. These include Bowlby's "internal working models" of attachment (Bowlby, 1973), Stern's "proto-narrative envelopes" and "schemas of being-with" (Stern, 1995), Sander's "themes of organization" (Sander, 1997), and Trevarthen's "relational scripts" (Trevarthen, 1993), among others. A formal description of how these strategies are represented remains an active field of inquiry. (pp. 5–6)

Using sources does not always involve direct quotations. Here key terms are quoted at the end of the paragraph, but research findings are presented as ideas in circulation that the authors put to use. In this example, direct quotations are kept to a minimum, yet acknowledgement of the research of others is a given.

Creating a Conversation

Imagine using sources to create a conversation. In *Conversations at the Frontier of Dreaming*, Ogden (2001b) demonstrates how this is artfully done as he elaborates the meaning of the word conversation:

And, as if by accident (but it is certainly not a matter of chance), the very word *conversation* is in conversation with itself, spawning metaphors as it goes. The word *conversation* is "fossil poetry" (Emerson, 1844, p. 231), derived from the conjunction of the Latin words *cum*, meaning with or together, and *versus*, meaning a row or furrow of earth; the movement of a plough turning back on itself as it ends one row and begins the next; and a line of poetry or other writing. *Conversation* is a word that has preserved in itself a chorus of accumulated meanings that speak both from the experience of opening the earth for purposes of impregnating/planting and from the experience of entering into language for purposes of communicating with ourselves and others. Thus, conversation is an act of engaging with another person in the work of creating man-made lines, lines of furrowed soil reflecting mankind's timeless effort to survive by taming and freeing the earth and Nature. At the same time, conversation is an act that reflects man's equally timeless effort to tame and to free himself (his own human nature) by transforming raw experience into words and gestures to communicate with others and with himself. There is nothing more fundamentally, more distinctively human than the need to converse. As innumerable observational studies of infants have demonstrated, we depend for our lives upon conversation (both in terms of our physical survival and in terms of our coming humanly to life). (pp. 3–4)

Ogden's sources are so well paired and incorporated into the structure of his prose that they become integral to his ideas and their expression. His sources may have served as inspiration for his ideas or as a stimulus for ideas that were already nascent. I suspect that his engagement with etymology and Emerson's language created something richer and more furrowed than what was in his mind before. As Ogden's phrases and sentences create their own "chorus of accumulated meanings," the evocativeness of his prose builds from line to line to carry this writer and his readers forward.

Maintaining Your Voice in the Company of Distinguished Others

How do you maintain your voice when your source is seminal and the material you quote arresting? Try to remember sources are there to augment your ideas. The key is to keep what you quote in proportion so it's clear you are orchestrating the conversation and haven't ceded your authority. Miller (2004) shows us how to do that when he discusses Jung's famous essay "The Transcend Function":

Given that the transcendent function is a bridge between the conscious and unconscious, it should come as no surprise that Jung wrote "The Transcend Function" in 1916 when he found himself actively engaging in making such a connection. After his break with Freud in or around 1912, Jung went through several years of what he himself called "a period of uncertainty" (1989c, p. 170). Jung stated flatly that "it would be no exaggeration to call it a state of disorientation" (p. 170) and that he "lived as if under constant inner pressure" (p. 173). In response to the disturbances, Jung meticulously reviewed, not once but twice, all the details of his life "with particular emphasis to childhood memories" (p. 173), but to no avail. This amounted to Jung's unsuccessful attempt to deal with the turmoil rationally with primary emphasis on the linear logic of consciousness. In a kind of surrender, Jung decided to submit to a conversation with the unconscious:

But this retrospection led to nothing but a fresh acknowledgement of my ignorance. Thereupon I said to myself, 'Since I know nothing at all, I shall simply do whatever occurs to me.' Thus I consciously submitted myself to the impulses of the unconsciousness. (p. 173)

Jung's capitulation was a seminal moment in depth psychology because it acknowledged for the first time the purposive, teleological nature of the unconscious. Indeed, that decision may be said to be the birth of the transcendent function in Jung's thinking, an explicit recognition of the fact that psychological growth requires a partnership between conscious and unconscious. (pp. 9–10)

Miller is completely at ease introducing Jung's voice. He can maintain his poise, because he maintains his purpose by establishing a sturdy paradigmatic frame around Jung's words. He keeps what he quotes contained either within the flow of his sentence or within a brief block quotation. Notice how he prepares his readers to understand what he quotes: He uses his own ideas to set up his block quotation and follows it with commentary. His source is not just cut and pasted in. Writers often make the mistake of thinking a block quotation can speak for itself, which often results in readers skipping it.

Exercise 15.4

Sources as Invited Guests

Consider sources as guests you invite into a conversation. If they have a large presence—like block quotations, provocative statements, or ideas from personalities with charisma or clout—your job is more challenging. In this exercise, you will be guided to host a variety of sources, gracefully including each according to its kind and your purpose.

a. With any of your writing projects in mind, gather very short quotations you could use to elaborate your ideas.
b. Practice working these smaller quotes into the flow of your sentences.
c. Identify relevant longer excerpts of five lines or more that would need to be formatted as block quotations. Try to find a few from influential sources who could monopolize the conversation if you let them.
d. Now frame these longer quotations with your ideas by introducing them and commenting on them after they make an appearance.

Point and Counterpoint

In his next two paragraphs, Miller (2004) uses primary sources to describe Jung's treacherous encounters with his unconscious and introduces concerns Jung and others had about Jung's stability after his break with Freud. Miller employs a footnote to reference secondary sources that are critical of Jung. His conclusion reflects the points and counterpoints he uses his sources to raise:

During the next several years Jung was buffeted by the turbulent forces of the unconscious. He dreamt prodigiously, was invaded by symbolic visions, and dialogued with fantasy figures. In response, Jung experimented with several forms of self-healing: using stones from the lakeshore behind his house to build a miniature town, journaling about his experience, and actively engaging in interactions with the visions that appeared to him. Jung describes the flow of unconscious images in overwhelming terms:

> An incessant steam of fantasies had been released, and I did my best not to lose my head but to find some way to understand these strange things. I stood helpless before an alien world; everything in it seemed difficult and incomprehensible. I was living in a constant state of tension; often I felt as if gigantic blocks of stone were tumbling down upon me. One thunderstorm followed another (1989c, p. 177).

His description of Jung's confrontations with the unconscious lead some to believe that Jung was substantially debilitated, even clinically impaired, during at least part of that time.[2] Indeed, Jung himself uses that kind of language: "At times [the inner pressure] became so strong that I suspected there was some psychic disturbance in myself" (1989c, p. 173). Whether or not the events in the several years following his rupture with Freud amounted to a breakdown, undoubtedly that period reflects an intense struggle by Jung to converse with and come to terms with the contents of the unconscious. (p. 10)

[2] Sandner (1992) refers to that as a period during which "a torrent of unconscious material came flooding in, temporarily overwhelming him" (p. 33). Dehing (1992) calls what Jung went through a "severe crisis" (p. 20). Angel (1992) flatly labels what Jung experienced a "breakdown" (p. 103).

When you acknowledge a counterargument, as Miller does, your writing reflects more complexity. Miller uses both primary and secondary sources to raise the question of whether Jung's struggle with his unconscious constituted a breakdown. The paragraph that follows the excerpt I just quoted identifies the profusion of essays Jung publishes in 1916 and shortly after, attesting to his emerging from this difficult period to articulate some of his core ideas. While the question of what happened to Jung remains open for Miller and others, what Jung accomplishes in the wake of his struggle is a testimony to his creativity. Miller lays all this out, strategically containing the sources he uses within the framework of his own ideas.

Exercise 15.5

Point and Counterpoint

a. Identify a source that challenges a point you've made or would like to make in one of your papers.
b. Introduce that challenging source into the progression of your ideas.
c. Refute that source or modify your ideas to take its counterargument into account, presenting a stronger argument of your own in its wake.
d. Repeat this process if you want to take on more than one challenging source or point, creating another dialogic progression.

When to Look and "See Where I Stole What"

Winnicott is thought to have been cavalier about stealing ideas from others for his own use. This perception actually misrepresents what he says in the opening of "Primitive Emotional Development" (1945):

> I shall not first give an historical survey and show the development of my ideas from the theories of others, because my mind does not work that way. What happens is that I gather this and that, here and there, settle down to clinical experience, form my own theories and then, last of all, interest myself in looking to see where I stole what. Perhaps this is as good a method as any. (p. 145)

Winnicott sees the infant's early development as characterized by the experience of being in bits and pieces. Thus his reference to gathering "this and that" from "here and there" reflects normal development. Ogden (2001a) notes that Winnicott is advocating that both infant *and writer* need not be concerned with the sources of meaning acquired in their development, since development should be anchored in feeling something real, not in the input of others:

> The individual's own lived experience must be the basis for creating coherence *for* one's self and integrity *of* oneself. Only after a sense of self has begun to come into being (for the infant and for the writer), can one acknowledge the contributions of others to the creating of oneself (and one's ideas). (Ogden, 2001a, p. 302)

Following Winnicott's theory of development, drafting your paper on the basis of what you know is as good a method as any for getting started. That way you can shape a coherent whole without fear of impingement. If you turn to the literature too soon, you could fall down a rabbit hole (as one writer called it), get distracted, or become overwhelmed and lose faith in your ability to think for yourself. Later you will need to turn to sources to find out what you borrowed or what you might still need. Going to sources when you have a firmer grip on your ideas also allows you to more confidently eliminate sources you don't need and reign in any temptation to hoard information, because you'll have a much better sense of what is relevant.

I want to make an important distinction between the process of writing your early drafts without worrying about tracking down sources and keeping track of your sources. Always use quotation marks in your notes so you can distinguish your words from your source and are less likely to inadvertently plagiarize. Record all reference information, *including page numbers*, so you won't have to go on a wild goose chase to find what's missing.

Writing a Literature Review

A literature review fulfills two primary functions: to identify relevant sources that demonstrate that your proposed work stands on solid ground and to establish a motive for your work (pp. 155–159) that shows that previous studies haven't gone far enough. You need to demonstrate precedents, an established vocabulary, relevant theoretical frames and show that more work still needs to be done. Your review needs to build a persuasive case for your project by demonstrating its legitimacy based on previous trends and current needs. The two functions go hand in hand.

Graduate students are often asked to complete their literature review as one of the first steps in writing a thesis or dissertation proposal. That may be difficult if you aren't sure of your ideas, which will become clearer as your work progresses. If you find yourself unable to craft a motive to organize your literature review, it may be too early in your thinking process to write one. Take more time to develop your own ideas so you can use them as a filter to sort through an abundance of sources.

The motive for your literature review works just like the motive for an introduction (pp. 155–158). The two are complementary. Craige's (2002) research-based article, "Mourning Analysis: The Post-Termination Phase," could have been submitted for a master's thesis. It is that substantial a piece of work. Her one-paragraph introduction establishes the motive for her paper (my p. 156). Her literature review begins in the second paragraph of her paper and runs for six pages out of forty-three. Below I quote the first three paragraphs of her review, the topic sentences of the subsequent paragraphs, and her review's closing paragraph, so you can see how it is structured as an argument. If you are writing a shorter literature review, the same structuring principles apply.

> Although the psychoanalytic literature on post-termination is sparse, there is a growing recognition of the importance of this phase. Rangell (1966) first designated post-termination as a discrete phase of the analytic process, as part of the cure. He recognized at least three post-termination processes, which occur simultaneously: resolving the transference neurosis, dissolving the analytic situation that fostered the development of the regressive transference, and reacting to the final loss of the analyst. In *The Fundamentals of Psychoanalytic Technique*, Etchegoyen (1991) devotes a brief section to the post-psychoanalytic process, which he views as "a natural and painful stage in which the analysis culminates" (p. 636). Discussing the ideas of other writers, Etchegoyen characterizes Rangell's position as follows: "Rangell feels that post-analysis is the cure of the transference neurosis, and he compares it with the surgical post-operative period in which the patient has to recover not only from the original illness but from the surgery itself" (p. 636). Etchegoyen goes on to discuss Guiard's important work (1979), published in Spanish, that takes Rangell's position a step further.
>
> According to Guiard, the post-termination phase is a mourning process during which the analysand must recover not only from the surgery but also from a new illness, the grief caused by the loss of the analyst, which must be faced alone. Guiard posits a post-termination process in three stages: "The

initial stage, in which the analyst is missed and his return is yearned for; then a stage of working through, in which the ex-analysand struggles for autonomy and accepts solitude; and finally the outcome, in which autonomy is achieved and the analyst's imago becomes more abstract" (quoted in Etchegoyen 1991, p. 637).

Mourning as a theme echoes throughout the analytic literature on termination. Many analysts who write about termination note that mourning the loss of the analyst does not reach completion until well after patient and analyst cease to meet (Buxbaum 1950; Weigert 1955; Reich 1950; Deutsch 1959; Ticho 1967; Loewald 1962; Blum 1989; Berenstein and Fondevila 1989; Rucker 1993; Orgel 2000). All of these writings are based on the psychoanalytic understanding of mourning as a normal response to any significant loss, including the loss of the analyst at termination, that is resolved by internalizing the lost loved object. Moore and Fine (1990) define mourning as the mental process by which one's psychic equilibrium is restored following the loss of a meaningful love object. Loewald (1962) suggests that how the analysand mourns and internalizes the analyst determines whether separation from the analyst will be experienced as deprivation and loss or as emancipation and mastery. (pp. 508–509)

Here are the topic sentences of the remaining paragraphs of her literature review and its closing paragraph:

Although many analytic writers view a period of mourning after termination as expectable, only one study (Lord, Ritvo, and Solnit 1978) addresses processes of mourning following termination, and it focuses on the unusual situation of analysands whose analysts died during the course of treatment. . . .

A few papers discuss whether the analyst is mourned at termination primarily as a transference object or as a real object. . . .

Several analytic papers focus on the development of the self-analytic function during the post-termination phase (Kramer 1959; Ticho 1967; Schlessinger and Robbins 1974, 1975, 1983; Berenstein and Fondevila 1989; Kantrowitz, Katz, and Paolitto 1990a, b). . . .

In the post-termination process, according to Ticho (1967), the self-analytic capacity is immediately put to the test in working through the remains of the transference neurosis and mourning the separation from the analyst. . . .

Other articles focus on the fate of the transference after termination (Pfeffer 1959, 1961, 1963, 1993; Schlessinger and Robbins 1974, 1975, 1983; Oremland, Blacker, and Norman 1975; Norman et al. 1976; Hurn 1973; Balkoura 1974). . . .

Other papers address the analyst's relationship to the patient after termination. Buxbaum (1950) introduced a procedure of keeping the "door open" after termination and even encouraged patients to be in touch occasionally to reduce the mourning reactions and the traumatic effects of ending analysis. . . .

Novick and Novick (2000) write that the analyst's role after termination is to maintain one's stance as analyst, available for future consultation if needed, while acknowledging continuing "respect, admiration, and objective love" for the patient after analysis (p. 214). . . .

Some writers, while not directly focusing on post-termination, recognize that significant positive changes in the patient may occur during that phase (Macalpine 1950; Milner 1950; Dewald 1964; Miller 1965; Menninger 1966; Novick 1982). Others note, however, that some patients experience serious difficulty after termination, even after having had a successful analysis. . . .

McLaughlin (1981), summarizing psychoanalytic follow-up research, writes that in successful outcomes analysands achieve better adaptation through internalizing the analyst's way of looking at things, as well as by creating a permanent new internal representation of the analyst. In unsatisfactory outcomes, however, the internal image of the analyst is "absorbed into the patient's old transferential difficulties" (p. 653). . . .

Formal psychoanalytic research efforts on the post-termination phase have been stymied because analysts are reluctant to contact former patients for follow-up sessions (Schachter 1990; Johan 1989). . . .

Conway (1999), the first analytic researcher to put the post-termination phase front and center, conducted a study of three subjects who had completed an analysis or psychoanalytic psychotherapy. . . .

No large-scale psychoanalytic research study has focused on the analysand's experience of the post-termination phase. Even though the psychoanalytic literature highlights the role of the mourning process after termination, no published research examines that process after successful termination. The present study explores reactions to the loss of the analytic relationship in the experience of a large group of candidates who have completed full psychoanalytic treatment. Additional studies will be needed to determine how well the present findings may be applied to a general population of analysands and to patients in less intensive psychotherapy. This research was modeled on the study reported in Kantrowitz's *The Patient's Impact on the Analyst* (1996), in which she used a questionnaire to develop an overview of the perspective of many individuals and then conducted interviews to explore their psychological experience in greater depth. This study measures the prevalence of mourning after termination, explores how analytic candidates typically negotiate the loss of their analyst, and considers cases in which the post-termination phase was particularly difficult for the analysand. (pp. 509–514)

In this closing paragraph, Craige clearly stakes her claim, distinguishes what she will do in her study to fill the gaps in current research, and marks out the territory that needs to be explored in future research.

Exercise 15.6

Writing a Literature Review

The key to writing an effective literature review is to use a motive to organize it and to set your review up as an argument rather than an annotated bibliography. Your argument has to persuade your readers that your proposed study didn't come out of the blue, is built on precedents, and serves an essential need.

a. List the core elements of your argument, starting with your motive. Write a sentence or two for each part of your argument, each on its own page.

b. List the sources you would cite for each of your core ideas, noting them in the appropriate pages you organized in *a* and underneath the sentences that state your ideas to remind you that your ideas, not your sources, should organize your paragraphs and lead them off as Craige (2002) demonstrates in her literature review.

c. Using the structure and notes you just created, write up each paragraph of your literature review, leading with your argument.

d. Bring your literature review to a close by addressing the so-what? factor (pp. 159–162) and underscoring the significance of the work you are about to do.

16 Conclusions

Endings are every bit as important as beginnings. The same kinds of caution therefore apply. They give the last impression, the taste that the reader carries away from the banquet. But we often make them too long, summarize facts that are already obvious, reargue a point already established, say abstractly what we have shown concretely—and by all these methods dilute the intensity our conclusion should have.

Donald Hall and Sven Birkerts, *Writing Well*

Conclusions are the most underutilized and underappreciated component of clinical papers. Their potentials are rarely realized, often because writers assume a simple summary of their paper's main points will suffice. The culture of some journals perpetuates this perception, but when your conclusion only repeats what you said in the body of your paper, you underestimate your readers and yourself. Your conclusion offers you an opportunity to build on what you've done, draw out the significance of your ideas, and point yourself and your readers in new directions.

By virtue of its placement, your conclusion comes with unique privileges that other parts of your paper do not possess. Like the end line of a poem, your conclusion has greater impact because of its position. At the end of your paper, you also have more freedom than you do when making your opening moves. In your conclusion, your ideas are not burdened by your readers' expectations that you will illustrate, explicate, and support what you propose. So you may generate implications and muse on possibilities based on the work you have already done without having to do more. Conclusions also bring important closure to your paper. Papers without a sense of closure just stop—like this thought stops right after liftoff.

Writing a strong conclusion may be among the most challenging and rewarding aspects of your writing process, because it can force your thinking to new levels. This chapter will help you meet that challenge as you come to understand, appreciate, and utilize the privileges and opportunities that a conclusion affords.

The Evolution of a Conclusion

Your conclusion will evolve from draft to draft as you develop your ideas. As often happens in writing your conclusion, you may initially lean on other sources before gaining your own footing. That's fine for starters. You could also use a summary of your ideas as a starting point, especially if your ideas are complex or your study is research based. Your goal is to find your own voice and end up with more than a summary.

We can follow this evolution through several drafts of Heather Craige's (2002) "Mourning Analysis." We've already looked at her introduction (my p. 156) and literature review (my pp. 223–225). Here's her abstract:

> One hundred twenty-one analytic candidates who had completed train-ing analysis responded to a survey about their post-termination experience. Seventy-six percent of respondents experienced a mourning process that lasted on average between six months and a year, while 24 per cent expe-rienced no discernible sense of painful loss. Twenty candidates were inter-viewed to obtain a deeper understanding of the mourning process that follows analysis. During the post-termination phase, the analysand's self-analytic capacity is tested in the struggle to contain and understand feelings about the loss of the analyst, as well as transference reactions triggered by that loss. After a "good-enough analysis," the analysand internalizes not only the ana-lyst's functions and attitudes toward him or her, but also a sustaining, positive internal image of the analyst. Four cases illustrate unexpected difficulties that may emerge during the post-termination phase when the loss of the analyst is experienced as a repetition of earlier, traumatic losses or as a rupture of an unanalyzed, selfobject transference. (p. 507)

Craige's final section, called "Discussion and Conclusion," opens with this short, strategically structured paragraph:

> In "Analysis Terminable and Interminable," Freud (1937) tells us that one cannot analyze an issue before it is ripe. This study demonstrates that the loss of the analyst may be anticipated but cannot be fully felt, mourned, or ana-lyzed during treatment. Those difficult tasks fall squarely on the analysand standing alone during the post-termination phase. The study also suggests that loss of the unique analytic relationship may be a more important compo-nent of post-termination mourning than has been appreciated. (p. 535)

Every sentence of this paragraph addresses the so-what? factor and underscores the significance of Craige's study.

In the next eight paragraphs, Craige spells out some of her ideas and refers to relevant sources, using all of these to support her findings and set her ideas off from others. She reflects on the implications of the "most sobering finding of this study . . . that 28% of candidates rated themselves disappointed with the results of their analysis" (p. 536). She identifies and responds to "an apparent paradox" that post-termination consultations with one's analyst presents: "How can one mourn a treatment that is not irrevocably over?" (p. 536). She also indicates areas for future research, including studying the termination process of analysands who are not analytic candidates, how a candidate's experience of post-termination changes over time, and what phenomena other than mourning may be central to this phase.

Let's look at Craige's final three paragraphs, which I read as her conclusion per se. To provide a benchmark for comparison, I have formatted the same key idea in bold in each of these versions and use italics in the third and final ones to indicate changes that are made from the previous draft. Craige's first draft is dated July 25, 1999:

> Conway's research suggests that there is no end to the post-termination phase because her subjects had a continuing mental relationship with their analysts. I would argue that the finding that most candidates continue to think about their analysts, wish to speak to their analysts during times of trouble, and ponder the meaning of their analytic experiences for years after termination is evidence that the analyst has become an internal object. Based on the experience of candidates, **the good-enough analyst can become a permanent fixture in the mind, providing a sustaining and helpful new internal object. In this way, once an analysand has mourned the loss of the daily relationship with the analyst, she may come to feel enriched rather than impoverished by the loss.** I would propose that while the internal objects endure and the need to understand the self is interminable, the post-termination phase does come to an end when the work of mourning is completed.

The structure of this paragraph is tight and clearly sets Craige's ideas off from Conway's. Craige makes effective use of Conway to establish that the post-termination phase does not end and that the analysand maintains an ongoing mental representation of his or her analyst. She will refute the first idea and build on the second. With Conway's idea of a mental representation in mind, Craige mentions three ways analysands use their analyst as an internal object. Craige's main thesis, highlighted in bold, draws out the significance and implications of the analysand's use of the analyst as a new object—specifically, that mourning the loss of the analytic relationship can lead to the new object becoming a source of enrichment and to the post-termination phase ending. What revisions, if any, would you make to her July draft? What might you encourage her to do?

Here's Craige's August 26, 1999, draft:

> This study concurs with the research findings of Pfeffer (1959, 1961, 1963, 1993), and Schlessinger and Robbins (1974, 1975, 1983) cited earlier; following a successful analysis, **the good-enough analyst can become a permanent fixture in the analysand's mind, providing a sustaining and helpful new internal object. In this way, once an analysand has mourned the loss of the daily relationship with the analyst, she may come to feel enriched rather than impoverished by the loss.** This study provides evidence, however, that the positive quality of this new object is not immutable. During the post-termination phase, there is a danger that the results of a good analysis can be ruined and the internal image of the analyst can change

from good enough to negative when the loss of the analyst is experienced as a repetition of earlier, traumatic losses or as a rupture of an unanalyzed, immature selfobject transference. This study demonstrates that it is often not possible to predict how an analysand will experience the loss of the analyst after termination. Even a skilled analyst may remain unaware of certain latent transferences that are only revealed after termination. Because of this uncertainty, the post-termination phase must be viewed as a vulnerable period in the life of the former analysand. The success or failure of the whole analysis may depend on the strength of the analysand's self-analytic capacity and on the analysand's openness to seeking additional help should the self-analytic capacity become overwhelmed. In this sense, the success of the entire analysis may rest on the way in which the analysand negotiates the work of mourning during the post-termination phase.

What differences do you notice between these two drafts? You may want to look before I point out what I see.

Craige has gained more confidence. We see her stating her own position earlier in her conclusion. She also develops more nuanced thoughts about the analyst as a new object whose positive qualities are recognized as vulnerable to erosion if the loss of the analyst repeats earlier trauma. As Craige details the hazards and uncertainties of the post-termination phase, she simultaneously underscores the importance of understanding it. The last sentence of this draft is a poignant addition to Craige's conclusion. What changes, if any, would you make to her August draft?

In her September 25, 1999, draft, you'll see that I have marked changes from the previous draft in italics:

In summary, this study establishes that following good-enough analysis, analysands typically experience a mourning process in the psychoanalytic sense of the word: they cope with the actual loss of the analyst by internalizing the analytic relationship as well as the analyst's functions and image. While a strong sense of loss of the unique analytic relationship is nearly universally experienced by respondents (94%), the conscious experience of mourning varied from non-discernible and not painful (24%) to highly painful (23%), with the majority of respondents experiencing a low to moderate degree of pain (52%). This study concurs with the research findings of Pfeffer (1959, 1961, 1963, 1993) and Schlessinger and Robbins (1994, 1975, 1983): following a successful analysis, **the good-enough analyst can become a permanent fixture in the analysand's mind, providing a sustaining and helpful new internal object. In this way, once an analysand has mourned the loss of the daily relationship with the analyst, she may come to feel enriched rather than impoverished by the loss.**

This study provides evidence, however, that the positive quality of this new object is not immutable. During the post-termination phase, there is a danger that the results of a good analysis may be *spoiled* and the internal image of the analyst may change from good enough to *bad* when the loss of the analyst is experienced as a repetition of earlier, traumatic losses or as a rupture of an unanalyzed, immature selfobject transference. It is often not possible to predict how an analysand will experience the loss of the analyst after termination. Even a skilled analyst may remain unaware of certain latent transferences that are only revealed after termination. *Furthermore, a patient's well-developed self-analytic capacity may be overwhelmed by "too much" internal or external stress after termination. Because of these sources of uncertainty, the post-termination phase should* be viewed as a vulnerable period in the life of the analysand. *Successfully meeting the tasks of the post-termination phase may rest* on the strength of the analysand's self-analytic capacity and on the analysand's openness to seeking additional help *if that capacity becomes overwhelmed. The benefits of the analysis may be consolidated or undermined depending on how* the analysand negotiates the work of mourning during the post-termination phase.

Craige begins her September draft with even more confidence. She leads with her own ideas and delays referencing others. She employs the problem/solution structure three times, giving this version a stronger sense of direction and more momentum. For example, if the analysand experiences a mourning process even after a good-enough analysis, then who or what helps the vulnerable analysand through that process in the absence of the analyst? In this version, we learn more about what's internalized. The new internal object incorporates the analytic relationship and the analyst's function and image.

Craige uses statistics to add more impetus to her motive, so when she presents her thesis, it carries more weight. When she notes that "the positive quality of the new object is not immutable," she sets up a second problem. She identifies the third when she says that the patient's self-analytic capacity may be overwhelmed in the post-termination phase. Details are added to fill out our understanding of what contributes to the analysand's vulnerability. Each time Craige builds a motive into her text and responds to the issues it raises, she creates a more assertive and dynamic conclusion. Underscoring the significance of her work, Craige's closing statement is also much more forceful than that of her previous draft.

Craige's published conclusion (submitted May 30, 1999) reflects mostly subtle changes from the previous draft with the exception of two important revisions:

> In summary, this study establishes that following good-enough analysis, analysands typically experience a mourning process in the psychoanalytic sense of the word—they cope with the loss of the analyst *as analyst* by internalizing the analytic relationship, as well as the analyst's functions and image. While a strong sense of loss of the unique analytic relationship was nearly universally experienced by respondents (94%), the conscious experience of mourning varied from indiscernible and not painful (24%) to highly painful (23%), with the majority of respondents experiencing a low-to-moderate degree of

pain (52%). This study concurs with the research findings of Pfeffer (1959, 1961, 1963, 1993) and Schlessinger and Robbins (1974, 1975, 1983), *which indicate that after* a successful analysis **the good-enough analyst becomes a permanent fixture in the analysand's mind, providing a sustaining and helpful new internal object. In this way, once an analysand has mourned the loss of the almost daily relationship with the analyst, she may come to feel enriched rather than impoverished by the loss.**

The positive quality of this new object, *however*, is not immutable. During the post-termination phase, the *internal image of the analyst may change from good-enough to bad, spoiling the results of a good analysis when the analysand experiences* the loss of the analyst as a repetition of earlier, traumatic losses or as a rupture of an unanalyzed selfobject transference. *Because some latent transferences emerge only after termination, even a skilled analyst may not be able to predict how an analysand will experience loss in the post-termination phase. Further,* a patient's well-developed self-analytic capacity may be overwhelmed by "too much" internal or external stress after termination.

Because of these *unknowns*, the post-termination phase should be viewed as a *period of vulnerability* in the life of the analysand. *Meeting the challenges of the post-termination phase rests* on the analysand's self-analytic capacity and on an openness to seeking additional help if needed. *An analysand who successfully navigates this potentially dangerous phase may gain an enhanced sense of resilience and accomplishment. Post-termination is thus a critical phase of the analytic process.* The benefits of the *entire* analysis may be *undermined or consolidated during this phase*, depending on how the analysand negotiates the work of mourning. (pp. 538–539)

Most of the changes Craige makes between her March draft and her final one reflect revisions that sharpen and tighten her points. Two new sentences in the last paragraph, however, do something more. They draw out the significance and implications of her research, adding depth to a conclusion that reveals more complexity in her thinking and her willingness to claim her own ideas with greater authority. Although Craige's conclusion begins with the not uncommon "in summary" and includes a review of the main findings of her research, it goes beyond that as it incorporates the problem/solution structure of a motive and addresses the so-what? factor, which gets increasing attention as her conclusion evolves.

Although you may not be able to develop your conclusion to its full potential until you have worked with your paper over time, reaching for that potential is important. Cook (1995) notes that conclusions aren't always read last. Readers may jump from an introduction to the conclusion, which then functions as "a second lead" (p. 123). Thus, your conclusion not only brings your paper to an effective close and creates what may be a lasting impression; it may also persuade readers to read your paper from start to finish.

Exercise 16.1

More than a Summary

a. Start by writing a summary of your core ideas for one of your writing projects.
b. Write some notes about the implications and significance of each of your core ideas, addressing the so-what? factor.
c. Use these notes to write a conclusion that is more than a summary, keeping Craige's work in mind.
d. Put your paper aside for at least a week, so you can return to it with fresh eyes. In the meantime, finish reading this chapter.
e. Read your conclusion after your break, then read your entire paper, and note how you could elaborate the implications and importance of your work.
f. Write another draft of your conclusion. Don't be afraid to revise it again, as Craige does, as your ideas and confidence evolve.

The Artist's Geometry

In his preface to *Roderick Hudson*, Henry James (1921) wrote about the "continuity" of relations in novels "of certain figures and things" (p. ix). He asks, "Where, for the complete expression of one's subject, does a particular relation stop—giving way to some other not concerned in that expression?" (p. x). His response applies to ending a clinical story: "Really, universally, relations stop nowhere, and the exquisite problem of the artist is eternally but to draw, by a geometry of his own, the circle within which they shall happily *appear* to do so" (p. x).

Exercise 16.2

Narrative Endings

I dip into a handful of good novels, short stories, and clinical papers to read their concluding paragraphs and to see what each tells me about endings. Try this exercise yourself. What do you learn?

Ending Clinical Narratives

When Jody Davies (1999) introduces us to Daniel, we learn that he is impervious to the cold even when he wears sandals in the winter (my pp. 166–167). As Davies brings the story of her clinical work with Daniel to a close, she returns to this motif not only to draw an elegant circle around her clinical narrative but also to demonstrate how Daniel's response to early trauma is no longer frozen. His sensitivities have changed:

I cannot provide any closure to this story. Daniel's is still a treatment in progress. But I will close with an exchange we had toward the beginning of this winter. Daniel was talking about something I could not quite attend to when suddenly I blurted out, "You're wearing boots!" Gone were the socks and the sandals. He grinned broadly. "I've been waiting to see how long it would take you to notice." "Has it been very long?" I felt a moment of concern. "Oh, I think I'll let you worry about that," he said, reaching for a healthier, more playful, even flirtatious version of his sadism. "So tell me about the boots," I continued. "I don't know. My feet have been getting cold lately," he shrugged. "That's amazing," I said, probably grinning too broadly. For Daniel countered much too quickly, "But don't get too excited. It's only the toes!" "Toes are good," I told him, "I'll take the toes, and we'll work from there." (p. 196)

A clinical paper could end here, in the narrative mode. Or it could continue with a discussion of what the paper's primary clinical material illustrates, a choice Davies makes when she presents "a few of the many, many relational matrices that organized themselves around this one particular clinical moment between Daniel and me" (p. 201) that is the focal point of her story. Her conclusion then extends her thinking into higher levels of abstraction as she discusses unconscious communications between analyst and analysand. Her closing paragraphs introduce the evocative metaphor of the analytic process as "a journey from self state to self state, between past and present, from unconscious to conscious modes of experience, oscillating in focus between self and other, [that] is a dizzying, destabilizing and occasionally overwhelming project" (p. 207). In the geometry of her paper, Davies draws four circles: one around the innermost clinical story, another around the interpretation of the transference/countertransference dynamics of that story, a third around her theoretical comments, and a fourth, the metaphor of a journey.

Like Davies, Rogers also draws a geometry of circles to end *A Shining Affliction* (chapter 3). She writes a final scene of her clinical story, a brief epilogue set six years later, and a note to her professional colleagues. As Davies and Rogers demonstrate, your conclusion gives you a chance to step away from your narrative and look at it from another perspective, approaching your material from a later date or through a different lens. Following chapter 86, Rogers steps back from the ending of her story to write an epilogue that recounts what happened to Ben, how she continues her analysis with Blumenfeld, never sees Melanie again, finishes her PhD, moves to Cambridge, MA, to work with Carol Gillian, and begins her own research and small private practice with young girls. She lets us glimpse her meeting with Blumenfeld the previous spring as they discuss her book and life's uncertainties. She tells us what has happened to her "little pieces," as Blumenfeld called them:

I have not seen or heard from Telesporus, or Emily, or Galle, or Margaret Mary, or Erin, or any of the others, except in my dreams. I am now taking a watercolor class with a wonderful Japanese man who points out light and shadows. "Look at autumn light. Paint the light." I see light on apples and bark, on the sidewalk, under a single twig. I have had to learn skills that once came to me without effort, those gifts from others within me lent to me during the time of a shining affliction. I feel their steady presence in my life and I am grateful to them for all that is alive in me. (p. 313)

In her epilogue's last paragraph, Rogers entwines narrative and meaning making without disrupting her narrative frame. In her afterword, her third ending, she shifts from the narrative to the paradigmatic mode to offer colleagues her "observations about clinical practice" (p. 320). She tells us how and why she decided to reveal her own story in telling Ben's and explains "the emotional truths at the heart of my relationship with Ben" (p. 320). She comments on what she learned from others about the not-uncommon failure of her relationship with Melanie and its implications for clinical practice. She writes about the therapeutic relationship and its vicissitudes while acknowledging the therapist's responsibilities for that relationship. She writes primarily at the second level of abstraction, of commentary and interpretation.

Rogers closes her afterword with these thoughts:

> As I write this sketch of my observations of clinical practice, I see that, rather obviously, they carry the story of the book as a whole. I hope that others—parents, teachers, patients of every age, but clinicians especially—will read this story as if standing outside a house at a window at night, peering into a room at once familiar and unfamiliar, and watching an unfolding drama that adumbrates their own knowledge of relationships in psychotherapy. (p. 320)

As you think of ending a paper that you have written in one of the narrative modes, what kind of closure do you want to create? This question is particularly germane to the lyric narrative, which privileges the uncertainties and unfinished business of the lyric present. Near the end of *Let's Take the Long Way Home* (2010), Caldwell writes about the Navajos, who resist closure in weaving their rugs:

> The old Navajo weavers used to insert an unmatched thread into each of their rugs, a contrasting color that runs to the outside edge. You can spot an authentic rug by this intentional flaw, which is called a spirit line, meant to release the energy trapped inside the rug and pave the way for the next creation.
>
> Every story in life worth holding on to has to have a spirit line. You can call this hope or tomorrow or the "and then" of narrative itself, but without it—without that bright, dissonant fact of the unknown, of what we cannot control—consciousness and everything with it would tumble inward and implode. The universe insists that what is fixed is also finite. (p. 184)

Narratives, including clinical narratives, end by the teller's hand drawing a necessary circle or spirit line.

Ending a Lyric Narrative

Barbara Pizer demonstrates that each lyric narrative may end in its own way. She ends "Passion, Responsibility, and 'Wild Geese'" (2005a) in the paradigmatic mode (my pp. 84–86). Her conclusion to "Maintaining Analytic Liveliness" (2007) is composed almost exclusively of dialogue from two sessions with Aaren. Pizer's work with him, as with Sam, is not over, yet these two sessions form a revealing sequence that shows us how Aaren's capacity to mentalize and relate to himself and others has deepened. Pizer (2007) concludes "Maintaining Analytic Liveliness" with this brief paragraph:

> Although I bring this small portion of our story to a close, it will go on in every which way, now and then, back and forth. Before I began this task, I asked Aaren if I could choose our work together—not simply for this presentation—but in order to focus on the paths of our experiencing and carry it forward with some meanings we may yet gather and track with greater clarity, to try and fuel the fire of what we begin to trust is a deep and meaningful liveliness between us. (p. 26)

Even though Pizer provides a hint of closure here, this paragraph's first sentence lets us know their story continues "in every which way." Intentionally, there are no summaries in this conclusion, little wrapping up, and paradoxically, the only nod to closure is simultaneously offset by an appreciation that this analytic couple's work continues.

Exercise 16.3

Ending Your Narrative

In this exercise, I will work with you as you develop a conclusion in the narrative or lyric narrative mode. You don't have to have a draft of a paper for this exercise. Notes or thoughts will do, but you will need to have a sense of the clinical work you would select to tell your story.

a. Think about where you want your story to end in terms of its narrative trajectory.
b. Think about what you want your readers to understand and appreciate about your clinical work. What would you like them to learn?
c. Write an ending that stays primarily within one of the narrative modes.
d. Now step back and consider your story from another perspective or a later date and write another ending from that new vantage point that extends rather than replaces the ending you had written before. Feel free to shift modes if you'd like to.

---

17 Revising

For if writing builds the house, nothing but revising will complete it. One writer
needs to be two carpenters: a builder with mettle, and a finisher with slow hands.
Susan Bell, *The Artful Edit*

Revising is an integral part of the writing process, but one that shouldn't be started
too early, because generating new material and revising it require different mind-
sets that "can get in each other's way. . . [and] push against each other (Elbow,
2000, p. xiv). You need "a fertile, inventive, yea-saying mentality. . . to come up
with lots of words and ideas" and a "critical, skeptical, nay-saying mentality [to]
critique, cut and revise" (Elbow, 2000, p. xiv). Because self-criticism can extin-
guish creativity and perfectionism may be paralyzing, don't evaluate your work
in progress too soon, especially against publication standards. Keep producing
sentences, paragraphs, and ideas instead. Your daring builder and careful finisher
(Bell, 2007, p. 2) can eventually work together, but give your builder a good head
start.

The "artful editor" is more a guide than a bully, a partner in conversation (Bell,
2007) than an autocrat. Inner critics rarely have the tact to be effective editors.
That's why I suggest that workshop participants park those critics down the street,
preferably in a tow-away zone, or give them the day off. The most adaptive ones
may be retrieved later and coached on how to behave. Others may need to be
retired or impounded for good. Francine Shapiro (2012) suggests putting negative
self-talk in the mouth of a cartoon character with a ridiculous voice and listening
to how that criticism sounds in a voice like that. One writing client laughed out
loud when a beeping Road Runner sped off with negative refrains trailing in a
cloud of dust.

When writing and revising, you may find it useful to "conjure a receptive reader"
whose imagined support can help you jumpstart your writing process, protect a
space in which your creativity can flourish, and sustain you when the going gets
rough (Slochower, 2006). Slochower (2006) finds that nearly "all formulations of
writer's block emphasize object-relational factors that interfere with the writing
process" (p. 46). As attachment theory suggests, attuned others (whether actual,
internalized, or never encountered and only imagined) may provide a safe base
from which you can explore your own mind and the minds and ideas of others.

At times you may prefer to write only for yourself—"to turn inward in a private act of recognition" (Slochower, 2006, p. 57)—so you can say what you want without fear of judgment or reprisal. Dianne Elise felt freer in writing "The Black Man and the Mermaid: Desire and Disruption in the Analytic Relationship" (2007) when she didn't think about publication:

> If I'd imagined from the start that I'd be publishing this paper, I'd never have been able to write the paper that did end up in print. . . . I only wanted my invited presentation on desire and disruption (an "offer" I couldn't refuse) "just to be fun". . . . without any intent to publish, I felt more creative freedom to be disclosing. . . . But "disrupting" one's professional community is dicey business. (October 13, 2012, email)

Are you more likely to take risks in writing when your inner critics are out to lunch, if you are held in the mind of another, when you imagine sweet success or promise yourself (cross your fingers behind your back and hope to die) never to let anyone else see what you have written?

However you get started, imagine an early draft as a safe place to rough out your project and put ideas into play. Thinking in terms of process rather than product can be liberating. Anne Lamott (1995) knows how imperfect beginnings are: "In fact, the only way I can get anything written at all is to write really, really shitty first drafts" (p. 22). Getting started and maintaining momentum are easier to do when you write often; use any time you can get, however limited; establish realistic expectations; become curious about what will turn up; and accept the imperfections of unfinished work.

Once your draft is underway, let your process unfold, writing by your own compass, intuitively and by ear. Some of you may try out different words, tighten sentences, or move them around as you go. These "ongoing edits" (Bell, 2007, p. 44) may create momentum, but they can also stymie, so notice if they propel or impede your progress. Whether you are revising your manuscript or reviewing another's, this chapter will guide you. The first step is to look for what works and has promise.

Exercise 17.1

Prospecting

Revising is often associated with fixing what's wrong and responding to comments written in red. I suggest you grab a highlighter, get a set of brightly colored pens, and make the red ones disappear. Now let's go prospecting, which in my book is not a strenuous activity.

a. Read your paper in one sitting to get a fresh impression of the whole without looking for anything in particular.[1] It's best if you do this after

---

[1]   Whatever I say about revising your paper may be applied to your reviewing and commenting on another author's work.

putting it aside for at least a few days. After you read your draft but without looking back on it, make a list of what you like.

b. On your next reading, use a vibrant color to mark what you find most intriguing, lively, arresting. It could be as small as a word, as large as an idea, or as pervasive as your voice.

c. Looking at your clinical material, use a new color to identify those narrative details and segments of your story that you find most compelling.

d. With a third color, underline those ideas (at any level of abstraction) that are the most valuable and highlight one or two as your top picks.

e. With a fourth color, circle your thesis or major claims wherever you find them.

f. With a fifth color, underline ideas that have potential but are not fully developed.

g. Review and reflect on what you noted and see where it leads you.

Macro, Meso, and Micro Revisions

I find it useful to think of revising in terms of scale. Since revisions you make on a larger scale will affect those down the line, the most efficient way to revise is to start at the macro level, then look at intermediate issues, and finally focus on the micro level. It's tempting to respond to whatever you see when you see it, to do too much rather than prioritize. I've been there, done that. As a teacher facing stacks of student papers, I know how long it takes to identify problems of every order of magnitude, how tiring it is, and how it's wasted effort. That's why I suggest you initially ignore the small stuff unless you are a natural ongoing editor and can revise at that level without losing momentum or diverting your focus from large and midsized matters.

Macro issues include choice of modes, voice, core ideas, motive, the so-what? factor, and your paper's overall structure. I associate meso issues with how you establish the temporal and conceptual axes of your paper; the structure of your argument; the integrity of the links you make to support your argument; how you define and use key terms; your paper's conceptual strength; your introduction; conclusion; use of sources; and how you institute disguise (chapter 18). Micro issues may be small in scale, but they have an enormous impact on readers and reviewers. They include the structure and effectiveness of sentences and paragraphs, your title and subheadings, copyediting and formatting details.

Time

Time is an effective silent partner when you put your manuscript away and come back to it fresh, days or weeks later. When you're in the thick of writing or all too familiar with your prose, it's hard to differentiate what's on the page from what you think is there. Even experienced writers have trouble getting out of their own head. If you've never put a manuscript aside and picked it up later, you may be surprised by how much easier it is to see the forest for the trees, decide which trees need pruning, and shape them instinctively. Before deliberately applying other techniques, let time work for you. It can jumpstart your revising process with the least effort.

Revising by Ear

Murray (1998) puts it simply: "My ear is a better editor than my eye" (p. 173). For Bell (2007), "*to edit is to listen*" (p. 2). When you revise by ear, you listen to the quality of the voice in the text (chapter 10). What does it convey? Is this the voice you want readers to hear? When you rework a part of your paper, listen to the voice in your revised text in context of what comes before and after your revisions. Have you maintained, improved, or unintentionally disrupted the music of your prose (Gass, 2009)? Reading aloud can help you detect how seamless your revisions are. It can also expose all kinds of flaws. In Ogden's (2005a) experience, "there is no better bullshit detector" (p. 26). Elbow (2012) tells his students that their writing will be more effective if it is "comfortable to say aloud. When it is, readers don't have to work as hard to understand your words. They seem to *hear* the meaning come up off the page" (p. 220). If you are writing in the evocative or enactive modes, the kind of music you create depends on what you want to evoke and/or enact. Go through your manuscript at least once concentrating only on your voice in the text, using chapter 10 as a guide.

Common Problems

Some writers make too many points for one paper; others too few. Some seem to be struggling to grasp a thesis; others have a thesis, but it's only tenuously connected to their clinical material. In other papers, the clinical material is such a perfect fit with theory that readers may question the author's credibility. Some writers have brilliant flashes of ideas, but they're not well worked out. They are short on critical thinking. A manuscript may be a source of information but doesn't pull readers in or employ a motive. Some writers are too dependent on their sources; their ideas seem derivative rather than distinctive.

If it's hard to get out of your own head and see what's on the page, how can you tell if, where, how, and why your manuscript works or falls short? One way is to take an active and strategic approach to revising. The exercises in this chapter will help you do that, although paradoxically they may appear to provide both too little guidance and too much. Too little because they can't anticipate all the questions a paper might present and too much because you'll find more exercises than you need for a given paper. Be selective and use what is relevant when it is relevant. Extrapolate. Use the exercises as models and create your own.

No matter how good a self-editor you are, inviting a colleague to read your paper when you are ready can be invaluable. The most experienced writers do that as a matter of course. If you're writing in the evocative or enactive modes, it's especially helpful. How else would you know how your writing affects your readers if you don't ask?

Exercise 17.2

"An Aerial View"

a. Take an "aerial view" of your paper (Murray, 1998, p. 180) and identify the claims it stakes out, the territory it explores, the boundaries of that territory, and what lies outside those boundaries.
b. What do you notice about the lay of the land?

Exercise 17.3

Another Big-Picture View

a. Another way to gain perspective on your paper is to preview it, reading only the title, abstract, epigraph, introduction, subheadings, and first sentence of each paragraph as they come up, and your conclusion.
b. Write a note to the author (especially if it's you), summarizing this paper on the basis of only what you previewed.
c. Compare what you know based on your preview with what you know about your entire paper. Are the differences matters of elaboration and detail? If not, do you need to bring some of your ideas out more prominently so your readers will spot them more easily, especially if they preview your paper before reading it through?

A Paper's Frame

Now let's review your introduction and conclusion, which should be closely related and highlight your main ideas, the impetus for your work (your motive), and its significance (the so-what? factor). Although I consider this meso-level work, midsized elements support and articulate macro issues. The two are intertwined. Distinctions between them are heuristic, sometimes only a matter of attention and emphasis.

Exercise 17.4

Introduction and Abstract

a. Based on your manuscript's introduction, list the expectations it sets up for readers.
b. Does the paper fulfill these expectations? Is there anything important in the paper that isn't anticipated in the introduction and needs to be?
c. Identify and label all the parts of your introduction.

d. Review chapter 11 to see if any essential components of an introduction are left out. Do you want to incorporate any that you left out?
e. Evaluate your introduction's effectiveness based on the principles and examples presented in chapter 11.
f. Be sure a strong motive is in place and that your paper adequately responds to it.
g. Is the sequence of ideas in your abstract, introduction, and body of your paper isomorphic; that is, are they presented in the same order?
h. What expectations are established in your abstract? Are they fulfilled? Have you included the most important key terms or concepts in your abstract? Review your abstract in the context of what you learned in chapter 11.

Exercise 17.5

Conclusion

a. Read your introduction and conclusion in tandem to see if they form a complementary pair. Does your conclusion address the issues raised in the introduction? Is the paper's motive resolved? Are the so-what? factors elaborated not just repeated?
b. Read your conclusion in light of what you learned in chapter 16. Have you taken full advantage of the opportunities a conclusion affords? Does your conclusion build on what is in your paper? Do the ideas in it go beyond those in your introduction?

Two Axes

Another way to parse your attention at the meso level is to focus on the individual axes of your paper and their intersections.

Exercise 17.6

Narrative Axis

a. Identify the narrative details and segments of your clinical story by drawing a colored line in the margin alongside this material. Switch colors if you tell the story of a different patient.
b. Think of this material as the data or evidence that illustrates and supports your interpretations and ideas along the conceptual axis of your paper. Is your evidence sufficient for the tasks at hand? If not, what do you need?

c. Gardner (1991/1983) notes that "fiction is made up of structural units: a passage of description, a passage of dialogue, an action" and that writers work unit by unit, "developing them one by one" (p. 127). Divide your paper into structural units, including those that are devoted to interpretations, concepts, and theories.

d. Identify and label the narrative techniques you employ, such as immediate scenes, narrative summary, flashback, foreshadowing, description, time tags, suspense, interior monologue, reverie, dialogue, imagery, etc.

e. What do you notice about your paper's structural units and your narrative techniques? Would your paper be more effective, for example, if you used an immediate scene in place of a narrative summary? Did you describe the setting and atmosphere if they are important or if doing so would add resonance? Can you identify opportunities to write more evocatively and/or enactively? Did you orient your readers with "time tags" (pp. 118, 149)?

f. Have you created a narrative that means more than it says and invites readers to participate in the creation of meaning?

g. If you are writing a lyric narrative, have you honored the principles of that mode (chapter 7)? Check, for example, how you handle verb tenses, if you get ahead of your story, if you pin meaning down on the basis of retrospective knowledge or honor the uncertainties of the lyric present.

h. Imagine your clinical story as fiction. How lively are the portraits you've drawn of your patient, your relationship, yourself? How specific, life-like, persuasive, compassionate, compelling? What emotions do they evoke?

i. Highlight the most important or charged moments in your clinical material, such as a conflict, impasse, key insight, or turning point.

j. Practice reading backwards, as I call it, to see if you have laid adequate groundwork for readers to appreciate these moments and your interpretations of them. What else, if anything, might need to be added?

k. Have you provided enough material for readers to come to their own conclusions about what you present? If not, do you want to?

Exercise 17.7

Conceptual Axis

a. Underline the key points in your paper.

b. Using a different colored pen, underline the primary evidence for each of your key points.

c. Using the template of the levels of abstraction as a worksheet, map the structure of your core ideas or arguments the way I did with Mitchell's (my pp. 111–112) and Gerson's (my pp. 187–188). If you are not writing in the paradigmatic mode, a conceptual structure may still be implied and may be mapped the same way.

d. Identify the work of your paper, i.e., where you do your most significant work, circling those key ideas on the template of the levels of abstraction you just filled out.

e. Linking the clinical material on the first level of abstraction to your ideas at the next level or two up is crucial to establishing the integrity of your paper and the persuasiveness of your interpretations and arguments. Review these connections, looking first at your worksheet and then back to the relevant sections of your paper. Will your readers feel your interpretations and conceptualizations are adequately supported? Do they appear to arise out of your clinical material or seem to be prefabricated or imposed upon it?

f. Review all the links you've drawn between each of the levels of abstraction. What do you notice? Have you leapfrogged over any levels? How high up have you gone? Are you ascending the levels of abstraction any higher than you need to go to accomplish the work of your paper and set it in an appropriate context?

g. Review chapter 13, noting which issues are most relevant to your paper. Then reread and revise your paper *one relevant issue at a time*, looking, for example, through the entire paper at your use of key terms or concepts. Limiting your focus will improve your acuity.

Situating Your Ideas

Some writers fail to cite enough sources to situate their ideas in the context of others, or they may lose their own voice when they do. Reviewing your use of sources is another important meso-level job.

Exercise 17.8

Sources

a. Review your use of sources in light of what you learned in chapter 15. Have you adequately acknowledged your debts and differentiated your ideas from others?

b. Do any of your sources take over? Does your voice get lost?

c. How well integrated are your sources? How do you prepare your readers for a quotation and then follow it up?

d. Check your use of block quotations (the long ones). Can you cut them down to fewer than five lines so they don't have to be formatted in a block? That way they are less likely to steal the show or be ignored.

e. If you have any block quotations left (and some may be useful), be sure you frame them with your own ideas, introducing them and following them up with your commentary.

Microediting

At some point in your writing process, it will be time to sweat the small stuff, because good writing depends on the choices you make at the micro level. Words are your medium. The ones you pick, those you leave out, and the ways you deploy words are your primary building materials. Once other things are pretty much in place at the macro and meso levels, finishers turn their attention to word choice, punctuation, sentence structure, paragraphs, title, epigraphs, subheadings, and eventually to copyediting, formatting, references, and copyright issues. If you don't address these issues, your readers and reviewers may not find their way to the worth of your paper. Microediting requires a tight focus on small stuff, but that small stuff is enormously important.

A good thesaurus, the latest edition of *The Chicago Manual of Style*, and some practical guides (e.g., Belcher, 2009; Booth, Columb, & Williams, 1995; Hale, 2001; Ross-Larson, 1996) can come in handy, but you may also want to consult thought-provoking writers like Fish (2011), Prose (2006), and Lukeman (2006), who pay close attention to the craft of sentences, paragraphs, and punctuation differently than guidebooks do. Think of the paragraph, for example, as punctuation (Lukeman, 2006, p. 159), "a form, a poetic form, a bit like a stanza" (Prose, 2006, p. 64) or "as a sort of literary respiration, with each paragraph as an extended—in some cases, very extended—breath" (Prose, 2006, p. 66), and you may think about your paragraphs in a new way and shape them differently.

You know how good friends can complete each other's sentences? Likewise, your mind can fill in a missing word when you read your own prose and is unlikely to get confused no matter how cluttered your sentences are. There's no shame in asking for help with any editing, but doing so too early in your writing process could feel like inviting a micromanager into your intimate space before you've arranged things yourself and feel at home.

Lagniappe, a Little Bit Extra

If you find it painful to cut things out of your manuscript, it might be easier if you deposit them in a scrap file. Then they're not gone forever. Another trick is to write as if you have to eliminate as many words as you can, trimming sentences and paragraphs that are "loose baggy monsters" to create more assertive prose if loose and baggy (Henry James's take on nineteenth-century serialized novels) isn't what you want to evoke or enact. I think of extraneous expressions as scaffolding. They seem to hold something up but obscure the lines of the building. "It is" or "there are" constructions are infamous examples. Other kinds of troublemakers include other weak verbs, misplaced modifiers, passive constructions, lack of parallelism, and too many nominalizations (see, for example, Bell, 2007; Belcher, 2009; Ross-Larson, 1996).

The more you help other writers edit their work and engage others in discussing yours, the better self-editor you will become. Learning to read as a writer (Prose,

2006) and analyzing the techniques of good prose will also sharpen your editorial skills. Editing, Bell (2007) writes, is about listening and making "choices rather than judgments" (p. 2). It's an art as well as a craft.

Exercise 17.9

Your Title

a. Readers form their first impression of your work when they read your title. Use it to engage and inform them. Grab their attention, spark their curiosity, and include key words that you want to show up in computer searches.
b. Effective titles are not all alike. Scan your book shelves and browse your favorite journals for inspiration. How does a title draw you in and help you anticipate what's to come? What kind of personality does it have? Even short titles have a voice.
c. Write a few variations of your working title: shorter, longer, with and without a subtitle. See which ones work best.

Exercise 17.10

Subheadings

The mode you write in will affect your use of subheadings and subdivisions (as it will affect almost everything else). What I say about them is aimed primarily at writing that is more conceptually organized.

a. Subheadings are guideposts that function like good leads and draw readers in. If you use them, what do they tell your readers? If they identify your paper's functional parts (e.g., literature review, clinical example, discussion), consider highlighting ideas instead (e.g., "The Artful Dodger and the Fixer-Upper," Naiburg, 2006, p. 451).
b. Notice the amount of text each subheading sets off. Too many subheadings may disrupt the flow of your ideas. Too few and your readers have to chunk unfamiliar material themselves and find their own resting places.

Exercise 17.11

Paragraphs

a. Review your paper by looking at the size *not the content* of your paragraphs. Paragraph breaks, like punctuation marks, do conceptual work. They signal logical relationships, help to articulate the structure of your ideas, and apportion material to facilitate absorption. They also create two windows of opportunity in which your ideas will receive special attention—at the beginning and end of each one.

b. Writers I work with tend to err on the side of making their paragraphs too long. Review paragraphs that are more than half a manuscript page. Dividing them may help your readers take in your ideas more easily as long as your divisions aren't arbitrary.

c. Narrative paragraphs may function differently than those that are conceptually organized. A shift in time, perspective, feeling, scene, or focus rather than the articulation of the structure of your thought may create the impetus for a new paragraph. Notice what prompts your paragraph breaks, if they make sense for the writing you are doing, and if, no matter what mode you are using, you take advantage of the beginning and end of each paragraph.

Giving Feedback

Let's imagine Peter asks you to help him with his manuscript. How does he view his draft's strengths and weaknesses, its challenges, vulnerabilities, and unfinished business? What does he think he needs from you *now*? His reflections can guide you in responding; set a collaborative tone; heighten his sensitivity to his readers; sharpen his editorial eye; and underscore the importance of his initiative, autonomy, and authority. Imagine that!

The best feedback you can give will be the result of mutual negotiations and shared expectations. Effective feedback is context dependent, specific, and selective. A little feedback goes a long way when it points to the most important issues, identifies problematic patterns, doesn't overwhelm the author, and supports his ability to sort things out for himself. Elbow (2001) finds that student writers can take in no more than three points about their writing per review. Nancy Sommers (2013), former Director of Harvard's Expository Writing Program, suggests limiting comments on student papers to one or two key points and identifying patterns of both strengths and weaknesses. You won't know how much Peter can absorb until you've worked with him. It's safer to start with a modest number of strategically selected comments that point to macro- and meso-level issues. Look for hinge points—those places, problems, or ideas on which so much hinges, because revisions at these points will have the most effect.

As psychotherapists, we know how important recognition is. Mitchell (1993a) writes that a patient needs "not clarification or insight so much as a sustained experience of being seen, personally engaged, and basically valued and cared about. . . . what today's analysis provides is the opportunity to freely discover and playfully explore one's own subjectivity, one's own imagination" (p. 25). As Elbow (2001) points out, "what writers need most is the experience of being heard and a chance for dialogue" (p. 3).

If you present your feedback as coming from one reader among others, you will be signaling that others might read Peter's paper differently. If your view is seen as a partial view from a particular perspective, albeit an attuned one, Peter will be freer to decide how to use what you offer (Elbow, 2001). Notice the difference between *I* statements and comments that masquerade as objective. "I feel the disorientation you experience with your patient. It feels real to me." "I lose the thread of your idea here." "I'm not sure how this detail fits in. Can you show me so I can see the connections you want to make?" *I* statements invite dialogue, confirming or seeking understanding. The following comments seem to come down from on high: "That's confusing." "Ambiguous." "Here's a gap in your thinking." "Your tone goes flat." Pronouncements like these risk cutting off conversation and shutting down a writer who feels judged.

Even when the writing demonstrates potential, "to be understood is more rewarding than to be praised. Being understood makes us want to take the trouble to try to articulate more of what is on our minds—and almost on our minds" (Elbow, 2000, pp. 31–32). When you review a manuscript, it's not only helpful to write select marginal comments but also to include a note to the author. That gives you a chance to demonstrate what you understand, address larger issues, and help the writer set priorities. Start with a healthy dose of recognition, which can make it easier for the writer to assimilate any criticism. End on a positive note, perhaps pointing to the paper's potential that has not been realized. Overall, try to balance positive and negative feedback. Imagining what it would be like to receive your comments may help you set the right tone.

"Felt Sense"

Elbow (2000) and Perl (2004) brought Gendlin's (1981) work with "felt sense" into composition studies. Whether you're writing a paper of your own or giving feedback, you may sense that what you've said isn't quite right, but it's as close as you can get at that time. Knowing that something isn't quite right creates the impetus for finding what you need. Rather than devalue what you've written or feel discouraged, check in with yourself, with your body's implicit knowledge, and search for words that are a better fit. You will probably have to do this several times, moving back and forth between nonverbal feelings and verbal articulation and between a verbal approximation and a felt sense of what you want to say.

Elbow (2000) exemplifies this technique when he describes giving feedback to a writer:

> "I was going to say 'Your essay was childish,' but that's not really right. It's not really childish. But somehow that's the word that came to mind. I wonder what I mean." And then pause quietly and look inside and wait for more words. Usually, more accurate words arise. I might end up with something like, "Yes, your essay isn't childish, but I feel a kind of stubborn or even obsessive quality in it, even though on the surface it seems very clear and reasonable. I feel a refusing-to budge quality that reminds me of a stubborn child." Till this point, I hadn't really known what I was trying to get at—what

my perception or reaction to the writing actually was. But having said this, I realize, yes, this is what I was noticing and wanting to say. I needed to say the wrong words to get to the right words. (pp. 137–138)

As Elbow demonstrates, you can use the "wrong words" to find better ones by creating a dialogue with yourself.

Getting Feedback

Some writers who receive feedback want to explain, justify, or defend themselves. In a workshop, one writer took up more of the allotted time apologizing than he gave his respondent to comment on what he had written. That's why I ask writers to let their respondents know the kind of feedback they want and ask writers to forgo apologizing or defending themselves. That way both partners can focus on what the writing is doing and how it affects a listener/reader. Respondents can be especially helpful if they begin on a positive note; ground their comments in the particulars of the text; focus on the large and mid-sized issues, especially the hinge points; and are selective in the comments they make.

Writing Groups

Participating in an ongoing writing group offers a number of perks—increased motivation to write; dedicated time to write and think as a writer in the company of other writers; opportunities to hone your skill as a reader; and the chance to discover how your manuscript is received. Group members may not always agree about a given manuscript, which is informative, especially if they trace their responses to the specific parts of the manuscript that prompt them.

Coming together as writers doesn't mitigate the challenge of forming and maintaining a working group (Bion, 1992a/1961). In fact, it may even heighten it. Group members may feel vulnerable as writers even if, or especially if, they are experienced psychotherapists. Protecting a writer's confidentiality, not just the patient's, and establishing safety support the work of a writing group as they would with any group. Use all you know about groups when participating. Whether you have a leader-led group or share the leadership among yourselves, you will profit from attending to the group's development. How you respond to each other's writing will evolve and also reflect the group's dynamics, your individual experience as writers and clinicians, and the particular manuscript that is on the table.

You may want to take advantage of the synergy of writing in the company of other writers and set some group time aside to write, doing some of the exercises in this book for starters. The first writing assignments I gave in my college classes called for only three pages of prose. You don't need much to spot patterns or gage a writer's craft, and a page limit may help writers spit their main points out. I think you may be surprised at how much readers and writers alike can learn from working on short pieces. I also suggest you build the revision process in, inviting writers to bring their revised and expanded work back to the group for additional comments.

If participants are not ready to share their writing with the group as a whole, they can work in pairs or comment on their writing process. It is important that participants know they are in charge of what they share and when and how they share it. Writers have difference tolerances for going public. To protect their creative space, some writers may want more time before they ask for input.

Whenever you review a participant's work in progress, keep in mind that you are probably much more accustomed to discussing clinical material as clinicians and feel more competent doing so than speaking from a reader's perspective. Directing attention to a manuscript rather than the clinical work it presents may take some effort. A writing group can't ignore the clinical work that's written up, but it can respond to it differently than it would if it were presented in supervision. You can shift your focus from the clinical work to how it's presented by offering criterion-based feedback and reader-based feedback. Criterion-based feedback is anchored in the craft of writing and aimed at what's required for the purposes of a particular paper. Reader-based feedback reflects readers' subjective responses (Elbow & Belanoff, 2003). In either approach, readers are most helpful to writers if they focus on the specifics of how a manuscript works or doesn't quite work for them and how it affects them. If a writer's presentation of clinical work is incomplete, puzzling, too self-confident, ambitious, or problematic in some other way, it is the clinician *as writer* you want to support.

Meeting Yourself on the Page

Writing is a recursive process (Perl, 1980) of generating new ideas, making connections, and revisiting and revising ones you've already made. While rereading what I've written, I usually rework it, because ongoing editing comes easily to me. Revising is my way back into my work and myself, a way to reconnect to the voice I am developing. No matter when you revise or how often, the writing process invites circling back, reviewing what you have, meeting yourself on the page, and reworking what you've written as your thoughts evolve—until you feel your paper is ready to be launched into the world and begin a more public life on its own.

18   Confidentiality and Disguise

Whatsoever things I see or hear concerning the life of men, in my attendance on the sick or even apart there-from, which ought not to be noised abroad, I will keep silence thereon, counting such things to be as sacred secrets.

Hippocratic Oath

Protecting the confidentiality of your patients and the analytic process may be the most vexing challenge you face as a writer, because a cascade of clinical, ethical, and writing issues are involved that are not easily untangled or resolved. How will you disguise your patient's identity without sacrificing the specifics on which understanding is based? How will you select clinical material without diluting its richness and complexity? Will you obtain your patient's written consent? How and when? If not, why? If you don't ask for your patients' consent, what are the risks and consequences of their discovering what you write? What constitutes informed consent in the context of transference/countertransference dynamics or the treatment of a child, family, group, or organization? How will you track the effects of asking (or not asking) your patients for their consent? How will writing affect your clinical work? How will the possibility of your patients' reading what you write affect what and how you write? How will the necessary compromises you make to protect confidentiality constrict the development of theory and practice? Will you share what you write with those you write about? How and when? How will your patients be affected by learning more about you from your writing?

How you struggle with these issues is constitutive of the clinical writing process just as confidentiality is "constitutive" of the analytic process (Lear, 2003, p. 4). While the clinical and ethical issues of confidentiality and disguise are beyond the scope of this book, other publications address these issues: e.g., *Writing about Patients: Responsibilities, Risks, and Ramifications* (Kantrowitz, 2006); *Confidentiality: Ethical Perspectives and Clinical Dilemmas* (Levin, Furlong, & O'Neil, Eds., 2003); *My Life as a Man* (Roth, 1993/1970); and articles by Aron (2000), Berman (1987, 2001), Bridges (2007), Furlong (1998, 2006), Gabbard (1997, 2000b), Gabbard and Williams (2001), Gerson (2000), Gobnik (2000), Goldberg (1997, 2004), Halpern (2003), Klumpner and Frank (1991), Kubler, (2003), Lipton (1991), S. Pizer (2000), Stoller (1988), Wilson and Harasemovitch

(2004), Tuckett (2000), Williams and Schaefer (2005). Kantrowitz's study is the most extensive to date and is based on her interviews with 141 analysts who wrote about their patients and thirty-seven patients who read what their therapists had written about them.

Disguise

While the need to protect your patient's identity is a given, how you do that is not. The standard is straightforward: "a case should be disguised sufficiently so that only the analyst and the patient would recognize who it is" (Gabbard, 2000b, p. 1074). But how you achieve that goal isn't as clear cut. To say a patient is in the arts without specifying which one isn't considered an effective solution, because a vague description doesn't rule out what you are trying to disguise (Gabbard, 2000b). Yet the use of thick disguise (altering identifying details, such as a specific medical condition, and/or adding bogus details) can mislead readers if they extrapolate on the basis of erroneous information (Kantrowitz, 2006; Klumpner & Frank, 1991; Lipton, 1991). Kantrowitz (2006) favors omitting details in lieu of changing them, yet writing that is too generic is not compelling or persuasive. How many details and the kinds of specifics your readers need depend on what you are trying to demonstrate. If your subject is sibling dynamics, the details of birth order and the number, age, and sex of your patient's siblings may be crucial to present. If you write about psychosomatic illness, substituting one symptom for another is fundamentally misleading. Whatever disguise you institute, you should preserve the integrity of your patient's psychodynamics and inner world (Kantrowitz & Gabbard, 2003), the dynamics of the treatment process, and your subjective experience.

A patient's age, class, ethnicity, religion, and race are often changed or left out, which misrepresents or erases important influences. Such a strategy of disguise has political implications and conservative consequences:

> For those of us psychoanalytic clinicians who also identify as social activists, the purpose of clinical illustration is not only about how to help the patient heal but also to challenge the inequalities of gender, race, class, and sexuality that have made so many ill in the first place. To accomplish the latter, case examples have to be specific as possible, particularly with regard to the very identifying elements most often altered by convention. This demand for specificity makes it extremely difficult to preserve confidentiality. (Layton, 1999, p. 326)

Six writers in *With Culture in Mind: Psychoanalytic Stories* (Dimen, 2011) demonstrate how you can identify the particular "political, social, and material contexts" needed to locate "the psychic and the social in a single clinical moment" (Dimen, 2011, p. 2) without giving away information that makes their patients identifiable. You might want to take a look.

Focus

As Lear (1998) demonstrates, you can avoid the quandary about changing identifying information by presenting tightly focused moments of clinical work so that little disguise is necessary if at all:

> One analysand, as he entered my office for the beginning of a session, would leave the outer door a fraction of an inch ajar. As his hand let the door handle go, it would make a gesture as delicate as any I have seen in a ballet. The next step in the pas de deux was being turned over to me: his fingers *told me* to finish the job and close the door. I, of course, said nothing; but as time passed and the analysand relaxed into his analysis, he eventually became puzzled by this gesture. Here is a small selection of the meanings that began to emerge as he associated to it: He liked getting me to do something; he enjoyed the feeling of control over me, for he knew that I would have to close the door. Leaving the door ajar meant that nothing he was going to say was going to be so important or private that it should not be heard by someone outside. He longed for us to be working together on a collaborative project, and if we both closed the door, we were a team. My noticing that he left the door ajar meant that I was sensitive. He was scared of what might happen inside the room and wanted to know that the emergency exit was open and ready for an escape. He was afraid that I might try to rape him from behind and he wanted to be sure that people outside could hear his screams. He was hoping that others might accidentally come into my office and then he would get a glimpse of what the rest of my life was like. He was hoping that others would come in and that he would be the object of their voyeuristic pleasure. He wanted others to know we were a couple. He wanted to be the star in a porno movie. He was teasing me, setting up a game that involved his wondering whether I would ever ask him about it. He was testing my analytic resoluteness. Closing the door meant sealing his fate. Closing the door meant there was no escape from facing his own mind. And so on. (p. 13)

Lear presents enough particulars to create "a sense of clinical reality, [but] there is nothing about the vignette that necessarily attaches it to a particular person" (Lear, 2003, p. 14). The thickness of Lear's description resides in the meanings he and his patient explore.

Exercise 18.1

Focus

a. Write up a focused moment of clinical work with a patient without instituting a disguise.

b. Review whatever identifying details you included to see whether your patient could be recognized by readers other than your patient and yourself.
c. Disguise or omit any identifying details that compromise your patient's anonymity.
d. After making any necessary revisions, ask a colleague to read your draft as I suggest (pp. 256–257).

A tight focus, however, cannot illuminate the course and movements of a treatment or convey a psychodynamic understanding of complex phenomena that require more elaboration (Gabbard, 2000b). Limiting the amount of clinical material to one session or less may also have the unintended consequence of reinforcing certain assumptions about what is most salient, e.g., that "everything we need to know will become evident in the transference" (Budd, 1997, p. 42). Kantrowitz (2006) worries that being so selective about the clinical material we write about may distort how analysis is represented and consequently how theory is shaped.

Composites

If you are writing about character structure, diagnostic categories, or characteristics that are shared across a group of patients, a composite based on several patients may suffice (Gabbard & Williams, 2001). Composites, like vignettes, function primarily as illustrations, are useful for educational purposes (Gabbard, 2000b), and are suitable for describing "phenomena that lend themselves to generalization" (Kantrowitz, 2006, p. 257). In *Hope and Dread in Psychoanalysis*, Mitchell (1993a) uses them along with examples that are not composites. To further protect confidentiality, readers don't know which are which. Some argue that a composite is not reliable, because it fictionalizes the analyst as well as the patient: The "particular vignette never actually took place," and "the analyst's behavior is hypothetical" just as the patient's is (Shapiro, 2004, p. 671; see also Goldberg, 1997, and Kantrowitz, 2006). While recognizing that "clinical essays have always occupied something of a middle ground between science and literature, or, if you would, reality and imagination" (Dimen, 2001, p. 406), using a composite for a case presentation or extended case study seems to me to be a more dubious choice than others, because it creates a grand fiction.

Exercise 18.2

Composites

a. Write the first of two composites, drawing on characteristics of a set of patients that share important similarities to illustrate an idea you might propose about this set of patients or their clinical process.

b. Write a second composite to illuminate the same point or a variation on it as Mitchell (2000) does when he writes about love and hate in the analyses of Fred, Gloria, Helen, and Ben or as Gabbard and Lester (1995) do when they write about analysts who commit boundary violations.

c. Write a third portrait that is not a composite but is closely based on a particular patient. Institute any disguises that are needed.

d. Without identifying which portraits are composites, ask one or more colleagues to read all three and look for anything that stands out as not persuasive or plausible or seems too revealing.

e. Consider revising your portraits and/or your disguises based on your readers' comments.

Skin in the Game

Analysts put skin in the game when they write more openly about themselves. Some write more personally; others reveal only what emerges explicitly in the analytic field. Warren Buffet used the term "skin in the game" when he argued that company leaders who put stockholders' money at risk should be willing to be at risk themselves by holding their company's stock. Doing so increases their stake in seeing things from the stockholders' perspective. Although she didn't use Buffet's language, one writer who obtains her patients' consent meant exactly that when she said she couldn't write about her patients without putting herself on the line.

Exercise 18.3

Skin in the Game

Did you put much skin in the game when you wrote about a focused clinical moment for exercise 18.1? If you didn't and you believe in the importance of doing so when you write, put more of yourself in and see how that feels. If you are inclined, you could write more about your internal states, reveries, associations, and somatic responses to the clinical work you present to see how comfortable you are with such disclosures.

Write with a Full Deck

I suggest you write almost all the drafts of your paper without instituting disguise so your mind has full access to everything it needs to do your best work. If you start adding or altering details or cordoning off segments of the treatment in your mind before you're written your paper through to its almost-final draft, you could inhibit or distort your own implicit, intuitive, and associative processes. Play with a full deck when you write, because you will have a much better chance of discovering something you don't already know and be more likely to write evocatively and enactively if you do.

Havens (1993) sees himself writing in the same way a painter works from nature: "I can only work from nature, as some painters say, from memories of the person held before my mind. I want those expressions to act on me. Otherwise I perceived what I expect, since the mind's first tendency is to capture the person in familiar images and concepts. Only when we return to nature with a fresh perspective do we begin to reach what has been suppressed" (p. 6). Havens (1993) explains that he disguises his patients with "details making them unrecognizable to many. But in another sense the cases are revealed, because the details chosen are meant to state an emotional truth, so that the patients recognize themselves" (p. 6). Thinking about what a disguise reveals in this sense could make the process of crafting one more like making an interpretation to your patient. But don't change or alter any identifying details or omit any until after you've worked everything else out. Once you've revised your manuscript to institute disguise, review it to make sure your disguise is sufficient, congruent, and credible. Adding disguise is not the last step in your writing process. Making sure everything fits together is.

Equivalents

When instituting a disguise, you need to look for equivalents for those identifying features or characteristics that need to be swapped to protect your patient's identity. At the same time, you need to preserve the integrity of what is most important to your clinical story. Each of you will find a way of doing both. What's most important for Havens (1996) to present authentically are "the details of my treatments and the speculations about what treatment can be" (p. ix). For Eigen (2004), it is the presentation of affects and the details of psychic realities. For Luepnitz (2002), "the main character of these stories is not the patient but the process—the talking cure" (pp. 11–12). In *Schopenhauer's Porcupines*, Luepnitz explains that she has "tried to describe the week-to-week unfolding of therapy—the setting of fees and the interpretation of dreams, the exhilarating detective work and the inevitable tedium, the wrong roads taken and the occasional thrill of arrival. Covering these facets of therapy remained more pressing than actual demographics, events, and faces" (pp. 11–12).

When in doubt about what to disguise or omit, ask a colleague to read your manuscript and look for any inconsistencies after you've instituted the necessary disguises. Don't explain what you've altered, so you don't betray your patient's confidentiality or bias your reader. Ask more generally if anything stands out as not credible or plausible, if any points seem inadequately illustrated, or if anything is too generic to be persuasive for the clinical story you are trying to tell. If your colleague points to anything that has been disguised (e.g., your patient's profession, a death in your patient's family), you may need to go back to the drawing board. It may not jeopardize the credibility of the clinical work you present if a patient's best friend died in a motor vehicle accident or rock climbing, if the person who died was a best friend, close cousin, or neighbor as long as the details you choose as a disguise support the emotional impact of what really happened.

If you've obtained your patient's consent to write about your clinical work, you may want to give your patient the option of reading your draft and commenting on the disguises you've chosen. Of course, comments, feelings, feedback, and fallout of all kinds may arise when you write about a patient and a patient reads or doesn't read your paper. Consent may be given and later rescinded (B. Pizer, 2014) or given and then doubted by your patient, causing you to drop that part of your writing project (S. Pizer, 2000). Instituting an effective disguise is an ethical imperative but not the only consideration to be negotiated with yourself and between you and your patient.

No single strategy of disguise fits every circumstance or can solve all the knotty dilemmas we face when writing about our patients. That complexity mitigates against instituting uniform procedures to protect confidentiality and challenges us to find our own solutions with each paper we write. Although the individual choices we make may be limiting, our collective efforts may yield a literature that contributes to our field and the vitality of our clinical work.

Afterword

I remember my Uncle Buddy, who survived the Battle of the Bulge and the Korean War but lost his fight with cancer when he was forty-eight. He assured us that he would take the fire when we went to visit his mother, who was a large presence in my life. It was simple, he said, he'd just wear unmatched socks.

Edward C. Whitmont used to say, "You never finish a book; you sacrifice it." That's how it feels, because I know where the spirit lines are that lead to things I still want to write. To make the necessary sacrifices to let my book go, I think of my uncle standing there to draw my grandmother's critical gaze.

I also know something that may apply to you as you near the end of a long writing project no matter who your grandmothers are. I know what I've learned and how, what it took to get here, and what was stirred up along the way. I know more about the wellsprings of my creativity and myself.

But how do you know something? Richard Poirier (1990/1977) asks in *Robert Frost: The Work of Knowing*. Like beans, for example. Thoreau shows us when he writes about his bean field at Walden. Frost shows us "in his poems of work and the work of his poems" (p. 278). "The answer is that you 'know' a thing and know that you know it only when 'work' begins to yield a language that puts you and something else, like a field, at a point of vibrant intersection" (Poirier, 1990/1977, p. 278).

References

Abrams, M. H. (1985). *A glossary of literary terms*. Fifth Edition. Fort Worth, TX: Harcourt Brace Jovanovich College Publishers.

Alberts, L. (2010). *Showing & telling: Learn how to show & when to tell for powerful & balanced writing*. Cincinnati, OH: Writer's Digest Books.

Altman, N. (2010). *The analyst in the inner city: Race, class, and culture through a psychoanalytic lens*. Second Edition. New York: Routledge.

Altman, N. & Davies, J. (2001). Editorial. *Psychoanalytic Dialogues 11 (6)*: 823.

Alvarez, A. (2005). *The writer's voice*. New York: Norton & Co.

Appignanesi, L. (2005). The sheep of reason: Adam Phillips examines the opposite of madness in *Going Sane*. *The Guardian*. February 18.

Aron, L. (2000). Ethical considerations in the writing of case histories. *Psychoanalytic Dialogues 14*: 1–51.

Atwood, M. (2002). *Negotiating with the dead: A writer on writing*. New York: Anchor Books.

Barth, R. (1978). *Image, music, text: Essays selected and translated by Stephen Heath*. New York: Hill and Wang.

Baxter, C. (1986). Charles Baxter. In R. Shapard & J. Thomas (Eds.), *Sudden fiction: American short-short stories* (229). Salt Lake City: Gibbs Smith Publishers.

Belcher, W. L. (2009). *Writing your journal article in 12 weeks: A guide to academic publishing success*. Los Angeles: Sage Publishers, Inc.

Bell, S. (2007). *The artful edit: On the practice of editing yourself*. New York: W.W. Norton.

Berman, J. (1987). *The talking cure: Literary representations of psychoanalysis*. New York: New York University Press.

Berman, J. (2001). Book review of *Tales from the Couch*: Writers on therapy: Jason Shinder. *Psychoanalytic Psychiatry 10*: 165–170.

Bion, W. (1984/1965). *Transformations*. London: Karnac.

Bion, W. (1992a/1961). *Experiences in groups and other papers*. London: Routledge.

Bion, W. (1992b). *Cogitations*. London: Karnac.

Bion, W. (2004/1964). *Second thoughts: Selected papers on psycho-analysis*. London: Karnac.

Birkerts, S. (2008). *The art of time in memoir: Then, again*. Minneapolis, MN: Graywolf Press.

Bollas, C. (1987). *The shadow of the object: Psychoanalysis of the unthought known*. New York: Columbia University Press.

Bollas, C. (1991/1987). *Forces of destiny: Psychoanalysis and human idiom*. London: Free Association Books.

Bollas, C. (1999). *The mystery of things*. London: Routledge.

Bollas, C. (2007). *The Freudian moment*. London: Karnac.

Bollas, C. (2009). *The evocative object world*. London: Routledge.

Boo, K. (2012). *Behind the beautiful forevers: Life, death, and hope in the Mumbai undercity*. New York: Random House.

Booth, W. (1961). *The rhetoric of fiction*. Chicago: University of Chicago Press.

Booth, W., Colomb, G., & Williams, J. (1995). *The craft of research*. Chicago: University of Chicago Press.

Boston Change Process Study Group. (2010). *Change in psychotherapy: A unifying pattern*. New York: W.W. Norton.

Bridges, N. A. (2007). Clinical writing about patients: Negotiating the impact on patients and their treatment. *Psychoanalytic Social Work 14*: 23–41.

Bromberg, P. M. (1998). *Standing in the spaces: Essays on clinical process, trauma and dissociation*. Hillsdale, NJ: Analytic Press.

Bromberg, P. M. (2006). *Awakening the dreamer: Clinical journeys*. Hillsdale, NJ: The Analytic Press.

Bromberg, P. M. (2011). *The shadow of the tsunami and the growth of the relational mind*. New York: Routledge.

Brooks, P. (1992/1984). *Reading for plot: Design and intention in narrative*. Cambridge, MA: Harvard University Press.

Brower, R. A. (2013/1951). *The fields of light: An experiment in critical reading*. Philadelphia: Paul Dry Books.

Bruner, J. S. (1966). *Toward a theory of instruction*. Cambridge, MA: The Belknap Press of Harvard University Press.

Bruner, J. S. (1986). *Actual minds, possible worlds*. Cambridge, MA: Harvard University Press.

Bruner, J. S. (1990). *Acts of meaning*. Cambridge, MA: Harvard University Press.

Bruner, J. S. (2002). *Making stories: Law, literature, life*. Cambridge, MA: Harvard University Press.

Bruner, J. S., et al. (1967). *Studies in cognitive growth: A collaboration at the Center for Cognitive Studies*. Hoboken, NJ: John Wiley & Sons.

Budd, S. (1997). Ask me no questions and I'll tell you no lies: The social organization of secrets. In I. Ward (Ed.), *The presentation of case material in clinical discourse* (29–44). London: Freud Museum.

Caldwell, G. (2010). *Let's take the long way home: A memoir of friendship*. New York: Random House.

Cambray, J. (2011). Moments of complexity and enigmatic action: A Jungian view of the therapeutic field. *Journal of Analytic Psychology 56 (3)*: 296–309.

Ciardi, J. (1959). *How does a poem mean?* Boston: Houghton Mifflin.

Coen, S. J. (2000). Why we need to write openly about our clinical cases. *Journal of the American Psychoanalytic Association 48*: 449–470.

Cohn, D. (1983/1978). *Transparent minds: Narrative modes for presenting consciousness in fiction*. Princeton, NJ: Princeton University Press.

Coltart, N. (1992). *Slouching towards Bethlehem. . ..* New York: The Guilford Press.

Coltart, N. (1993). *How to survive as a psychotherapist*. London: Sheldon Press.

Cook, M. J. (1995). *Leads and conclusions*. Cincinnati, OH: Writer's Digest Books.

Craige, H. (2002). Mourning analysis: The post-termination phase. *Journal of the American Psychoanalytic Association 50*: 507–550.

Culler, J. (2001). Comparing poetry. ACLA Presidential Address. *Comparative Literature 53 (3)*: vii–xviii, xi.

D'Agata, J. (Ed.). (2003). *The next American essay*. Minneapolis, MN: Graywolf Press.

D'Agata, J. (Ed.). (2009). *The lost origins of the essay*. St. Paul, MN: Graywolf Press.

Davies, J. M. (1999). Getting cold feet, defining "safe-enough" borders: Dissociation, multiplicity, and integration in the analyst's experience. *Psychoanalytic Quarterly 68*: 184–208.

Davies, J. M. (2012/2004). Whose bad objects are we anyway? Repetition and our elusive love affair with evil. In L. Aron & A. Harris (Eds.), *Relational psychoanalysis. Vol. 5: Evolution of process* (163–181). New York: Routledge.

Derrida, J. (1978). Coming into one's own. In G. Hartman (Ed.), *Psychoanalysis and the question of the text* (114–148). Baltimore: Johns Hopkins University Press.

Dimen, M. (2001). Perversion is us? Eight notes. *Psychoanalytic Dialogues 11 (6)*: 825–860.

Dimen, M. (Ed.). (2011). *With culture in mind: Psychoanalytic stories*. New York: Routledge.

Dybek, S. (1986). Stuart Dybek. In R. Shapard & J. Thomas (Eds.), *Sudden fiction: American short-short stories* (241–242). Salt Lake City: Gibbs Smith Publishers.

Eigen, M. (1992). *Coming through the whirlwind: Case studies in psychotherapy*. Wilmette, IL: Chiron Publications.

Eigen, M. (1998). *The psychoanalytic mystic*. London: Free Association Books.

Eigen, M. (2001). *Ecstasy*. Middleton, CT: Wesleyan University Press.

Eigen, M. (2002). *Rage*. Middleton, CT: Wesleyan University Press.

Eigen, M. (2004). *The sensitive self*. Middleton, CT: Wesleyan University Press.

Eigen, M. (2005). *Emotional storm*. Middleton, CT: Wesleyan University Press.

Eigen, M. (2009). *Flames from the unconscious: Trauma, madness, and faith*. London: Karnac.

Elbow, P. (1973). *Writing without teachers*. London: Oxford University Press.

Elbow, P. (1981). *Writing with power: Techniques for mastering the writing process*. New York: Oxford University Press.

Elbow, P. (1994). What do we mean when we talk about voice in texts? In K. Blake Yancey (Ed.), *Voices on voice: Perspectives, definitions, inquiry* (1–35). Urbana, IL: National Council on Teachers of English.

Elbow, P. (2000). *Everyone can write: Essays toward a hopeful theory of writing and teaching writing*. New York: Oxford University Press.

Elbow, P. (2001). *About responding to student writing*. http://www.marist.edu/writingcenter/workshop.html.

Elbow, P. (2012). *Vernacular eloquence: What speech can bring to writing*. New York: Oxford University Press.

Elbow, P. & Belanoff, P. (2003). *Being a writer: A community of writers revisited*. Boston: McGraw Hill.

Elise, D. (2007). The black man and the mermaid: Desire and disruption in the analytic relationship. *Psychoanalytic Dialogues 17*: 791–809.

Ellenberger, H. (1970). *The discovery of the unconscious: The history and evolution of dynamic psychiatry*. New York: Basic Books.

Epstein, R. (1999). Generativity theory. In S. R. Pritzker & M. A. Runco (Eds.), *Encyclopedia of creativity*. Vol. 1 (759–766). Waltham, MA: Academic Press.

Feiner, A. H. (1987). Notes on the dynamics of the problems of editing psychoanalytic journals. *Contemporary Psychoanalysis 23*: 676–688.

Ferro, A. & Basile, R. (2009). The universe of the field and its inhabitants. In A. Ferro & R. Basile (Eds.), *The analytic field: A conceptual concept* (5–29). London: Karnac.

Fish, S. (2011). *How to write a sentence and how to read one.* New York: Harper.

Flax, J. (1996). Taking multiplicity seriously: Some implications for psychoanalytic theorizing and practice. *Contemporary Psychoanalysis 32*: 577–593.

Foehl, J. C. (2010). The play's the thing: The primacy of process and the persistence of pluralism in contemporary psychoanalysis. *Contemporary Psychoanalysis 46*: 48–86.

Fonagy, P. (2001). *Attachment theory and psychoanalysis.* New York: The Other Press.

Fosshage, J. L. (2000). The meanings of touch in psychoanalysis: A time for reassessment. *Psychoanalytic Inquiry 20*: 21–43.

Franck, F. (1973). *The Zen of seeing: Seeing/drawing as meditation.* New York: Vintage Books.

Freud, S. (1933). *The new introductory lectures on psycho-analysis.* W. J. H. Sprott (Trans.). New York: W.W. Norton & Company.

Frost, R. (1995). *Robert Frost: Collected poems, prose, & plays.* Eighth Printing. New York: The Library of America.

Furlong, A. (1998). Recovered memories of trauma: Transferring the present to the past: C. Brooks Brenneis. *Canadian Journal of Psychoanalysis 6*: 325–329.

Furlong, A. (2006). Further reflections on the impact of clinical writing on patients. *International Journal of Psychoanalysis 87*: 747–768.

Gabbard, G. O. (1997). Case histories and confidentiality. *International Journal of Psychoanalysis 78*: 820–821.

Gabbard, G. O. (2000a). What can neuroscience teach us about transference? *Canadian Journal of Psychoanalysis 9*: 1–18.

Gabbard, G. O. (2000b). Disguise or consent? Problems and recommendations concerning the publication and presentation of clinical material. *International Journal of Psychoanalysis 81*: 1071–1086.

Gabbard, G. O. & Lester, E. P. (1995). *Boundaries and boundary violations in psychoanalysis.* New York: Basic Books.

Gabbard, G. O. & Westen, D. (2003). Rethinking therapeutic action. *International Journal of Psychoanalysis 84*: 823–841.

Gabbard, G. O. & Williams, P. (2001). Preserving confidentiality in the writing of case reports. *International Journal of Psychoanalysis 82*: 1067–1068.

Galatzer-Levy, R. M. (1995). Psychoanalysis and dynamic systems theory: Prediction and self similarity. *Journal of the American Psychoanalytic Association 43*: 1085–1113.

Gardner, J. (1991/1983). *The art of fiction: Notes on craft for young writers.* New York: Vintage Books.

Gardner, L. (2013). *Rhetorical investigations: B. G. Vico and C. G. Jung.* London: Routledge.

Gardner, M. R. (1994). Is that a fact? Empiricism revised, or a psychoanalyst at sea. *International Journal of Psychoanalysis 75*: 927–937.

Gass, W. H. (2009/1996). *Finding a form.* Champaign, IL: Dalkey Archive Press.

Gass, W. H. (2012). *Life sentences: Literary judgments and accounts.* New York: Alfred A. Knopf.

Geertz, C. (1994/1988). *Works and lives: The anthropologist as author.* Stanford, CA: Stanford University Press.

Geertz, C. (2000/1973). *The interpretation of cultures: Selected essays by Clifford Geertz.* New York: Basic Books.

Geertz, C. (2000). *Available light: Anthropological reflects on philosophical topics.* Princeton, NJ: Princeton University Press.

Gendlin, E. T. (1981/1978). *Focusing.* New York: Bantam Books.

Gerson, S. (2000). The therapeutic action of writing about patients: Commentary on papers by Lewis Aron and by Stuart A. Pizer. *Psychoanalytic Dialogues 10*: 261–266.

Gerson, S. (2009). When the third is dead: Memory, mourning, and witnessing in the aftermath of the Holocaust. *International Journal of Psychoanalysis 90*: 1341–1357.

Ghent, E. (1990). Masochism, submission, surrender—Masochism as a perversion of surrender. *Contemporary Psychoanalysis 26*: 108–136.

Gide, A. (1973). *The counterfeiters.* New York: Vintage Books/Random House.

Gilbert, S. M. & Gubar, S. (1984/1979). *The madwoman in the attic: The woman writer and the nineteenth-century literary imagination.* New Haven: Yale University Press.

Gilligan, C. (1982). *In a different voice: Psychological theory and women's development.* Cambridge, MA: Harvard University Press.

Gilligan, C. (2011). *Joining the resistance.* Cambridge, UK: Polity.

Gilligan, C., Rogers, A. G., & Tolman, D. L. (Eds.). (1991). *Women, girls & psychotherapy: Reframing resistance.* New York: Harrington Park Press/Haworth Press.

Gobnik, A. (2000). Man goes to see a doctor. In J. Shinder (Ed.), *Tales from the couch: Writers on therapy* (18–37). New York: William Morrow, An Imprint of HarperCollins Publishers.

Goldberg, A. (1997). Writing case histories. *International Journal of Psychoanalysis 78*: 435–438.

Goldberg, A. (2004). A risk of confidentiality. *International Journal of Psychoanalysis 85*: 301–310.

Goldberg, N. (1986). *Writing down the bones: Feeling the writer within.* Boston, MA: Shambhala.

Goldman, D. (1993). *In search of the real: The origins and originality of D. W. Winnicott.* Northvale, NJ: Jason Aronson, Inc.

Goldner, V. (2005). The poem as transformational third: Commentary on paper by Barbara Pizer. *Psychoanalytic Dialogues 15*: 105–117.

Goldstein, H. (1998). On writing for publication. *Families in Society: The Journal of Contemporary Human Services 79 (5)*: 451–454.

Goodman, N. (1978). *Ways of worldmaking.* Indianapolis: Hackett Publishing Co.

Gornick, V. (2001). *The situation and the story: The art of personal narrative.* New York: Farrar, Straus, and Giroux.

Grand, S. (2000). *The reproduction of evil: A clinical and cultural perspective.* Hillsdale, NJ: The Analytic Press.

Grand, S. (2003). Unsexed and ungendered bodies. *Studies in Gender and Sexuality 4*: 313–341.

Grand, S. (2010). *The hero in the mirror: From fear to fortitude.* New York: Routledge.

Grand, S. (2013). God at an impasse: Devotion, social justice, and the psychoanalytic subject. *Psychoanalytic Dialogues 23 (4)*: 449–463.

Grebow, H. (2008). A tale of two minds: Mentalization and adult analysis. *International Journal of Psychoanalytic Self Psychology 3*: 16–33.

Grebow, H. (2009). Seamstress of the psyche: Mending implicit patterns: The craft and artistry of psychoanalysis. *International Journal of Psychoanalytic Self Psychology 4*: 265–267.

Grebow, H. (2010). Seeing with our senses: An exploration of the origins of analytic knowing. *International Journal of Psychoanalytic Self Psychology 5*: 307–333.

Greenberg, J. R. (1986). Theoretical models and the analyst's neutrality. *Contemporary Psychoanalysis 22*: 87–106.

Greenblatt, S. (1997). The touch of the real. *Representations 59*: 15–30.

Güner, F. (2010). The leading psychoanalysts talks fashion, therapy, and about becoming an art curator. *The Arts Desk*. April 17.

Hale, C. (2001). *Sin and syntax: How to craft wickedly effective prose*. New York: Broadway Books.

Hall, D. & Birkerts, S. (1991). *Writing well*. Seventh Edition. New York: HarperCollins.

Halpern, J. (2003). Beyond wishful thinking: Facing the harm that psychotherapists can do by writing about their patients. *Journal of Clinical Ethics 14*: 118–136.

Harris, A. (1991). Gender as contradiction. *Psychoanalytic Dialogues 1*: 197–224.

Hart, J. (2006). *A writer's coach: The complete guide to writing strategies that work*. New York: Anchor Books.

Harvey, G. (1996). *Elements of the academic essay*. http://hybrid.commons.gc.cuny.edu/files/2012/11/GordonHarvey-Elements-of-the-Academic-Essay.doc

Harvey, G.(2008). *Writing with sources: A guide for Harvard students*. Second Edition. Indianapolis: Hackett Publishing Company.

Havens, L. (1987). *Approaches to the mind: Movement of the psychiatric schools from sects toward science*. Cambridge, MA: Harvard University Press.

Havens, L. (1993). *Coming to life: Reflections on the art of psychotherapy*. Cambridge, MA: Harvard University Press.

Havens, L. (1994). *Learning to be human*. Reading, MA: Addison-Wesley Publishing Company.

Havens, L. (1996/1989). *A safe place: Laying the groundwork of psychotherapy*. Cambridge, MA: Harvard University Press.

Heaney, S. (1980). *Preoccupations: Selected prose 1968–1978*. New York: Farrar, Straus, and Giroux.

Heaney, S. (1998). Song. In *Opened ground: Selected poems 1966–1996* (173). New York: Farrar, Straus and Giroux.

Heaney, S. (2002*). Finders and keepers: Selected prose 1971–2001*. New York: Farrar Straus Giroux.

Heilbrun, C.L. (1988). *Writing a woman's life*. New York: Ballantine Books.

Hillman, J. (1977/1975). *Re-visioning psychology*. New York: Harper & Row.

Hillman, J. (2004). Gods, disease, and politics. *Parabola: The Search for Meaning 29 (4)*: 70–75.

Hogenson, G. (2004). Archetypes: Emergence and the psyche's deep structure. In J. Cambray & L. Carter (Eds.), *Analytic psychology: Contemporary perspectives in Jungian analysis* (32–55). Hove, England: Brunner-Routledge.

Ipp, H. (2010). Nell—A bridge to the amputated self: The impact of immigration on continuities and discontinuities of self. *International Journal of Self Psychology 5*: 373–386.

Iser, W. (1980/1974). The reading process: A phenomenological approach. In J.P. Tompkins (Ed.), *Reader-response criticism: From formalism to post-structuralism* (50–69). Baltimore: Johns Hopkins University Press.

Jacobs, T.J. (2008). Discussion of contributions to *Psychoanalytic Inquiry* issue on analytic writing. *Psychoanalytic Inquiry 28*: 510–517.

James, H. (1921) *Roderick Hudson*. London: Macmillan and Co. (Preface originally published in the 1907–1909 New York Edition of James's fiction)

Johnson, M. (2007). *The meaning of the body: Aesthetics of human understanding*. Chicago: University of Chicago Press.

Kahane, C. (1995). *Passions of the voice: Hysteria, narrative, and the figure of the speaking woman*. Baltimore: Johns Hopkins University Press.

Kantrowitz, J. (2006). *Writing about patients: Responsibilities, risks, and ramifications.* New York: The Other Press.

Kantrowitz, J. & Gabbard, G. (2003). Writing about patients I: Analysts' ways of protecting confidentiality and conflictual views about their methods. Presentation, American Psychoanalytic Association Annual Meeting, June 21, Boston.

Kidder, T. & Todd, R. (2013). *Good prose: The art of nonfiction.* New York: Random House.

Kirsch, A. (2012). In praise of style. *The New York Times Book Review.* January 22, p. 13.

Kluger, J. (2013, September 23). The art of living. *Time 182 (13)*: 44–50.

Klumpner, G. H. & Frank, A. (1991). On methods of reporting clinical material. *Journal of the American Psychoanalytic Association 39*: 537–551.

Knoblauch, S. (2000). *The musical edge of therapeutic dialogue.* Hillsdale, NJ: The Analytic Press.

Knox, J. (2003). *Archetypes, attachment, analysis: Jungian psychology and the emergent mind.* Hove, England: Brunner-Routledge.

Knox, J. (2004). Development aspects of analytical psychology: New perspectives from cognitive neuroscience and attachment theory. In J. Cambray & L. Carter (Eds.), *Analytic psychology: Contemporary perspectives in Jungian analysis* (56–82). Hove, England: Brunner-Routledge.

Korzybski, A. (1994/1933) *Science and sanity: An introduction to non-Aristotelian systems and general semantics.* Fifth Edition. Englewood, NJ: Institute of General Semantics.

Krauss, N. (2006). *The history of love.* New York: W.W. Norton & Company.

Kubler, A. (2003). From the Editor. *Fort Da 9*: 1–3.

Kuhn, T. S. (1970/1962). *The structure of scientific revolutions.* Second Edition. Chicago: University of Chicago Press.

Lakoff, G. (1990). *Women, fire, and dangerous things: What categories reveal about the mind.* Chicago: University of Chicago Press.

Lakoff, G. & Johnson, M. (1999). *Philosophy in the flesh: The embodied mind and its challenge to Western thought.* New York: Basic Books.

Lakoff, G. & Johnson, M. (2003/1980). *Metaphors we live by.* Chicago: University of Chicago Press.

Lakoff, G. & Turner, M. (1989). *More than cool reason: A field guide to poetic metaphors.* Chicago: University of Chicago Press.

Lamott, A. (1995). *Bird by bird: Some instructions on writing and life.* New York: Anchor Books.

Layton, L. (1999). Social factors in the case study. *Journal for the Psychoanalysis of Culture and Society 4 (2)*: 325–327.

Lear, J. (1998). *Love and its place in nature.* New Haven: Yale University Press.

Lear, J. (2003). Confidentiality as a virtue. In C. Levin, A. Furlong, & M. K. O'Neil (Eds.), *Confidentiality: Ethical perspectives, and clinical dilemmas* (4–17). Hillsdale, NJ: The Analytic Press.

Levin, C., Furlong, A., & O'Neil, M.K. (Eds.). (2003). *Confidentiality: Ethical perspectives and clinical dilemmas.* Hillsdale, NJ: The Analytic Press.

Lichtenberg, J., Lachmann, F. & Fosshage, J. (2011). *Psychoanalysis and motivational systems: A new look.* New York: Routledge.

Lipton, E. L. (1991). The analyst's use of clinical data, and other issues of confidentiality. *Journal of the American Psychoanalytic Association 39*: 967–985.

Loewald, H. W. (1980). *Papers on psychoanalysis.* New Haven: Yale University Press.

Lopate, P. (1995). Introduction. In P. Lopate (Ed.), *The art of the personal essay: An anthology from the classical era to the present* (xxiii–liv). New York: Anchor Books.

Luepnitz, D. A. (2002). *Schopenhauer's porcupines: Intimacy and its dilemmas, five stories of psychotherapy*. New York: Basic Books.

Lukeman, N. (2006). *A dash of style: The art and mastery of punctuation*. New York: W.W. Norton.

Lunsford, A., Ruszkiewicz. J, & Walters, K. (2010). *Everything's an argument/with readings*. Boston: Bedford/St. Martins.

Lyons-Ruth, K. (1999). The two-person unconscious. *Psychoanalytic Inquiry 19*: 576–617.

Mahony, P. (1984). Further reflections on Freud and his writing. *International Journal of Psychoanalysis 32*: 847–864.

Mahony, P. (1986). *Freud and the rat man*. New Haven: Yale University Press.

Mahony, P. (1987/1981). *Freud as a writer*. Expanded Edition. New Haven: Yale University Press.

Manning, S. (2013). My father is a river. Unpublished writing exercise.

Maso, C. (2000). *Break every rule: Essays on language, longing & moments of desire*. Washington, DC: Counterpoint.

McClanahan, R. (1999). *Word painting: A guide to writing more descriptively*. Cincinnati: Writer's Digest Books.

McDougall, J. (1991/1985). *The theaters of the mind: Illusion and truth on the psychoanalytic stage*. New York: Brunner/Mazel.

McGleughlin, J. (2001). Letter to a patient or . . . Unpublished manuscript.

McGleughlin, J. (2011). The analyst's necessary vertigo. *Psychoanalytic Dialogues 21*: 630–642.

McGleughlin, J. (2013). To be seen is to be disappeared: When recognition of trauma betrays the trauma itself. Presentation, Division 39, Spring Meeting, Boston.

McLaughlin, J. T. (1993). Work with patients: The impetus for self-analysis. *Psychoanalytic Inquiry 13*: 365–389.

McLaughlin, J. T. (2005). *The healer's bent: Solitude and dialogue in the clinical encounter*. New York: Routledge.

McLuhan, M. (1994/1964). *Understanding media: The extensions of man*. Cambridge, MA: MIT Press.

Miller, J. C. (2004). *The transcendent function: Jung's model of psychological growth through dialogue with the unconscious*. Albany, NY: SUNY Press.

Miller, Jr., J. E. (Ed.). (1972). *Theory of fiction: Henry James*. Lincoln: University of Nebraska Press.

Miner, E. (1990). *Comparative poetics: An intercultural essay on theories of literature*. Princeton, NJ: Princeton University Press.

Mitchell, J. (2003). *Siblings: Sex and violence*. Cambridge, UK: Polity.

Mitchell, S. A. (1988). *Relational concepts in psychoanalysis: An integration*. Cambridge, MA: Harvard University Press.

Mitchell, S. A. (1993a). *Hope and dread in psychoanalysis*. New York: Basic Books.

Mitchell, S. A. (1993b). Aggression and the endangered self. *Psychoanalytic Quarterly 62*: 351–382.

Mitchell, S. A. (2000). *Relationality: From attachment to intersubjectivity*. Hillsdale, NJ: Analytic Press.

Molino, A. (Ed.). (1997). *Freely associated: Encounters in psychoanalysis with Christopher Bollas, Joyce McDougall, Michael Eigen, Adam Phillips, Nina Coltart*. London: Free Association Books.

Morris, H. (1992). Translating transmission: Representation and enactment in Freud's construction of history. In J.H. Smith & H. Morris, H. (Eds.), *Telling facts: History and narration in psychoanalysis* (48–102). Baltimore: Johns Hopkins University Press.

Morris, H. (1993). Narrative representation, narrative enactment, and the psychoanalytic construction of history. *International Journal of Psychoanalysis 74*: 33–54.

Murfin, R. (1992). What is deconstructionism? In P. Beidler (Ed.), *Henry James: The turn of the screw* (179–192). Boston: Bedford Books.

Murray, D.M. (1998). *The craft of revision*. Third Edition. Fort Worth, TX: Harcourt Brace College Publishers.

Naiburg, S. (2000). *Clinical writing for journal publication*. Smith College School of Social Work, Master's Thesis.

Naiburg, S. (2003). Mentors at the gate: Editors talk about clinical writing for journal publication. *Clinical Social Work Journal 31 (3)*: 295–313.

Naiburg, S. (2006). Between fate and destiny: Oedipus and reactive certainty in the consulting room. *Psychoanalytic Dialogues 16 (4)*: 445–463.

Nelson, K. (Ed.). (1989). *Narratives from the crib*. Cambridge, MA: Harvard University Press.

Norton, S. (2009). *Developmental editing: A handbook for freelancers, authors, and publishers*. Chicago, University of Chicago Press.

Ogden, B.H. & Ogden, T.H. (2012). *The analyst's ear and the critic's eye: Rethinking psychoanalysis and literature*. New York: Routledge.

Ogden, T.H. (1985). On potential space. *International Journal of Psychoanalysis 66*: 129–141.

Ogden, T.H. (1997). *Reverie and interpretation: Sensing something human*. Northvale, NJ: Jason Aronson, Inc.

Ogden, T.H. (1998). A question of voice in poetry and psychoanalysis. *Psychoanalytic Quarterly 67*: 426–448.

Ogden, T.H. (2001a). Reading Winnicott. *Psychoanalytic Quarterly 70*: 299–323.

Ogden, T.H. (2001b). *Conversations at the frontier of dreaming*. Northvale, NJ: Jason Aronson, Inc.

Ogden, T.H. (2002). A new reading of the origins of object relations theory. *International Journal of Psychoanalysis 83*: 767–782.

Ogden, T.H. (2003). On not being able to dream. *International Journal of Psychoanalysis 84*: 17–30.

Ogden, T.H. (2004). This art of psychoanalysis. *International Journal of Psychoanalysis 85*: 857–877.

Ogden, T.H. (2005a). On psychoanalytic writing. *International Journal of Psychoanalysis 66*: 15–29.

Ogden, T.H. (2005b). *This art of psychoanalysis: Dreaming undreamt dreams and interrupted cries*. London: Routledge.

Ogden, T.H. (2009). *Rediscovering psychoanalysis: Thinking and dreaming, learning and forgetting*. London: Routledge.

Ogden, T.H. (2012). *Creative readings: Essays on seminal analytic works*. London: Routledge.

O'Hagan, S. (2005). That way sanity lies. *The Observer*. February 12.

Oliver, M. (1994). *A handbook of poetry: A prose guide to understanding and writing poetry*. San Diego: Harcourt, Inc.

Orange, D. (1995). *Emotional understanding: Studies in psychological epistemology*. New York: Guilford Press.

Orange, D. M. (2003). Why language matters to psychoanalysis. *Psychoanalytic Dialogues* 13: 77–103.

Panksepp, J. (1998). *Affective neuroscience: The foundations of human mind and animal emotions.* Oxford: Oxford University Press.

Panksepp, J. (2009). Brain emotional systems and qualities of mental life: From animal models of affect to implications for psychotherapeutics. In D. Fosha, D. Siegel, & M. Solomon (Eds.), *The healing power of emotion: Affective neuroscience, development, and clinical practice* (1–26). New York: W.W. Norton & Company.

Perl, S. (1980). Understanding composition. *College Composition & Communication 31*: 363–369.

Perl, S. (2004). *Felt sense: Writing with the body.* Portsmouth, NH: Boynton/Cook Publishers.

Phillips, A. (1988). *Winnicott.* Cambridge, MA: Harvard University Press.

Phillips, A. (1994). *On flirtation: Psychoanalytic essays on the unconscious life.* Cambridge, MA: Harvard University Press.

Phillips, A. (1995). *Terrors and experts.* London: Farber and Farber.

Phillips, A. (1998). *The beast in the nursery: On curiosity and other appetites.* New York: Pantheon Books.

Phillips, A. (2001a). Clutter: A case history. In *Promises, promises: Essays on psychoanalysis and literature* (59–71). New York: Basic Books.

Phillips, A. (2001b). *Promises, promises: Essays on psychoanalysis and literature.* New York: Basic Books.

Phillips, A. (2002). Introduction. In A. Phillips (Ed.) and A. Bance (Trans.), *Sigmund Freud: Wild analysis* (vii–xxv). London: Penguin Books.

Phillips, A. (2014). The art of nonfiction No. 7: Adam Phillips. (Interviewed by P. Holdengräber). *The Paris Review 208*: 28–54.

Pickering, J. (2012). Bearing the unbearable: Ancestral transmission through dreams and moving metaphors in the analytic field. *Journal of Analytic Psychology 57*: 576–596.

Pizer, B. (2003). When the crunch is a (k)not: A crimp in relational dialogue. *Psychoanalytic Dialogues 13 (2)*:171–192.

Pizer, B. (2005a). Passion, responsibility, and 'Wild Geese': Creating a context for the absence of conscious intentions. *Psychoanalytic Dialogues 15 (1)*: 57–84.

Pizer, B. (2005b). "Eva, get the goldfish bowl": Affect and intuition in the analytic relationship. Paper presented at the Toronto Institute for Contemporary Psychoanalysis.

Pizer, B. (2007). Maintaining analytic liveliness: "The fire and the fuel" of growth and change. Paper presented at the Spring Meeting, Division of Psychoanalysis (39), American Psychological Association, Toronto.

Pizer, B. (2012). The repetition compulsion and body words: Transforming the unspeakable in psychoanalytic work. Stephen A. Mitchell Memorial Lecture. Toronto Institute for Contemporary Psychoanalysis.

Pizer, B. (2014). A clinical exploration of moving anger forward: Intimacy, anger, and creative freedom. *Psychoanalytic Dialogues 24*: 14–28.

Pizer, S. (2000). A gift in return: The clinical use of writing about a patient. *Psychoanalytic Dialogues 10 (2)*: 247–266.

Plaut, F. (1999). The writing of clinical papers: The analyst as illusionist. *Journal of Analytic Psychology 44*: 375–393.

Poe, E. A. (1846). *The philosophy of composition.* http://xroads.virginia.edu/~HYPER/poe/composition.html.

Poirier, R. (1990/1977). *Robert Frost: The work of knowing.* Stanford, CA: Stanford University Press.

Pontalis, J.-B. & Quinney, A. (Trans.). (2003). *Windows.* Lincoln: University of Nebraska Press.

Prose, F. (2006). *Reading like a writer: A guide for people who love books and for those who want to write them.* New York: HarperCollins.

Psychoanalytic Social Work. (1999). Guidelines for review of manuscripts.

Quinney, A. (2003). Translator's introduction. In J.-B. Pontalis & A. Quinney (Trans.), *Windows* (v–xv). Lincoln: University of Nebraska Press.

Racker, H. (1957). The meaning and uses of countertransference. *Psychoanalytic Quarterly 26*: 303–357.

Richards, I. A. (1947). Literature, oral-aural and optical. In J. P. Russo (Ed.), *I. A. Richards, Complementarities: Uncollected essays* (201–208). Manchester: Carcanet New Press.

Rico, G. L. (1983). *Writing the natural way: Using your right-brain techniques to release your expressive powers.* Los Angeles: J. P. Tarcher, Inc.

Rodenburg, P. (2002). *Speaking Shakespeare.* New York: Palgrave Macmillan.

Rogers, A. (1995). *A shining affliction: A story of harm and healing in psychotherapy.* New York: Penguin Books.

Rogers, A. (2007). *The unsayable: The hidden language of trauma.* New York: Ballantine Books.

Ross-Larson, B. (1996). *Edit yourself: A manual for everyone who works with words.* New York: W. W. Norton.

Roth, P. (1993/1970). *My life as a man.* New York: Holt, Rinehart & Winston.

Rowland, S. (2005). *Jung as a writer.* London: Routledge.

Russell, P. L. (1994). Process with involvement: The interpretation of affect. In L. Lifson (Ed.), *Understanding therapeutic action: Psychodynamic concepts of cure* (201–216). Hillsdale, NJ: The Analytic Press.

Russell, P. L. (1998). Trauma and the cognitive function of affects. In J. G. Teicholz & D. Kriegman (Eds.), *Trauma, repetition, and affect: The work of Paul Russell.* (23–47). New York: The Other Press.

Russell, P. L. (2006/1975). The theory of the crunch. *Smith Studies in Social Work 76 (1/2)*: 9–21.

Ryle, G. (1990/1971). *Collected papers, Vol. 2, Collected essays, 1929–1968.* London: Routledge.

Said, E. W. (1985). *Beginnings: Intention and method.* New York: Columbia University Press.

Sandler, J. (1983). Reflections on some relations between psychoanalytic concepts and psychoanalytic practice. *International Journal of Psychoanalysis 64*: 35–45.

Sanville, J. (1999) Playing in time and space: An interview with Jean Sanville. In J. Edward & E. Rose (Eds.), *The social work psychoanalyst's casebook: Clinical voices in honor of Jean Sanville* (1–22). Hillsdale, NJ: The Analytic Press.

Scharff, J. S. (2000). On writing from clinical experience. *Journal of the American Psychoanalytic Association 48*: 421–447.

Shapiro, F. (2012). *Getting past your past: Take control of your life with self-help techniques from EMDR therapy.* New York: Rodale Books.

Shapiro, S. A. (2004). The impossibility of case histories: A review of *The Impossibility of Sex* by Susie Orbach. *Contemporary Psychoanalysis 40*: 669–675.

Shapiro, T. (1994). Psychoanalytic facts: From the editor's desk. *International Journal of Psychoanalysis 75*: 1225–1232.

Sharpe, S. A. & Rosenblatt, A. D. (1994). Oedipal sibling triangles. *Journal of the American Psychoanalytic Association 42*: 491–523.

Sidoli, M. (1993). Naming the nameless. In M. Stein (Ed.), *Mad parts of sane people in analysis* (87–104). Wilmette, IL: Chiron Publications.

Slochower, J. A. (2006). *Psychoanalytic collisions*. Mahwah, NJ: The Analytic Press.

Solomon, D. (2005). The rescue artist. *The New York Times Magazine*. February 27, pp. 40–45.

Sommers, N. (2013). *Responding to student writing*. Boston: Bedford/St. Martin's.

Spence, D. (1982). *Narrative truth and historical truth: Meaning and interpretation in psychoanalysis*. New York: W.W. Norton & Company.

Spence, D. (1994). In search of signs of healing—the quest for clinical evidence. *Contemporary Psychoanalysis 32*: 287.

Stein, S. (1995). *Stein on writing*. New York: St. Martin's Griffin.

Stein, S. (1999). *How to grow a novel: The most common mistakes writers make and how to overcome them*. New York: St. Martin's Griffin.

Stern, D. B. (1997). *Unformulated experience: From dissociation to imagination in psychoanalysis*. Hillsdale, NJ: The Analytic Press.

Stern, D. B. (2005). Narrative writing and soulful metaphors: Commentary on paper by Barbara Pizer. *Psychoanalytic Dialogue 15 (1)*: 85–93.

Stern, D. B. (2010). *Partners in thought: Working with unformulated experience, dissociation, and enactment*. New York: Routledge.

Stern, D. N. (2004). *The present moment in psychotherapy and everyday life*. New York: W.W. Norton & Co.

Stewart, G. (1990). *Reading voices: Literature and the phonotext*. Berkeley: University of California Press.

Stoller, R. J. (1988). Patients' responses to their own case reports. *Journal of the American Psychoanalytic Association 36*: 371–391.

Suchet, M. (2011). Crossing over. *Psychoanalytic Dialogues 21 (2)*: 172–191.

Sullivan, H. S. (1950). The illusion of personal individuality. *Psychiatry 13*: 317–332.

Sweetnam, A. (2001). Talking about talking about patients. *Psychoanalytic Dialogues 11 (6)*: 861–884.

Symington, N. (1983). The analyst's act of freedom as agent of therapeutic change. *The International Review of Psycho-Analysis 10*: 283–291.

Symington, N. & J. Symington. (1996). *The clinical thinking of Wilfred Bion*. New York: Routledge.

Tanner, T. (1965). *The reign of wonder: Naivety and reality in American literature*. Cambridge, UK: Cambridge University Press.

Targan, B. (1986). The short-short story: Étude. In R. Shapard & J. Thomas (Eds.), *Sudden fiction: American short-short stories* (248–249). Salt Lake City, UT: Gibbs Smith Publishers.

Target, M. & Fonagy, P. (1996). Playing with reality: II. The development of psychic reality from a theoretical perspective. *International Journal of Psychoanalysis 77*: 459–479.

Toulmin, S. (1992). *Cosmopolis: The hidden agenda of modernity*. Chicago: Chicago University Press.

Toulmin, S. (2000). *Return to reason*. Cambridge, MA: Harvard University Press.

Toulmin, S. (2003/1958). *The uses of argument*. Updated Edition. Cambridge, UK: Cambridge University Press.

Toulmin, S., Rieke, R., & Janik, A. (1979). *An introduction to reasoning*. New York: Macmillan Publishing Co.

Tuckett, D. (1993). Some thoughts on the presentation and discussion of the clinical material of psychoanalysis. *International Journal of Psychoanalysis, 74*: 1175–1189.

Tuckett, D. (1994). Developing a grounded hypothesis to understand a clinical process: The role of conceptualisation in validation. *International Journal of Psychoanalysis 75*: 1159–1180.

Tuckett, D. (1998). Evaluating psychoanalytic papers: Towards the development of common editorial standards. *International Journal of Psychoanalysis 79*: 431–448.

Tuckett, D. (2000). Reporting clinical events in the *Journal*: Towards the construction of a special case. *International Journal of Psychoanalysis 81*: 1065–1069.

Vendler, H. (1995). *Soul says: On recent poetry*. Cambridge, MA: Belknap Press of Harvard University Press.

Voigt, E. B. (2009). *The art of syntax: Rhythm of thought, rhythm of song*. Minneapolis, MN: Graywolf Press.

Waelder, R. (1962). Psychoanalysis, scientific method, and philosophy. *Journal of the American Psychoanalytic Association 10*: 617–637.

Walk, K. (2008). *Teaching with writing: A guide for faculty and graduate students*. Princeton Writing Program. www.princeton.edu/writing.

Weisel-Barth, J. (2006). Thinking and writing about complexity theory in the clinical setting. *International Journal of Psychoanalytic Self Psychology 1 (4)*: 365–388.

Westen, D. (1999). The scientific status of unconscious processes: Is Freud really dead? *Journal of the American Psychoanalytic Association 47*: 1061–1106.

Westen, D. (2002). The language of psychoanalytic discourse. *Psychoanalytic Dialogues 12 (6)*: 857–898.

Wharton, B. (1999). Response to Plaut: 'The writing of clinical papers: the analyst as illusionist.' *Journal of Analytical Psychology 44*: 395–398.

White, H. (1981). The value of narrativity in the representation of reality. In W.J.T. Mitchell (Ed.), *On narrative* (1–23). Chicago: University of Chicago Press.

Williams, P. (2010). *The fifth principle*. London: Karnac.

Williams, P. (2013). *Scum*. London: Karnac.

Williams, P. & Schaefer, M. (2005). On confidentiality. *Fort Da 11*: 74–87.

Wilson, M. & Harasemovitch, J. C. (2004). On confidentiality. *Fort Da 10*: 39–53.

Winer, R. (1994). *Close encounters: A relational view of the therapeutic process*. Northvale, NJ: Jason Aronson, Inc.

Winnicott, D. W. (1958/1945). Primitive emotional development. In D. W. Winnicott, *Through pediatrics to psychoanalysis: Collected papers* (145–155). New York: Basic Books.

Winnicott, D. W. (1974). Fear of breakdown. *International Review of Psycho-Analysis 1*: 103–107.

Witkin, S. (2000). Taking social work into the new millennium. *Social Work 45 (1)*: 5–7.

Wright, S. (2009). Going home: Migration as enactment and symbol. *Journal of Analytical Psychology 54*: 475–492.

Yancey, K. B. (1994). Introduction: Definition, intersection, and difference—Mapping the landscape of voice. In K. B. Yancey (Ed.), *Voices on voice: Perspectives, definitions, inquiry* (vii–xxiv). Urbana, IL: National Council of Teachers of English.

Young-Bruehl, E. (2003). Winnicott: Life and work. By F. Robert Rodman. *International Journal of Psychoanalysis 84*: 1661–1665.

Index

Page numbers in *italics* refer to figures and numbers in **bold** refer to exercises.